CONTENTS

FOREWORD TO THE FIRST EDITION

Perhaps the only justification for writing is that it tries to answer the question we asked ourselves one day, which will not let us rest until it receives an answer. The great books—I mean: the *necessary* books—are those that can answer the questions that other men, darkly and without formulating them clearly, ask. I do not know if many have lost any sleep over the question that gave rise to this book; and I strongly doubt that my answer will meet with general approval. But if I am not sure of the scope and validity of my reply, I am sure of my personal need for it. From the time when I began to write poems, I wondered whether it was worth while to do so: would it not be better to transform life into poetry than to make poetry from life? And poetry—cannot its proper object be, more than the creation of poems, the creation of poetic instants? Can there be a universal communion in poetry?

In 1942 José Bergamín, who was then among us, decided to observe the fourth centenary of the birth of Saint John of the Cross with a series of lectures, and he invited me to participate. He thus gave me an opportunity to bring my ideas to a sharper focus and to sketch an answer to the question that had been tormenting me since adolescence. Those reflections were published under the title of "Poetry of Solitude and Poetry of Communion" in the review *El Hijo Pródigo* [The Prodigal Son], no. 5. The present book is merely the maturing, the development, and, here and there, the correction of that distant text.

A praiseworthy custom decrees that, at the beginning of works such as this, the author shall state the names of those to whom he owes special gratitude. My debts are many and I have tried to indicate them throughout this book, without omitting any. That is why I shall not list them now. Nevertheless, I wish to make one exception and mention the name of Alfonso Reyes. His stimulus has been twofold: on the one hand, his friendship and his example have encouraged me; on the other, the books he has written on themes related to those of the present volume—*The Literary Experience, Demarcation*, and so many unforgettable essays included in other works—made clear what seemed obscure, transparent the opaque, easy and well ordered the intricate and tangled. In a word: they lighted my way.

Octavio Paz

Mexico, August 1955

FOREWORD TO THE SECOND EDITION

This newly revised and enlarged edition of *The Bow and the Lyre* incorporates all the changes that appear in the French version of the book and other, more recent changes. The most important of these are the enlargement of the chapter "Verse and Prose" (in the part on the modern poetic movement) and the new Epilogue, "Signs in Rotation," which replaces the old one. This new chapter is the point of contact between *The Bow and the Lyre* and other writings not included in this volume: *Recapitulations* (1965) and *The New Analogy* (1967). Do all these changes indicate that the question to which the "Foreword to the First Edition" alludes has not been answered? The answer changes because the question changes. Immobility is an illusion, a mirage of movement; but movement, in turn, is another illusion, the projection of The Same that is reiterated in each of its changes and thus unceasingly reiterates its changing question—always the same.

Octavio Paz

Delhi, May 1967

Introduction

1. Poetry and Poem

POETRY IS KNOWLEDGE, salvation, power, abandonment. An operation capable of changing the world, poetic activity is revolutionary by nature; a spiritual exercise, it is a means of interior liberation. Poetry reveals this world; it creates another. Bread of the chosen; accursed food. It isolates; it unites. Invitation to the journey; return to the homeland. Inspiration, respiration, muscular exercise. Prayer to the void, dialogue with absence: tedium, anguish, and despair nourish it. Prayer, litany, epiphany, presence. Exorcism, conjuration, magic. Sublimation, compensation, condensation of the unconscious. Historic expression of races, nations, classes. It denies history: at its core all objective conflicts are resolved and man at last acquires consciousness of being something more than a transient. Experience, feeling, emotion, intuition, undirected thought. Result of chance; fruit of calculation. Art of speaking in a superior way; primitive language. Obedience to rules; creation of others. Imitation of the ancients, copy of the real, copy of a copy of the Idea. Madness, ecstasy, logos. Return to childhood, coitus, nostalgia for paradise, for hell, for limbo. Play, work, ascetic activity. Confession. Innate experience. Vision, music, symbol.

Analogy: the poem is a shell that echoes the music of the world, and meters and rhymes are merely correspondences, echoes, of the universal harmony. Teaching, morality, example, revelation, dance, dialogue, monologue. Voice of the people, language of the chosen, word of the solitary. Pure and impure, sacred and damned, popular and of the minority, collective and personal, naked and clothed, spoken, painted, written, it shows every face but there are those who say that it has no face: the poem is a mask that hides the void—a beautiful proof of the superfluous grandeur of every human work!

How can we not recognize in each of these formulas the poet who justifies them and who, in making them incarnate, gives them life? They are expressions of something lived and suffered, and we have no choice but to cling to them—condemned to abandon the first for the second and the second for the one that follows. Their very authenticity shows that the experience that justifies each of these concepts transcends them. Then one must interrogate the direct testimonies of the poetic experience. The unity of poetry can only be grasped by means of the naked contact with the poem.

When we question the poem about the existence of poetry, are we not arbitrarily confusing poetry and poem? Aristotle said that "there is nothing in common, except metrics, between Homer and Empedocles; and thus the former is rightly called a poet and the latter a physiologist." And so it is: not every poem—or to be exact: not every work constructed according to the laws of meter—contains poetry. But are those metrical works real poems or artistic, didactic, or rhetorical artifacts? A sonnet is not a poem, but a literary form, except when that rhetorical mechanism—stanzas, meters, and rhymes—has been touched by poetry. There are machines for rhyming but not for poetizing. There is also poetry without poems; landscapes, persons, and events are often poetic: they are poetry without being poems. Now, when poetry is given as a condensation of chance or when it is a crystallization of powers and circumstances alien to the poet's creative will, we are in the presence of the poetic. When—active or passive, awake or sleeping—the poet is the wire that conducts and transforms the poetic current, we face something radically different: a work. A poem is a work. Poetry is polarized, assembled, and isolated in a human product:

painting, song, tragedy. The poetic is poetry in an amorphous state; the poem is creation, poetry standing erect. Poetry is isolated and revealed completely only in the poem. It is licit to question the poem about the existence of poetry if one ceases to conceive the poem as a form capable of being filled with any content. The poem is not a literary form but the meeting place between poetry and man. A poem is a verbal organism that contains, stimulates, or emits poetry. The form and the substance are the same.

As soon as we turn our eyes away from the poetic to focus them on the poem, we are astonished at the multitude of forms assumed by the being that we thought was unique. How can we lay hold on poetry if each poem reveals itself as something different and irreducible? The science of literature tries to reduce the staggering plurality of the poem to genres. Because of its very nature, the attempt suffers from a twofold insufficiency. If we reduce poetry to a few forms—epic, lyric, dramatic—what shall we do with novels, prose poems, and those strange books called *Aurélia*, *Les Chants de Maldoror*, or *Nadja*? If we accept all the exceptions and intermediate forms—decadent, savage, or prophetic—the classification becomes an infinite catalogue. All verbal activities, to keep within the sphere of language, are susceptible to a change of sign and to transformation into a poem: from interjection to logical discourse. This is not the only limitation, or the most serious one, of the classifications of rhetoric. To classify is not to understand. And even less to comprehend. Like all classifications, nomenclatures are working tools. But they are tools that do not serve when one wants to use them for tasks more subtle than mere external arrangement. A large part of criticism is nothing but this ingenuous and abusive application of the traditional nomenclatures.

A similar reproach must be made to the other disciplines utilized by criticism, from stylistics to psychoanalysis. The former aims to tell us what a poem is by studying the poet's verbal habits. The latter, by interpreting his symbols. The stylistic method can be applied to Mallarmé and also to a collection of almanac verses. The same is true of psychologists' interpretations, biographies, and the other studies that attempt to explain, and sometimes succeed in explaining to us the why, how, and wherefore of a poem. Rhetoric, stylistics, sociology, psychol-

ogy, and the other literary disciplines are indispensable if we wish to
study a work, but they can tell us nothing about its ultimate nature.

The dispersion of poetry into a thousand heterogeneous forms could
induce us to construct an ideal type of poem. The result would be a
monster or a ghost. Poetry is not the sum of all poems. Each poetic
creation is a self-sufficient unit. The part is the whole. Each poem is
unique, irreducible, and unrepeatable. And so one feels inclined to
agree with Ortega y Gasset: there is no justification for calling such
diverse objects as Quevedo's sonnets, La Fontaine's fables, and the
Spiritual Canticle by the same name.

At first glance, this diversity appears to result from history. Each
language and each nation engender the poetry that the moment and
their particular genius dictate. But the historical criterion does not
solve problems, it multiplies them. The same diversity prevails within
each period and each society: Nerval and Hugo are contemporaries, as
are Velázquez and Rubens, Valéry and Apollinaire. If it is only by an
abuse of language that we apply the same name to the Vedic poems
and to Japanese haiku, is it not also an abuse to use the same noun for
experiences as diverse as those of Saint John of the Cross and his in-
direct profane model, Garcilaso? The historical perspective—a conse-
quence of our fatal remoteness—causes us to standardize landscapes
that are rich in antagonisms and contrasts. Distance makes us forget
the differences that separate Sophocles from Euripides, Tirso from
Lope. And those differences do not result from historical variations,
but from something much more subtle and elusive: the human person.
Thus, it is not so much historical knowledge but rather biography that
could give us the key for understanding the poem. And here a new
obstacle intervenes: in each poet's production each work is also
unique, isolated, and irreducible. *La Galatea* or *El viaje del Parnaso*
does not explain *Don Quixote de la Mancha*; *Iphigenie* is something
essentially different from *Faust*; *Fuente-Ovejuna*, from *La Dorotea*.
Each work has a life of its own, and the *Eclogues* are not the *Aeneid*.
Occasionally, one work denies another: the *Preface* to Lautréamont's
unpublished poems casts an ambiguous light on *Les Chants de Mal-
doror*; *Une Saison en Enfer* proclaims that the alchemy of the word of
Les Illuminations is madness. History and biography can give us the

tonality of a period or a life, sketch the limits of a work and describe, from without, the configuration of a style; they are also capable of explaining the general sense of a tendency and even of ascertaining the why and how of a poem. But they cannot tell us what a poem is. The only note that is common to all poems is that they are works, human products, like the paintings of artists and the chairs of carpenters.

Now, poems are works in a very strange way: between one and another there is not that relationship of filiation that exists so palpably with tools. Technique and creation, tool and poem are different realities. The technique is method and its worth is in proportion to its effectiveness, that is, to the extent that it is a method susceptible to repeated application: its value lasts until a new method is devised. The technique is repetition that improves or deteriorates; it is heritage and change: the gun replaces the bow. The *Aeneid* does not replace the *Odyssey*. Each poem is a unique object, created by a "technique" that dies at the very moment of creation. The so-called "poetic technique" is not transmissible, because it is not made of formulas but of inventions that only serve their creator. It is true that the style—conceived as the common manner of a group of artists or a period—approximates to the technique, both in the sense of heritage and change and in that of being a collective method. The style is the starting point of every creative intent; and for this very reason, every artist aspires to transcend that common or historical style.

When a poet acquires a style, a manner, he stops being a poet and becomes a constructor of literary artifacts. To call Góngora a baroque poet may be correct from the standpoint of literary history, but not if one wants to penetrate his poetry, which is always something more. It is true that the Cordovan's poems constitute the supreme example of the baroque style; but we must not forget that the expressive forms characteristic of Góngora—what we now call his style—were first merely inventions, unpublished verbal creations that did not become methods, habits, and formulas until later. The poet utilizes, adapts, or imitates the common fund of his epoch—that is, the style of his time —but he transmutes all those materials and produces a unique work. Góngora's best images—as Dámaso Alonso has shown admirably— stem precisely from his capacity to transfigure the literary language of his predecessors and contemporaries. Sometimes, of course, the poet is conquered by the style. (A style that is never his, but of his time: the poet does not have a style.) Then the failed image becomes common property, booty for future historians and philologists. Of these stones and others like them are built those structures that history calls artistic styles.

I do not mean to deny the existence of styles. Nor do I say that the poet creates from nothing. Like all poets, Góngora leans on a language. That language was something more precise and radical than speech: a literary language, a style. But the Cordovan poet transcends that language. Or in other words: he resolves it into unrepeatable poetic acts: images, colors, rhythms, visions: poems. Góngora transcends the baroque style; Garcilaso, the Tuscan; Rubén Darío, the modernist. The poet feeds on styles. Without them, there would be no poems. Styles are born, grow, and die. Poems endure, and each one of them constitutes a self-sufficient unit, an isolated specimen, that will never be repeated.

The unrepeatable and unique nature of the poem is shared by other works: paintings, sculptures, sonatas, dances, monuments. To all of them can be applied the distinction between poem and utensil, style and creation. For Aristotle, painting, sculpture, music, and the dance are also poetic forms, like the tragedy and the epic. And thus in speaking of the absence of moral qualities in the poetry of his contemporaries, as an example of this omission he cites the painter Zeuxis and not a tragic poet. In fact, over and above the differences that separate a painting from a hymn, a symphony from a tragedy, they possess a creative element that causes them to revolve in the same universe. In their own way, a painting, a sculpture, a dance are poems. And this way does not differ much from that of the poem made of words. The diversity of the arts does not hinder but rather emphasizes their unity.

The differences between word, sound, and color have placed the essential unity of the arts in doubt. The poem is made of words, ambiguous beings that are color and sound and are also meaning; the painting and the sonata are composed of simpler elements: forms, notes, and colors that mean nothing in themselves. The starting point of the plastic and sonorous arts is non-meaning; that of the poem, an amphibious organism, is the word, a meaningful entity. I find this distinction more subtle than real. Colors and sounds also have meaning. It is not by accident that critics speak of plastic and musical languages. And before these expressions were used by the initiated, people knew and practiced the language of colors, sounds, and signs. Moreover, there is no need to dwell on the insignia, emblems, knocks, calls, and other forms of nonverbal communication used by certain groups. In all of them the meaning is inseparable from their plastic or sonorous qualities.

In many cases, colors and sounds have a greater evocative power than speech. Among the Aztecs the color black was associated with darkness, cold, drought, war, and death. It also alluded to certain gods: Tezcatlipoca, Mixcóatl; to a space: the north; to a time: Técpatl; to flint; to the moon; to the eagle. To paint something black was like expressing or invoking all these representations. Each of the four colors meant a space, a time, some gods, some stars, and a destiny. One was born under the sign of a color, as Christians are born under a patron saint. It may not be otiose to add another example: the dual function of rhythm in the civilization of ancient China. When one tries to explain the notions of Yin and Yang—the two alternating rhythms that form the Tao—one resorts to musical terms. A rhythmical conception of the cosmos, the couplet Yin and Yang is philosophy and religion, dance and music, rhythmic movement impregnated with meaning. And similarly, it is not an abuse of figurative language, but an allusion to the significative power of sound, to use expressions like harmony, rhythm, or counterpoint to describe human actions. Everyone uses these words, knowing that they have sense, diffuse intentionality. There are no colors or sounds in themselves, stripped of meaning: touched by the hand of man, their nature changes and they enter the world of works. And all works end as meaning; whatever man touches is tinged with intentionality: it is a going toward. . . . Man's world is the world of meaning. It tolerates ambiguity, contradiction, madness, or confusion, but not lack of meaning. The very silence is populated by signs. Thus, the arrangement of buildings and their proportions respond to a certain intention. There is no lack of meaning—in fact, the opposite is true—in the vertical thrust of the Gothic, the tense balance of the Greek temple, the roundness of the Buddhist stupa or the erotic vegetation that covers the walls of the sanctuaries of Orissa. All is language.

The differences between the spoken or written language and the others—plastic or musical—are very profound, but not so profound that they make us forget that all are, essentially, language: expressive systems endowed with significative and communicative force. Painters, musicians, architects, sculptors, and other artists use as materials of composition elements that are not radically different from those used by the poet. Their languages are different, but they are a language. And it is easier to translate Aztec poems into their architectural and sculptural equivalents than into the Spanish tongue. The Tantric texts or the Kavya erotic poetry speak the same language as the sculptures of Konarak. The language of Sor Juana's *Primero sueño* does not differ markedly from that of the Sagrario Metropolitano of Mexico City. Surrealist painting is closer to the poetry of that movement than to cubist painting.

To say that it is impossible to escape from meaning is like enclosing all works—artistic or technical—in the leveling universe of history. How can one find a sense that is not historical? Neither by their materials nor by their meanings do works transcend man. They are all an "in order to" and a "toward" that lead to a concrete man, and he in turn acquires meaning only within a precise history. Morality, philosophy, customs, arts—everything, in short, that constitutes the expression of a given period partakes of what we call style. Every style is historical, and all the products of a period, from its simplest tools to its most disinterested works, are impregnated with history, that is to say, with style. But those affinities and kinships conceal specific differences. Within a style it is possible to discover what separates a poem from a tractate in verse, a painting from an educational print, a piece of furniture from a sculpture. That distinctive element is poetry. It alone can show us the difference between creation and style, a work of art and a utensil.

Whatever his activity and profession may be, artist or artisan, man transforms raw material: colors, stones, metals, words. The transmuting operation works as follows: the materials leave the blind world of nature to enter the world of works, that is, of meanings. Then what happens to the material stone when man uses it to carve a statue and to build a staircase? Although the stone of the statue is no different from that of the staircase and both are related to an identical system of meanings (for example: both are part of a medieval church), the transformation of the stone in the sculpture is of a different nature from that which changed it into a staircase. The fate of language in the hands of prose writers and poets can show us the meaning of that difference.

The highest form of prose is discourse, in the literal sense of the word. In discourse words aspire to be constituted as univocal meaning. This work implies reflection and analysis. At the same time, it involves an unattainable ideal, because the word refuses to be mere concept, bare meaning. Each word—aside from its physical properties—contains a plurality of senses. Thus, the prose writer's activity is directed against the very nature of the word. And therefore it is not true that M. Jourdain spoke in prose without knowing it. Alfonso Reyes rightly points out that one cannot speak in prose without having complete consciousness of what one is saying. One could also add that prose is not spoken: it is written. The spoken language is closer to poetry than to prose; it is less reflective and more natural, and that is why it is easier to be a poet without knowing it than a prose writer. In prose the word tends to be identified with one of its possible meanings, at the expense of the others: a spade is called a spade. This is an analytical operation and is not performed without violence, since the word possesses a number of latent meanings, it is a certain potentiality of senses and directions. The poet, on the other hand, never assaults the ambiguity of the word. In the poem language recovers its pristine originality, mutilated by the subjugation imposed on it by prose and everyday speech. The reconquest of its nature is total and it affects the sonorous and plastic values as well as the expressive ones. The word, free at last, shows all its entrails, all its meanings and allusions, like a ripe fruit or a rocket exploding in the sky. The poet sets his matter free. The prose writer imprisons his.

The same occurs with forms, sounds, and colors. Stone triumphs in the sculpture, is abased in the staircase. Color sparkles in the painting;

the movement of the body, in the dance. Matter, conquered or de-formed in the utensil, recovers its splendor in the work of art. The poetic operation is the reverse of technical manipulation. Thanks to the former, matter reconquers its nature: color is more color, sound is completely sound. In poetic creation there is no victory over matter or over the instruments, as the vain aesthetic of artisans wishes, but a setting free of matter. Words, sounds, colors, and other materials undergo a transmutation as soon as they enter the circle of poetry. Without ceasing to be tools of meaning and communication, they turn into "something else." That change—unlike what happens in technol-ogy—does not consist in an abandonment of their original nature, but in a return to it. To be "something else" means to be the "same thing": the thing itself, that which it is, really and originally.

Moreover, the stone of the statue, the red of the painting, the word of the poem, are not purely and simply stone, color, word: they are the incarnation of something that transcends and surpasses them. Without losing their primary values, their original weight, they are also like bridges that take us to another shore, doors that open on an-other world of meanings inexpressible by means of mere language. An ambivalent being, the poetic word is completely that which it is—rhythm, color, meaning—and it is also something else: image. Poetry changes stone, color, word, and sound into images. And this second quality, that of being images, and the strange power they have to arouse in the listener or spectator constellations of images, turns all works of art into poems.

Nothing precludes our regarding plastic and musical works as poems, if they are able to meet the two stated conditions: on the one hand, to return their materials to that which they are—sparkling or opaque matter—and thus to deny the world of utility; on the other hand, to be transformed into images and thus to become a peculiar form of communication. Without ceasing to be language—sense and transmission of sense—the poem is something that is beyond lan-guage. But that thing that is beyond language can only be reached through language. A painting will be a poem if it is something more than pictorial language. Piero della Francesca, Masaccio, Leonardo, or Uccello do not deserve, or suffer, to be classified as anything but poets.

In them the concern for the expressive resources of painting, that is, for the pictorial language, is resolved in works that transcend that same language. The investigations of Masaccio and Uccello were utilized by their heirs, but their works are something more than those technical discoveries: they are images, unrepeatable poems. To be a great painter means to be a great poet: one who transcends the limits of his language.

In short, the artist is not served by his tools—stone, sound, color, or word—like the artisan, but serves them to recover their original nature. A servant of language, whichever one it may be, he transcends it. This paradoxical and contradictory operation—which will be analyzed later—produces the image. The artist is a creator of images: a poet. And it is their capacity as images that permits the *Spiritual Canticle* and the Vedic hymns, haiku, and Quevedo's sonnets to be called poems. As images, words, without ceasing to be themselves, transcend language as a given system of historical meanings. The poem, without ceasing to be word and history, transcends history. And without examining more closely the essence of this transcending of history, it can be concluded that the plurality of poems does not deny, but rather affirms, the unity of poetry.

Each poem is unique. All poetry, with greater or lesser intensity, is latent in each work. Therefore, the reading of a single poem will tell us, more surely than any historical or philological research, what poetry is. But the experience of the poem—its re-creation through reading or recitation—also reveals a disconcerting plurality and heterogeneity. The reading almost always presents itself as the revelation of something alien to the poetry properly so called. The few contemporaries of Saint John of the Cross who read his poems gave more attention to their exemplary value than to their fascinating beauty. Many of the passages we admire in Quevedo left seventeenth-century readers cold, while the things that repel or bore us were what they found charming. Only by an effort at historical understanding do we divine the poetic function of the historical enumerations in Manrique's *Coplas*. At the same time, we are moved, perhaps more deeply than his contemporaries were, by the allusions to his time and to the immediate past. And it is not only history that makes us read the same text with different eyes. For some the poem is the experience of abandonment; for others, of rigor. Young boys read verses to help themselves express or know their feelings, as if the dim, intuited features of love, heroism, or sensuality could only be contemplated clearly in the poem. Every reader seeks something in the poem. And it is not unlikely that he will find it: he already had it in him.

It is not impossible that, after this first and deceptive contact, the reader may reach the center of the poem. Let us imagine that encounter. In the flux and reflux of our passions and occupations (always divided, always I and my double and the double of my other self), there is a moment when everything comes to terms. The opposites do not disappear, but are fused for an instant. It is a little like suspended animation: time has no importance. The Upanishads teach that this reconciliation is *ananda* or bliss with the One. Of course, few are capable of reaching this state. But all of us, at some time, even for a fraction of a second, have glimpsed something similar. One does not have to be a mystic in order to know this truth. We have all been children. We have all loved. Love is a state of union and participation, open to men: in the amorous act consciousness is like the wave that, after overcoming the obstacle, before breaking rises to a crest in which everything—form and movement, upward thrust and force of gravity—achieves a balance without support, sustained by itself. Quietude of movement. And just as we glimpse a fuller life, more life than life, through a beloved body, we discern the fixed beam of poetry through the poem. That instant contains every instant. Without ceasing to flow, time stops, overflowing itself.

A magnetic object, a secret meeting place of many opposing forces, the poem gives us access to the poetic experience. The poem is a possibility open to all men, regardless of their temperament, their mentality or their disposition. Now, the poem is just this: a possibility, something that is only animated by the contact with a reader or a listener. There is one note common to all poems, without which they would never be poetry: participation. Each time the reader truly relives the poem, he reaches a state that we can call poetic. The experience can take this form or that, but it is always a going beyond oneself, a breaking of the temporal walls, to be another. Like poetic creation, the experience of the poem is produced in history, is history, and, at the same time, denies history. The reader struggles and dies with Hector, doubts and kills with Arjuna, recognizes the rocks of the native coast with Odysseus. He relives an image, denies succession, overflows time. The poem is mediation: thanks to it original time, father of the times, becomes incarnate in an instant. Succession becomes pure present, a spring that nourishes itself and transmutes man. The reading of the poem reveals a marked similarity to poetic creation. The poet creates images, poems; and the poem makes of the reader an image, poetry.

The three parts into which this book has been divided propose to answer these questions: Is there a poetic utterance—the poem—irreducible to any other form of expression? What do poems say? How is the poetic utterance communicated? Perhaps it may not be unnecessary to repeat that nothing affirmed here should be regarded as mere theory or speculation, because it is the testimony of an encounter with some poems. Although this work has been elaborated more or less systematically, the natural distrust caused by writings of this kind can justly be mitigated. If it is true that alien residues—philosophical, moral, or others—intrude in every attempt to understand poetry, it is also true that the suspicious character of all poetics seems to be redeemed when it rests on the revelation that once, for a few hours, a poem gave us. And although we may have forgotten those words and although even their savor and meaning have disappeared, we still keep alive the sensation of some minutes so full that they were time overflowing, a high tide that broke the dikes of temporal succession. For the poem is a means of access to pure time, an immersion in the original waters of existence. Poetry is nothing but time, rhythm perpetually creative.

The Poem

2. Language

Man's first attitude toward language was confidence: the sign and the object represented were the same. The sculpture was a double of the model; the ritual formula a reproduction of reality, capable of reengendering it. To speak was to re-create the object alluded to. The exact pronunciation of the magic words was one of the principal conditions of their efficacy. The necessity to preserve the sacred language explains the birth of grammar, in Vedic India. But centuries later men observed that an abyss had opened between things and their names. The sciences of language won their autonomy as soon as the belief in the identity between the object and its sign had ceased. The first task of thought was to establish a precise and unique meaning for words; and grammar became the first step of logic. But words rebel at definition. And the battle between science and language has not yet ended.

The history of man can be reduced to the history of the relations between the words and the thought. Every period of crisis begins or coincides with a criticism of language. Suddenly there is a loss of faith in the efficacy of the word: "I held Beauty on my knees and she was bitter," says the poet. Beauty or the word? Both: without words beauty is ungraspable. Objects and words bleed from the same wound. All societies have passed through these crises of their foundations which are, likewise and above all, crises of the meaning of certain words. One frequently forgets that, like all other human creations, empires and states are made of words: they are verbal acts. In Book XIII of the *Analects*, Tzu-Lu asks Confucius: "If the Duke of Wei called you to administer his country, what would be your first act?" The Master replied, "The reform of language."

We do not know where evil begins, if in words or in things, but when words are corrupted and meanings become uncertain, the sense of our acts and works is also uncertain. Things lean on their names and vice versa. Nietzsche begins his criticism of values by confronting words: what, really, is the meaning of virtue, truth, or justice? When he revealed the meaning of certain sacred and immutable words—precisely those that were the cornerstones of Western metaphysics—he undermined its foundations. All philosophical criticism begins with an analysis of language.

The ambiguity of every philosophy stems from its fatal subjection to words. Almost all philosophers affirm that words are crude instruments, incapable of laying hold upon reality. Now, is it possible to have a philosophy without words? Symbols, even the purest and most abstract, like those of logic and mathematics, are also language. Moreover, the signs must be explained and there is no means to explain them other than language. But let us imagine the impossible: a philosophy having a symbolic or mathematical language without reference to words. Man and his problems—the essential theme of every philosophy—would not be accommodated by it. For man is inseparable from words. Without them, he is ungraspable. Man is a being of words. And vice versa: every philosophy that is served by words is condemned to the servitude of history, because words are born and die, like men. And so, at one extreme, the reality that words cannot express; at the other, the reality of man, which can only be expressed with words. Therefore we must examine the pretensions of linguistic science, beginning with its principal postulate: the notion of language as an object.

If every object is, in some way, a part of the knowing subject—the fatal limit of knowledge and simultaneously the only possibility of cognition—what can be said of language? The limits between object and subject appear particularly nebulous here. The word is man himself. We are made of words. They are our only reality or, at least, the only testimony of our reality. There is no thought without language, nor object of knowledge either: the first thing man does in the presence of an unknown reality is to name it, baptize it. What we know not is the unnamed. All learning begins as the teaching of the true names of things and ends with the revelation of the key word that will open the doors of wisdom for us. Or with the confession of ignorance: silence. And even silence says something, for it is pregnant with signs. We cannot escape from language. Of course, specialists can isolate language and change it into an object. But it is an artificial being plucked from its original world since, unlike what happens with other objects of science, words do not live outside us. We are their world and they ours. In order to lay hold upon language our only recourse is to use it. The nets for catching words are made of words. By this I do not mean to deny the value of linguistic studies. But the discoveries of linguistics must not make us forget its limitations: language, in its ultimate reality, eludes us. That reality consists in being something indivisible and inseparable from man. Language is a condition of man's existence and not an object, an organism, or a conventional system of signs that we can accept or reject. In this sense the study of language is one part of a total science of man.[1]

To affirm that language is man's exclusive property contradicts a very ancient belief. Let us remember how many fables begin: "When

[1] Today, fifteen years after this paragraph was written, I would not say exactly the same thing. Linguistics, chiefly due to N. Trubetzkoy and Roman Jakobson, has succeeded in isolating language as an object, at least on the phonological level. But if, as Jakobson himself says, linguistics has joined sound to language (phonology), it has not yet accomplished the complementary operation: to join meaning to sound (semantics). From this standpoint my statement is still valid. Moreover, I would point out that the discoveries of linguistics—for example, the conception of language as an unconscious system and one that obeys strict laws, independent of our will—are changing this science more and more into a central discipline in the study of man. As part of this general science of signs proposed by Lévi-Strauss, linguistics touches on cybernetics at one extreme and anthropology at the other. Thus it will perhaps be the point of contact between the exact and the human sciences.

the animals could talk. . . ." It may seem surprising, but this belief
was resuscitated by science in the last century. Many persons still main-
tain that animal communication systems are not essentially different
from those used by man. For some scholars it is not a misspent meta-
phor to speak of the language of the birds. In fact, the two distinguish-
ing marks of speech are present in the animal languages: meaning—
reduced, naturally, to the most elemental and rudimentary level—and
communication. The animal cry alludes to something, says something:
it has meaning. And that meaning is picked up and, as it were, under-
stood by other animals. Those inarticulate cries constitute a system of
common signs, endowed with meaning. Words have the selfsame
function. Therefore, speech is merely the development of animal lan-
guage, and words can be studied like any other object of natural
science.

One might object to this idea because of the incomparable complexi-
ty of human speech and the absence of abstract thought in animal lan-
guage. These are differences of degree, not of essence. More decisive,
to me, is what Marshall Urban calls the tripartite function of words:
words indicate or designate, they are names; they are also instinctive
or spontaneous replies to a material or psychic stimulus, as in the case
of interjections and onomatopoeia; and they are representations: signs
and symbols. Meaning is indicative, emotive, and representative. The
three functions appear in every verbal expression, at different levels
and with varying intensity. There is no representation that does not
contain indicative and emotive elements; and the same must be said of
indication and emotion. Although these are inseparable elements, the
symbolic function is the foundation of the other two. Without repre-
sentation there is no indication: the sounds of the word *bread* are
sonorous signs of the object to which they allude; without them the
indicative function could not take place: the indication is symbolic.
And similarly: the cry is not only an instinctive reply to a particular
situation but an indication of that situation by means of a representa-
tion: word, shout. In short, "the essence of language is the representa-
tion, *Darstellung*, of one element of experience by means of another,
the bipolar relation between the sign or the symbol and the thing

signified or symbolized, and the consciousness of that relation."[2] Having thus characterized human speech, Marshall Urban asks the specialists whether the three functions are present in animal cries. Most experts affirm that "the phonetic scale of monkeys is completely 'subjective' and can only express emotions, never designate or describe objects." The same can be said of their facial expressions and other bodily gestures. It is true that in some animal cries there are faint signs of indication, but the existence of the symbolic or representative function has never been proved. And so there is a hiatus between animal and human language. Human language differs radically from animal communication, in a qualitative not quantitative way. Language is man's exclusive property.[3]

Hypotheses that tend to explain the genesis and development of language as the gradual passage from the simple to the complex—for example, from interjection, cry, or onomatopoeia to indicative and symbolic expressions—seem equally lacking in foundation. Primitive languages display a great complexity. In almost all archaic languages there are words that of themselves constitute phrases and complete sentences. The study of primitive languages confirms what cultural anthropology reveals: as we probe into the past we do not find simpler societies, as was thought in the nineteenth century, but rather disconcertingly complex ones. The transition from the simple to the complex may be a constant in the natural sciences, but not in the sciences of culture. Although the hypothesis of the animal origin of language founders in the face of the irreducible character of meaning, it does have the great originality of including "language in the sphere of expressive movements."[4] Before he speaks, man gesticulates. Gestures and movements have meaning. And in meaning the three elements of language—indication, emotion, and representation—are present. Man

[2] Wilbur Marshall Urban, *Language and Reality*, Lengua y Estudios Literarios (Mexico City: Fondo de Cultura Económica, 1952).

[3] Today I would not state the differences between animal and human communication so categorically. Certainly there is a break or hiatus between them, but both are part of that universe of communication—intuited by all poets under the form of the universal analogy—which cybernetics has discovered.

[4] Urban, *Language and Reality*.

speaks with his hands and face. The cry approaches representative and indicative meaning when it is combined with those gestures and movements. Perhaps the first human language was the imitative and magical pantomime. Governed by the laws of analogical thought, corporal movements imitate and recreate objects and situations.

No matter how speech may have originated, specialists seem to agree on the "primarily mythical nature of all words and forms of language." Modern science impressively confirms the idea of Herder and the German romantics: "It seems clear that from the beginning language and myth have existed in an inseparable correlation. . . . Both are expressions of a basic tendency toward the formation of symbols: the radically metaphorical principle that is at the root of every function of symbolization."[5] Language and myth are vast metaphors of reality. The essence of language is symbolic because it consists in the representation of one element of reality by another, as occurs with metaphors. Science verifies a belief common to all poets of all times: language is poetry in a natural state. Each word or group of words is a metaphor. And it is also a magic instrument, that is, a thing susceptible to being changed into something else and transmuting what it touches: the word *bread*, touched by the word *sun*, actually becomes a star; and the sun, in turn, becomes a luminous food. The word is a symbol that gives off symbols. Man is man because of language, because of the original metaphor that caused him to be another and separated him from the natural world. Man is a being who has created himself in creating a language. By means of the word, man is a metaphor of himself.

The constant production of images and rhythmical verbal forms is a proof of the symbolizing character of speech, of its poetic nature. Language tends spontaneously to be crystallized in metaphors. Words constantly collide and throw out metallic sparks or form phosphorescent pairs. New stars continually populate the verbal sky. Each day words and phrases appear at the surface of language, still dripping moisture and silence from their cold scales. At the same moment others disappear. Suddenly the wasteland of a worn-out language is covered

[5] Ibid.

with unexpected verbal flowers. Luminous creatures inhabit the thickets of speech. Voracious creatures, above all. At the heart of language rages a civil war without quarter. All against one. One against all. Vast ever-moving throng, constantly breeding, intoxicated with itself! From the lips of children, madmen, scholars, cretins, lovers, or recluses gush images, puns, expressions sprung from the nothing. For an instant they shine or sparkle; then they are extinguished. Made of flammable matter, words begin to burn as soon as they touch the imagination or the fancy. But they are incapable of keeping their fire. Speech is the substance or food of the poem, but it is not the poem. The distinction between the poem and those poetic expressions—invented yesterday or repeated for a thousand years by a people who have kept their traditional knowledge intact—is rooted in this: the poem is an attempt to transcend language; on the other hand, poetic expressions exist on the same plane as speech and result from the interplay of words in men's mouths. They are not creations, works. Speech, social language is concentrated in the poem, is articulated and raised. The poem is language standing erect.

Today no one regards the people as the author of the Homeric epics, nor can anyone defend the idea of the poem as a natural secretion of language. Lautréamont meant something else when he prophesied that poetry would one day be made by everyone. Nothing is more dazzling than this prospect. But, as happens with every revolutionary prophecy, the advent of that future state of total poetry presupposes a return to the original time. In this case, to the time when to speak was to create. Or rather: a return to the identity between the object and the name. The distance between the word and the object—which is, precisely, that which obliges each word to become a metaphor of the thing it designates—is the result of another distance: as soon as man acquired consciousness of himself, he broke away from the natural world and made himself another world inside himself. The word is not identical to the reality it names because between man and things—and, more deeply, between man and his being—consciousness of himself intervenes. The word is a bridge by which man tries to traverse the distance that separates him from external reality. But that distance is a part of human nature. To obliterate it, man must renounce his humanity, either by returning to the natural world, or by transcending the limitations that his condition imposes on him. Both temptations, latent throughout all history, are now presented to modern man with greater exclusivity. Therefore contemporary poetry oscillates between two poles: on the one hand, it is a profound affirmation of the magic values; on the other, a revolutionary vocation. Both directions express man's revolt against his own condition. Thus, "to change man," means to renounce being a man: to sink forever into animal innocence or to free oneself from the weight of history. In order to achieve the second alternative it is necessary to reverse the terms of the old relation, so that it will not be the historical existence that determines consciousness, but the other way around. The revolutionary endeavor appears as a recuperation of the alienated consciousness and, likewise, as the conquest that this recuperated consciousness makes of the historical world and of nature. In control of historical and social laws, consciousness would determine existence. Then mankind would have taken its second mortal leap. By means of the first, man left the natural world, ceased to be an animal and stood up: he contemplated nature and contemplated himself. In taking the second, he would return to the original unity, not losing consciousness but making it the real foundation of nature. Although this is not man's only attempt to recover the lost unity of consciousness and existence (magic, mysticism, religion, and philosophy have proposed and propose other ways), its merit resides in the fact that it is a way open to all men and one that is reputed to be the purpose or meaning of history. And here one would have to ask: if the primordial unity between the world and man were reconquered, would not words be superfluous? The end of alienation would also be the end of language. Utopia, like mysticism, would terminate in silence. Well, whatever we may think of this idea, it is evident that the fusion—or rather the reunion—of the word and the object, the name and the thing named, requires man's prior reconciliation with himself and with the world. Until this change occurs, the poem will continue to be one of the few resources by which man can go beyond himself to find out what he is, profoundly and originally. Therefore, the spark of the poetic cannot be confused with the more daring and decisive endeavors of poetry.

The fact that it is impossible to entrust poetic creation to the pure dynamism of language is corroborated as soon as one perceives that there is not a single poem in which a creative will has not intervened. Yes, language is poetry and each word conceals a certain metaphorical charge that is ready to explode as soon as the secret mechanism is tripped, but the creative force of the word resides in the man who utters it. Man sets language in motion. The notion of a creator, a necessary antecedent of the poem, seems to be opposed to the belief in poetry as something that escapes the control of the will: Everything depends on what is understood by will. First of all, we must abandon the static conception of the so-called faculties as we have abandoned the idea of a separate soul. One cannot speak of psychic faculties— memory, will, etc.—as if they were separate and independent entities. The psyche is an indivisible whole. If it is not possible to trace the limits between body and spirit, neither is it possible to discern where the will ends and pure passivity begins. In each of its manifestations the psyche expresses itself totally. In each function all the others are present. Immersion in states of absolute receptivity does not imply the abolition of the will. The testimony of Saint John of the Cross—"desiring nothing"—takes on an immense psychological value here: the nothing itself becomes active, by the force of the desire. Nirvana offers the same combination of active passivity, of movement that is repose. States of passivity—from the experience of inner emptiness to the opposite one of congestion of being—require the exercise of a will determined to destroy the duality between object and subject. The perfect yogi is the one who, motionless, sitting in an appropriate posture, "staring impassively at the end of his nose," is so much a master of himself that he forgets himself.

We all know how difficult it is to reach the shores of distraction. This experience runs counter to the prevailing tendencies of our civilization, which proposes abstraction, retraction, and even contraction as archetypes of human behavior. A man who is distracted denies the modern world. In doing this, he gambles everything. Intellectually his decision is no different from that of the person who commits suicide because of his eagerness to find out what is on the other side of life. The distracted person asks himself, "What is on the other side of wakefulness and reason?" Distraction means: attraction for the reverse of this world. The will does not disappear; it simply changes direction: instead of serving the analytical powers, it prevents them from confiscating psychic energy for their own purposes. The poverty of our psychological and philosophical vocabulary in this subject contrasts with the richness of poetic expressions and images. Let us remember Saint John's "silent music" or Lao-Tse's "emptiness is plenitude." Passive states are by no means experiences of silence and emptiness, but of positive and full moments: from the center of being flows a stream of images. "My heart is sprouting flowers in the middle of the night," the Aztec poem says. Paralysis of the will attacks only one part of the psyche. The passivity of one area stimulates the activity of the other and makes it possible for the imagination to be victorious over the analytical, discursive or reasoning tendencies. In no case does the creative will disappear. Without it, the doors of identification with reality remain inexorably closed.

Poetic creation begins as violence to language. The first act in this operation is the uprooting of words. The poet wrests them from their habitual connections and occupations: separated from the formless world of speech, words become unique, as if they had just been born. The second act is the return of the word: the poem becomes an object of participation. Two opposing forces inhabit the poem: one of elevation or uprooting, which pulls the word from the language; the other of gravity, which makes it return. The poem is an original and unique creation, but it is also reading and recitation: participation. The poet creates it; the people, by recitation, re-create it. Poet and reader are two moments of a single reality. Alternating in a manner that may aptly be called cyclical, their rotation engenders the spark: poetry.

The two operations—separation and return—require that the poem be sustained by a common language. Not by popular or colloquial speech, as is supposed now, but by the language of a community: city, nation, class, group or sect. The Homeric poems were "composed in a literary and artificial dialect that was never actually spoken" (Alfonso Reyes). The great texts of Sanskrit literature belong to periods when this language had ceased to be spoken, except among small groups. In

Kalidasa's theater, the noble characters speak Sanskrit; the plebeians, Prakrit. Now, popular or of the minority, the language that sustains the poet possesses two distinguishing marks: it is a living language and a common one. That is, a language used by a group of men to communicate and perpetuate their experiences, passions, hopes and beliefs. No one can write a poem in a dead language, except as a literary exercise (and then it is not a poem, because a poem is fully realized only in participation: without a reader it is only half a work). Nor does the language of mathematics, physics, or any other science offer sustenance to poetry: it is a common language, but not a living one. No one sings in formulas. It is true that scientific definitions can be utilized in a poem (Lautréamont used them with genius). But then a transmutation, a change of sign is produced: the scientific formula ceases to serve the demonstration and tends instead to destroy it. Humor is one of poetry's best weapons.

In creating the language of European nations, legends and epic poems helped to create those same nations. And in a profound sense they founded them: they gave them consciousness of themselves. Indeed, by means of poetry, the common language was changed into mythical images endowed with archetypal value. Roland, the Cid, Arthur, Lancelot, Parsifal are heroes, models. The same can be said—with certain decisive reservations—of the epic creations that coincide with the birth of bourgeois society: novels. Of course, the distinctive quality of the modern age, from the standpoint of the poet's social situation, is his marginal position. Poetry is a food that the bourgeoisie —as a class—have been incapable of digesting. And so they have tried, time and time again, to domesticate it. But as soon as a poet or a poetic movement gives in and agrees to return to the social order, a new creation appears that constitutes, sometimes without intending to do so, a criticism and a scandal. Modern poetry has become the food of the dissidents and exiles of the bourgeois world. A split society and a poetry in rebellion go hand in hand. Yet even in this extreme case the close relation between the social language and the poem is not broken. The poet's language is that of his community, whatever the latter may be. Between the two is established a reciprocal play of influences, a system of communicating vessels. Mallarmé's is a language for the initiated. Readers of the modern poets are united by a kind of complicity and form a secret society. But what is characteristic of our time is the destruction of the balance precariously maintained throughout the nineteenth century. The poetry of sects is approaching its end because the tension has become intolerable: the social language is constantly being degraded into a desiccated jargon of technicians and journalists; and, at the other extreme, the poem is turning into a suicidal exercise. We have come to the end of a process begun at the dawn of the modern age.

Many contemporary poets, wishing to cross the barrier of emptiness that the modern world puts before them, have tried to seek out the lost audience: to go to the people. But now there are no people: there are organized masses. And so, "to go to the people" means to occupy a place among the "organizers" of the masses. The poet becomes a functionary. This change is quite astonishing. The poets of the past had been priests or prophets, lords or rebels, clowns or saints, servants or beggars. It behooved the bureaucratic state to make of the creator a high-ranking employee of the "cultural front." The poet has a "place" in society today. But does poetry?

Poetry lives on the deepest levels of being, while ideologies and everything that we call ideas and opinions constitute the most superficial layers of consciousness. The poem feeds on the living language of a community, on its myths, its dreams and its passions, that is, its strongest and most secret tendencies. The poem establishes the people because the poet retraces the course of language and drinks from the original source. In the poem society is face to face with the foundations of its existence, with its initial word. When he uttered this original word, man created himself. Achilles and Odysseus are something more than two heroic figures: they are the Greek destiny creating itself. The poem is mediation between society and that which founds it. Without Homer, the Greek people would not be what they were. The poem reveals to us what we are and invites us to be that which we are.

Modern political parties turn the poet into a propagandist and thus degrade him. The propagandist disseminates the concepts of the hierarchs among the "mass." His task is to transmit certain directives from the higher to the lower level. His radius of interpretation is very

limited (clearly any deviation, even an involuntary one, is dangerous).
The poet, on the other hand, works from the lower to the higher level:
from the language of his community to that of the poem. At once, the
work returns to its sources and becomes an object of communion. The
relation between the poet and his people is organic and spontaneous.
Now everything opposes this process of constant re-creation. The peo-
ple split up into classes and groups; then they become petrified in
blocs. The common language is changed into a system of formulas.
With the lines of communication closed, the poet finds himself with-
out a language to lean on and the people without images in which to
recognize themselves. This situation must be accepted honestly. If the
poet abandons his exile—the only possibility of authentic rebellion—
he also abandons poetry and the possibility that this exile will be trans-
formed into communion. Because between the propagandist and his
audience a twofold error is established: he believes he is speaking the
language of the people; and the people, that they are listening to the
language of poetry. The gesticulating loneliness of the tribune is total
and irrevocable. It—and not the loneliness of the one who struggles
alone to find the common word—is indeed a loneliness with no exit
and no future.

Some poets believe that a simple verbal change is enough to recon-
cile poem and social language. Some resuscitate folklore; others lean
on colloquial speech. But folklore, preserved in museums or in isolated
regions, stopped being a language several centuries ago: it is a curiosi-
ty or a nostalgia. And as for the lacerated speech of the big cities: it is
not a language, but the residue of something that was a coherent and
harmonious whole. The speech of the city tends to become petrified in
formulas and slogans and thus suffers the same fate as popular art,
changed into an industrial artifact, and that of man himself, who from
a person is transformed into a mass. The exploitation of folklore, the
use of colloquial language or the inclusion of deliberately antipoetic or
prosaic passages in a text of high tension are literary resources that
have the same meaning as the use of artificial dialects by the poets of
the past. In every case they are characteristic procedures of the so-
called poetry of the minority, like the geographical images of the Eng-
lish "metaphysical" poets, the mythological allusions of Renaissance

writers or the irruptions of humor in Lautréamont and Jarry. Touch-
stones encrusted in the poem to emphasize the authenticity of the rest,
their function is not unlike that of the use, in painting, of materials
that traditionally did not belong to that world. Not in vain has *The
Waste Land* been likened to a collage. The same can be said of certain
of Apollinaire's poems. All of this possesses poetic effectiveness, but it
does not make the work more comprehensible. The sources of compre-
hension are different: they are rooted in the common bond of the lan-
guage and values. The modern poet does not speak the language of
society nor does he commune with the values of the present civiliza-
tion. The poetry of our time cannot escape from loneliness and rebel-
lion, except by a change of society and of man himself. The action of
the contemporary poet can only be exerted on individuals and groups.
In this limitation, perhaps, lies his present effectiveness and his future
fecundity.

Historians affirm that periods of crisis or stagnation automatically
produce a decadent poetry. They thus condemn hermetic, solitary or
difficult poetry. On the contrary, moments of historical ascendancy
are characterized by an art of plenitude, to which the whole society
accedes. If the poem is written in what is called the language of all, we
are in the presence of an art of maturity. Clear art is great art. Art that
is obscure and for the few, decadent. Certain pairs of adjectives ex-
press this duality: human and inhuman, popular and minority, classic
and romantic (or baroque) art. These periods of splendor are almost
always made to coincide with the political or military apogee of the
nation. As soon as peoples have great armies and invincible leaders,
great poets appear. Other historians maintain that this poetic greatness
occurs a little earlier—when the armies sharpen their teeth—or a lit-
tle later—when the grandsons of the conquerors digest the winnings.
Dazzled by this idea, they form radiant pairs: Racine and Louis XIV,
Garcilaso and Charles V, Shakespeare and Elizabeth. And other ob-
scure, crepuscular pairs, like Luis de Góngora and Philip IV, Lyco-
phron and Ptolemy Philadelphus.

With regard to the obscurity of the works, it must be said that every
poem presents difficulties at the outset. Poetic creation always encount-
ers the resistance of the inert and horizontal. Aeschylus was accused

of obscurity. Euripides was hated by his contemporaries and was regarded as unclear. Garcilaso was called un-Spanish and cosmopolitan. The romantics were accused of being hermetic and decadent. The "modernists" faced the same criticism. The truth is that the difficulty of every work lies in its novelty. Separated from their habitual functions and united in an order that is not the order of conversation or discourse, words offer an irritating resistance. All creation engenders ambiguity. Poetic enjoyment is not produced until certain difficulties, analogous to the difficulties of creation, are overcome. Participation implies a re-creation; the reader reproduces the poet's actions and experiences.

Moreover, almost all periods of crisis or social decadence are fertile in great poets: Góngora and Quevedo, Rimbaud and Lautréamont, Donne and Blake, Melville and Dickinson. If we are to follow the historical criterion, Poe was the expression of Southern decadence and Rubén Darío of the extreme prostration of Spanish-American society. And how can one explain Leopardi at the height of the Italian dissolution and the German romantics in a shattered Germany at the mercy of the Napoleonic armies? Much of the Hebrews' prophetic poetry coincided with the periods of slavery, dissolution, or decadence of Israel. Villon and Manrique wrote in what has been called the "autumn of the Middle Ages." And what is there to say of the "society of transition" in which Dante lived? The Spain of Charles IV produced Goya. No, poetry is not a mechanical reflection of history. The relations between them are more subtle and complex. Poetry changes, but it does not progress or decay. Societies decay.

In times of crisis the bonds that make society an organic whole are broken or weakened. In periods of fatigue, they are immobilized. In the former case, society is dispersed; in the latter, it is petrified under the tyranny of an imperial mask and the official art is born. But the language of sects and small communities is propitious for poetic creation. The group's situation of exile gives its words a particular tension and value. Every sacred language is secret. And conversely: every secret language—not excluding that of plotters and conspirators—borders on the sacred. The hermetic poem proclaims the greatness of poetry and the wretchedness of history. Góngora is a testimony of the

health of the Spanish language, just as the Conde-Duque de Olivares
is of the decadence of an empire. A society's fatigue does not neces-
sarily imply the extinction of the arts nor does it provoke the poet's
silence. Instead, it may have the opposite effect: it may stimulate the
appearance of solitary poets and works. Each time a great hermetic
poet appears, or movements of poetry in revolt against the values of
a determinate society, it must be suspected that the society, not the
poetry, is suffering from incurable ills. And those ills can be meas-
ured by considering two circumstances: the absence of a common lan-
guage and the society's deafness to the solitary song. The poet's lone-
liness reveals the social decline. Creation, always at the same height,
shows the lowering of the historical level. And thus the difficult poets
sometimes seem superior to us. This is due to an error of perspective.
They are not higher; it is simply that the world around them is lower.[6]

The poem leans on the social or communal language, but how is the
transition effected and what happens to the words when they leave
the social sphere and become the words of the poem? Philosophers,
orators, and writers choose their words. The philosopher, according
to their meanings; the others, with regard to their moral, psychological
or literary effectiveness. The poet does not choose his words. When
one says that a poet seeks his language, he does not mean that the poet
goes through libraries or markets picking up old and new turns of
phrase but that, indecisive, he vacillates between the words that really
belong to him, that have been inside him from the beginning, and the
others learned in books or in the street. When a poet finds his word,
he recognizes it: it was already in him. And he was already in it. The
poet's word is confused with his very being. He is his word. At the
moment of creation, the most secret part of our selves comes to the
surface of consciousness. Creation consists in bringing forth certain
words that are inseparable from our being. Those words and not
others. The poem is made of necessary and irreplaceable words. That
is why it is so difficult to correct a work that has already been made.
Every correction implies a re-creation, a turning backward to our in-
ner selves. The fact that it is impossible to translate poetry also stems

[6] On "Poetry, Society, and State," see Appendix I.

from this circumstance. Each word of the poem is unique. There are no synonyms. Unique and irremovable: it is impossible to wound one word without wounding the whole poem; impossible to change a comma without upsetting the whole edifice. The poem is a living whole, made of irreplaceable elements. And thus the true translation can only be a re-creation.

To affirm that the poet uses only the words that were already in him does not contradict what has been said about the relations between poem and common language. To dissipate this ambiguity it is enough to remember that, by its very nature, all language is communication. The words of the poet are also those of his community. Otherwise they would not be words. Every word implies two persons: the one who speaks and the one who hears. The verbal universe of the poem is not made of the dictionary's words, but the community's. The poet is not a man rich in dead words, but in living ones. Personal language means common language revealed or transfigured by the poet. The highest of the hermetic poets defined the poem's mission as follows: "To give a purer sense to the words of the tribe." And this is true even in the most superficial sense of the phrase: a return to the etymological meaning of the word and, likewise, an enrichment of language. Many words that now seem common and current to us are inventions, Italianisms, neologisms, and Latinisms of Juan de Mena, Garcilaso, or Góngora. The words of the poet are also the words of the tribe or will be one day. The poet transforms, re-creates, and purifies the language; and later, he shares it. But what is this purification of the word by poetry, and what is meant by the affirmation that the poet is not served by words, but is their servant?

Words, phrases, and exclamations that root out our pain, pleasure, or any other feeling are reductions of language to its mere affective value. The words thus uttered cease to be, strictly speaking, instruments of relation. Croce observes that they are not properly verbal expressions: they lack the voluntary and personal element and they overabound in the almost mechanical spontaneity with which they are produced. They are set phrases, from which every personal nuance is absent. It is not necessary to accept the Italian philosopher's opinion to realize that, even if they are true expressions, they lack an indispensable dimension: that of being vehicles of relation. Every word implies a speaker. And the least that can be said of those expressions and phrases with which our affectivity is mechanically released is that in them the speaker is diminished and almost obliterated. The word suffers a mutilation: that of the hearer.

Valéry says in one of his writings that "the poem is the development of an exclamation." Between *development* and *exclamation* there is a contradictory tension; and I should add that this tension *is* the poem. If one of the two terms disappears, the poem returns to mechanical interjection or becomes an eloquent amplification, description, or theorem. The *development* is a language that creates itself in the face of that crude and properly inexpressible reality to which the exclamation alludes. Poem: ear that listens to a mouth that says what the exclamation did not say. The cry of pain or joy indicates the object that wounds or gladdens us; it indicates it but conceals it: it says *there it is*, it does not say *what* or *who* it is. The reality indicated by the exclamation remains unnamed: it is there, neither absent nor present, about to appear or to vanish forever. It is an imminence—of what? The *development* is not a question or an answer: it is a summons. The poem—mouth that speaks and ear that hears—will be the revelation of that which the exclamation indicates without naming. I say revelation and not explanation. If the *development* is an explanation, reality will not be revealed but elucidated and language will suffer a mutilation: we shall have ceased to see and hear and we shall only understand.

The opposite extreme is the use of language for the purpose of immediate exchange. Then words cease to have precise meanings and lose many of their plastic, sonorous, and emotive values. The speaker does not disappear; on the contrary, he is affirmed to excess. What grows thin and weak is the word, which becomes a mere medium of exchange. All its values are extinguished or decreased, at the expense of the relation value.

In the case of the exclamation, the word is a cry hurled at the void: it dispenses with the speaker. When the word is an instrument of abstract thought, the meaning devours everything: listener and verbal pleasure. A vehicle of exchange, it is degraded. In all three cases it is reduced and specialized. And the cause of this common mutilation is that language becomes for us a tool, an instrument, a thing. Each time we are served by words, we mutilate them. But the poet is not served by words. He is their servant. In serving them, he returns them to the plenitude of their nature, makes them recover their being. Thanks to poetry, language reconquers its original state. First, its plastic and sonorous values, generally disdained by thought; next, the affective values; and, finally, the expressive ones. To purify language, the poet's task, means to give it back its original nature. And here we come to one of the central themes of this reflection. The word, in itself, is a plurality of meanings. If by the action of poetry the word recovers its original nature—that is to say, its possibility of meaning two or more things at the same time—the poem seems to deny the very essence of language: meaning or sense. Poetry would be a futile and, at the same time, a monstrous undertaking: it depriving man of his most precious possession, language, and giving him in return a sonorous unintelligible babbling! What is the meaning of the words and phrases of the poem, if indeed they have a meaning?

3. Rhythm

WORDS BEHAVE LIKE capricious and autonomous beings. They always say "this and that" and, at the same time, "the other." Thought does not resign itself; unable to avoid their use, again and again it tries to reduce them to its own laws; and again and again language rebels and breaks the dikes of syntax and the dictionary. Lexicons and grammars are works condemned to remain unfinished. Language is always in motion, although man, because he is at the center of the maelstrom, is rarely aware of this incessant changing. That is why grammar, as if it were something static, affirms that language is a combination of words and that these words constitute the simplest unit, the linguistic cell. In reality, the vocable never occurs in isolation; no one speaks in disconnected words. Language is an indivisible whole; it is not formed of the sum of its words, as society is not the total of the individuals who compose it. An isolated word is incapable of constituting a meaningful unit. The disconnected word is not, properly, language; nor is a succession of vocables arranged haphazardly. Before language can be produced, the signs and sounds must be associated in such a way that they will imply and transmit a meaning. In the phrase the potential plurality of meanings of the separate word is transformed into a certain and unique, although not always rigorous and univocal, direction. Thus, it is not the word, but the phrase or sentence, that constitutes the simplest unit of speech. The phrase is a self-sufficient whole; as in a microcosm, all language dwells therein. Like the atom, it is an organism separable only by violence. And indeed, only by the violence of grammatical analysis is the phrase broken up into words. Language is a universe of meaningful units, that is, of phrases.

To verify the truth of these affirmations one has only to observe the writing of those who have not been trained in grammatical analysis. Children are incapable of isolating words. The teaching of grammar begins by showing them how to divide phrases into words and words into syllables and letters. But children have no consciousness of words; they have a very acute consciousness of phrases: they think, speak, and write in meaningful blocks and find it hard to understand that a phrase is made of words. Those who can scarcely write display the same tendency. As they write, they separate or join the words at random: they do not know for certain where one word ends and another begins. But when they speak, on the contrary, illiterate persons pause in all the right places: they think in phrases. Similarly, whenever we forget ourselves or become excited or lose control of ourselves, the natural language regains its rights and two or more words are joined on paper, not according to the rules of grammar but obeying the command of the thought. Whenever we are distracted, language reappears in its natural state, as it was prior to grammar. It could be argued that certain isolated words form meaningful units of themselves. In certain primitive languages the unit seems to be the word; the demonstrative pronouns of some of these languages do not merely indicate this or that, but "this one who is standing," "that one who is so close you could touch him," "that girl who is absent," "this visible man," and so on. But each of these words is a phrase. And so the isolated word is not language, even in the simplest tongues. Those pronouns are phrase-words.[1]

---

[1] Modern linguistics seems to contradict this opinion. Nevertheless, as we shall see, the contradiction is not absolute. To Roman Jakobson "the word is a constituent part of a higher contexture, the phrase, and simultaneously a contexture of other smaller

The poem possesses the same complex and indivisible character as language and its cell: the phrase. Every poem is a self-contained totality: it is a phrase or a group of phrases forming a whole. Like other men, the poet does not express himself in disconnected words, but in compact and inseparable units. The cell of the poem, its simplest nucleus, is the poetic phrase. But, unlike what occurs with prose, the unit of the phrase, that which constitutes it as such and makes it language, is not the sense or significative direction, but the rhythm. This disconcerting property of the poetic phrase will be studied later; but first it is essential to describe the manner in which the prosaic phrase—common speech—is transformed into a poetic phrase.

No one can escape from a belief in the magical power of words. Not even those who view them with suspicion. Reserve toward language is an intellectual attitude. We weigh and measure words only at certain moments; when that instant has passed, we have faith in them again. To trust language is man's spontaneous and original attitude: a thing is its name. Faith in the power of words is a reminiscence of our most ancient beliefs: nature is animate; each object has a life of its own; words, which are the doubles of the objective world, are also animate. Language, like the universe, is a world of calls and responses; flux and reflux, union and separation, inspiration and expiration. Some words attract, others repel each other, and all correspond. Speech is a cluster of living beings, moved by rhythms like the rhythms that rule the stars and the plants.

-----

constituent parts, the *morphemes* (minimal units endowed with meaning) and *phonemes*." The phonemes, in turn, are bundles or clusters of *differential traits*. Each differential trait as well as each phoneme stands against the other particles in a relation of opposition or contrast: phonemes "designate a mere otherness." Now, although they lack a meaning of their own, phonemes "partake of meaning" since their "function is to differentiate, establish, separate or emphasize" the morphemes and thus to distinguish them from each other. In turn, the morpheme only achieves an effective meaning in the word, and the word in the phrase or the phrase-word. So then, differential traits, phonemes, morphemes, and words are signs that are fully meaningful only in a context. Finally, the context has meaning and is intelligible only within a key that is common to the speaker and the listener: language. The semantic units (morphemes and words) and phonological units (differential traits and phonemes) are linguistic elements because they belong to a system of meanings that contains them. The linguistic units do not constitute language but vice versa: language constitutes them. Each unit, whether on the phonological or the significative level, is defined by its relation with the other parts: "language is an indivisible whole."

Everyone who has practiced automatic writing—insofar as this endeavor is possible—knows the strange and dazzling associations of language left to its own spontaneity. Evocation and convocation. "Les mots font l'amour," says André Breton. And a spirit as lucid as Alfonso Reyes issues a warning to the poet who is too sure of his dominion over language: "One day the words will band together against you and rise up in revolt all at the same time. . . ." But it is not necessary to resort to these literary testimonies. Dream, delirium, hypnosis, and other states of relaxation of consciousness favor the free flow of phrases. The current seems endless: one phrase leads us to another. Drawn by the river of images, we touch the shores of pure existence and divine a state of unity, of final reunion with our being and with the being of the world. Incapable of setting dikes against the tide, consciousness vacillates. And suddenly everything issues in a final image. A wall looms up before us: we return to silence.

Contrary states—extreme tension of consciousness, acute perception of language, dialogues in which intelligences clash and sparkle, transparent galleries multiplied to infinity by introspection—are also favorable for the sudden appearance of phrases fallen from heaven. No one has summoned them; they are like a reward for vigilance. After the striving of reason that opens the way, we reach a zone of harmony. Everything becomes easy, everything is a tacit reply, an awaited allusion. We feel that the ideas rhyme. Then we perceive that thoughts and phrases are also rhythms, calls, echoes. To think is to sound the right note, to vibrate as soon as the light wave touches us. Anger, enthusiasm, indignation, everything that takes us out of ourselves has the same liberating virtue. Unexpected phrases, possessing an electric force, appear: "she fulminated him with her glance," "thunder and lightning gushed from his mouth." The element fire governs all those expressions. Oaths and evil words explode like atrocious suns. There are curses and blasphemies that cause the cosmic order to tremble. Afterward, man feels surprise and remorse for what he said. The one who spoke those phrases was not really he, but "another": he was "beside himself." Amorous dialogues show the same character. Lovers "take the words out of each other's mouths." Everything coincides: pauses and exclamations, laughter and silence. The dialogue is not merely an accord: it is a harmonious chord. And the lovers themselves feel like two happy rhymes uttered by an invisible mouth.

Language is man, but it is something more. This could be the starting point for an examination of these troubling properties of words. But the poet does not ask himself how language is made and if that dynamism is his or only a reflex. With the innocent pragmatism of all creators, he confirms a fact and utilizes it: words come and flock together without being summoned by anyone; and their unions and separations are not the result of pure chance: an order governs the affinities and repulsions. At the heart of every verbal phenomenon there is a rhythm. Words unite and separate in accordance with certain rhythmic principles. If language is a continual push and pull of phrases and verbal associations governed by a secret rhythm, the reproduction of that rhythm will give us power over words. The dynamism of language leads the poet to create his verbal universe by utilizing the same forces of attraction and repulsion. The poet creates by analogy. His model is the rhythm that moves every language. The rhythm is a magnet. In reproducing it—by means of meter, rhyme, alliteration, paronomasia, and other procedures—he summons the words. Sterility gives way to a state of verbal abundance; when the inner sluices are opened, the phrases pour out like fountains or jets of water. The difficult thing, says Gabriela Mistral, is not to find rhymes but to avoid their abundance. Poetic creation consists, to a marked degree, in this voluntary utilization of rhythm as an agent of seduction.

The poetic process is not different from conjuration, enchantment, and other magical procedures. And the poet's attitude is very similar to the magician's. Both utilize the principle of analogy; both act for utilitarian and immediate ends: they do not ask themselves what language or nature is, but use them for their own purposes. It is not difficult to add another trait: magicians and poets, unlike philosophers, technicians, and sages, draw their powers from themselves. To do their work it is not enough for them to possess a body of knowledge, as is the case with a physicist or a chauffeur. Every magical operation requires an inner force, achieved by a painful effort at purification. The sources of magic power are twofold: formulas and other methods of enchantment, and the enchanter's psychic power, his spiritual refinement that permits him to bring his rhythm in tune with the rhythm of the cosmos. The same occurs with the poet. The language of the poem is in him and only to him is it revealed. The poetic revelation involves an inner search. A search that in no way resembles introspection or analysis; more than a search, a psychic activity capable of bringing on the passivity that favors the outcropping of images.

The magician is often compared to the rebel. The seduction his figure still exerts on us results from his having been the first to say no to the gods and yes to the human will. All other rebellions—those, precisely, by which man has become man—stem from this first rebellion. In the figure of the wizard there is a tragic tension that is absent in the man of science and the philosopher. The latter serve knowledge, and in their world the gods and natural forces are merely hypotheses and unknown quantities. For the magician, the gods are not hypotheses, nor, as for the believer, realities that must be appeased or loved, but powers that must be seduced, conquered, and used. Magic is a dangerous and sacrilegious enterprise, an affirmation of human power vis-à-vis the supernatural. Separated from the human herd, facing the gods, the magician is alone. His greatness and, almost always, his final sterility is rooted in that aloneness. On the one hand, it is a testimony of his tragic decision. On the other, of his pride. Indeed, every magic that is not transcended—that is, not transformed into a gift, into philanthropy—consumes itself and ends by consuming its creator. The magician sees men as instruments, forces, nuclei of latent energy. One form of magic consists in the dominion over self for ultimate dominion over others. Princes, kings, and leaders surround themselves with magicians and astrologers, the precursors of political advisers. The formulas for magic power are fatally bound up with tyranny and the domination of men. The magician's is a solitary rebellion, because the essence of magical activity is the quest for power. The similarities between magic and technology have frequently been pointed out, and some think that the former is the remote source of the latter. Whether or not this hypothesis is valid, it is obvious that the characteristic mark of modern technology—like that of ancient magic—is the cult of power. Standing opposite the magician is Prometheus, the loftiest figure created by Western imagination. Neither magician, nor philosopher, nor sage: hero, stealer of fire, philanthropist. The Promethean revolt embodies the revolt of mankind. Implicit in the chained hero's alone-ness throbs the return to the world of men. The magician's solitude is a solitude with no return. His revolt is sterile because magic—that is to say, the quest for power by power—ends by annihilating itself. And this, precisely, is the drama of modern society.

The ambivalence of magic can be summed up as follows: on the one hand, it tries to put man in an active relation with the cosmos, and in this sense it is a sort of universal communion; on the other, its practice merely implies the quest for power. "Why?" is a question that magic does not ask and one that it cannot answer without being transformed into something else: religion, philosophy, philanthropy. In short, magic is a conception of the world but it is not an idea of man. That is why the magician is a figure torn between his communication with the cosmic forces and his inability to reach man, except as one of those forces. Magic affirms the brotherhood of life—an identical current runs through the universe—and denies the brotherhood of men.

Certain creations of modern poetry are inhabited by the same tension. Mallarmé's work is, perhaps, the supreme example. Never have words been more fully packed and fraught with themselves; so much so, that we scarcely recognize them, like those tropical flowers that look black by dint of their redness. Each word shimmers, such is its clarity. But it is a mineral clarity: it reflects and engulfs us, without giving off cold or heat. A language as sublime as this deserved the baptism of fire of the theater. Only on the stage could it have been consumed and consummated fully and, thus, truly incarnated. Mallarmé tried it. Not only has he left us a number of poetic fragments that are theatrical attempts, but a reflection on that impossible and en-visioned theater. But there is no theater without a common poetic word. The tension of Mallarmé's poetic language is consumed in itself. His myth is not philanthropic; he is not Prometheus, the one who gives fire to men, but Igitur: the one who contemplates himself. His clarity ends by igniting him. The arrow returns to strike the one who shoots it, when the target is our own questioning image. Mallarmé's greatness lies not just in his attempt to create a language that would

be the magic double of the universe—the Work conceived as a Cosmos
—but above all in the consciousness of the impossibility of transform-
ing that language into theater, into a dialogue with man. If the work
is not resolved into theater, it has no alternative but to end in the blank
page. The magical act is transmuted into suicide. By the path of the
magical language the French poet arrives at silence. But every human
silence contains an utterance. We remain silent, Sor Juana said, not
because we have nothing to say, but because we do not know how to
say all that we should like to say. Human silence is a being still and,
therefore, it is implicit communication, latent meaning. Mallarmé's
silence says *nothing* to us, which does not mean that it says nothing. It
is the silence that precedes silence.

The poet is not a magician, but his conception of language as a
"society of life"—as Cassirer defines the magical vision of the cosmos
—brings him close to magic. Although the poem is not an enchant-
ment or conjuration, in the manner of spells and sortileges the poet
awakens the secret powers of language. The poet bewitches the lan-
guage by means of rhythm. One image sprouts from another. Thus,
the predominant function of rhythm distinguishes the poem from all
other literary forms. The poem is a mass of phrases, a verbal order,
founded on rhythm.

If we beat a drum at regular intervals, the rhythm will appear as
time divided into equal parts. This abstraction could be represented
graphically by a line of dashes: - - - - - - - - - -. The rhythmic intensity
will depend on the speed with which the beats fall on the drumhead.
Shorter intervals will produce increased violence. The variations will
also depend on the combination of beats and intervals. For example:
-I--I-I--I-I--I-I--I-I--, and so on. Even reduced to this outline, rhythm is
something more than measure, something more than time divided into
parts. The succession of beats and pauses reveals a certain intention-
ality, something like a plan. Rhythm provokes an expectation, arouses
a yearning. If it is interrupted, we feel a shock. Something has been
broken. If it continues, we expect something that we cannot identify
precisely. Rhythm engenders in us a state of mind that will only be
calmed when "something" happens. It puts us in an attitude of wait-

ing. We feel that the rhythm is a moving toward something, even though we may not know what that something is. Every rhythm is a sense of something. So then, rhythm is not exclusively a measure devoid of content but a direction, a sense. Rhythm is not measure, but original time. And measure is not time, but a way to calculate it. Heidegger has shown that every measure is a "mode of making time present." Calendars and clocks are ways to mark our steps. This presentation implies a reduction or abstraction of the original time: the clock presents time and in order to present it, divides it into equal parts devoid of meaning. Temporality—which is man himself and which, therefore, gives meaning to what he touches—is prior to the presentation and that which makes it possible.

Time is not outside us, nor is it something that passes before our eyes like the hands of the clock: we are time and it is not the years that pass but we ourselves. Time has a direction, a sense, because it is we ourselves. Rhythm performs an operation contrary to that of clocks and calendars: time ceases to be abstract measure and returns to that which it is: something concrete and possessed of direction. Continual flow, perpetual going beyond, time is a permanent transcending itself. Its essence is the *more*—and the negation of that more. Time affirms meaning in a paradoxical way: it possesses a meaning—the going beyond, always outside itself—that does not cease to deny itself as meaning. It destroys itself and, in destroying itself, repeats itself, but each repetition is a change. Always the same and the negation of the same. Thus, it is never mere measure, empty succession. When rhythm unfolds before us, something passes with it: we ourselves. In the rhythm there is a "going toward," which can only be elucidated if, at the same time, what we are is elucidated. Rhythm is not measure, or something that is outside us, but we ourselves are the ones who flow in the rhythm and rush headlong toward "something." Rhythm is meaning and it says "something." Thus, its verbal or ideological content is not separable. What the poet's words say is already being said by the rhythm on which those words rest. What is more: those words are the natural outgrowth of the rhythm, as the flower from the stem. The relation between rhythm and poetic word is no different from that which prevails between dance and musical rhythm: it cannot be said that the rhythm is the sonorous representation of the dance; nor that the dance is the corporal translation of the rhythm. All dances are rhythms; all rhythms, dances. The dance is already in the rhythm, and vice versa.

Rituals and mythical tales show that it is impossible to dissociate the rhythm from its meaning. Rhythm was a magical procedure with an immediate purpose: to bewitch and imprison certain forces, to exorcise others. It also served to commemorate or, more precisely, to reproduce certain myths: the appearance of a demon or the arrival of a god, the end of one time or the beginning of another. A double of the cosmic rhythm, it was a creative force, in the literal sense of the word, capable of producing what man desired: rainfall, plenty in the hunt, or the enemy's death. Dancing already contained the representation, in the germ; the dance and the pantomime were also a drama and a ceremony: a ritual. Rhythm was a rite. Moreover, we know that rite and myth are inseparable realities. The presence of the rite is found in every mythical story because the tale is merely the translation into words of the ritual ceremony: the myth relates or describes the rite. And the rite makes the story immediate; by means of dances and ceremonies the myth is incarnated and repeated: the hero returns among men once again and conquers demons, the earth is covered with verdure and the radiant face of the disinterred girl appears, the time that ends is born again and a new cycle begins.

The tale and its representation are inseparable. Both are already in the rhythm, which is drama and dance, myth and rite, story and ceremony. The twofold reality of the myth and the rite rests on the rhythm, which contains them. Again it becomes evident that, far from being empty and abstract measure, rhythm is inseparable from a specific content. It is the same with verbal rhythm: the phrase or "poetic idea" does not precede the rhythm, nor does the latter precede the former. They are one and the same. The phrase and its possible meaning are already latent in the verse. That is why there are heroic and light, dancing and solemn, gay and funereal meters.

Rhythm is not measure: it is a vision of the world. Calendars, morality, politics, technology, arts, philosophies, in short everything we call culture is rooted in rhythm. It is the source of all our creations.

Binary or tertiary rhythms, rhythms antagonistic or cyclical, nourish institutions, beliefs, arts, and philosophies. History itself is rhythm. And every civilization can be reduced to the development of a primordial rhythm. The ancient Chinese saw (perhaps it may be more accurate to say heard) the universe as the cyclical combination of two rhythms: "Now Yin—then Yang: that is the Tao." Yin and Yang are not ideas, at least in the Western sense of the word, as Granet observes; nor are they mere sounds and notes: they are emblems, images that contain a concrete representation of the universe. Endowed with a dynamism creative of realities, Yin and Yang alternate, and in alternating they engender the whole. Nothing in that whole has been suppressed or removed; every aspect is present, alive, and in possession of its particularities. Yin is winter, the season of women, the house, and the shadow. Its symbol is the door, that which is closed and hidden and matures in darkness. Yang is light, agricultural work, hunting and fishing, fresh air, the time of men, openness. Heat and cold, light and darkness, "time of plenitude and time of decrepitude: masculine time and feminine time—a dragon aspect and a serpent aspect—that is life." The universe is a bipartite system of contrary, alternating, and complementary rhythms. Rhythm rules the growth of plants and empires, of crops and institutions. It governs morality and etiquette. The libertinism of princes alters the cosmic order; but then, at certain periods, so does their chastity. Courtesy and good government are rhythmic forms, like love and the change of seasons. Rhythm is a sharp image of the universe, a visible embodiment of the cosmic legality: Yi Yin—Yi Yang. "Now Yin—then Yang: that is the Tao."[2]

The Chinese are not the only people who have perceived the universe as union, separation, and reunion of rhythms. All of man's cosmological conceptions stem from the intuition of an original rhythm. At the heart of every culture there is a fundamental attitude toward life that, before being expressed in religious, aesthetic, or philosophical creations, is manifested as rhythm. Yin and Yang for the Chinese; quaternary rhythm for the Aztecs; dual for the Hebrews. The Greeks conceive the cosmos as a struggle and combination of opposites. Our

[2] Marcel Granet, *La pensée chinoise* (Paris, 1938).

culture is impregnated with ternary rhythms. From logic and religion
to politics and medicine they seem to be ruled by two elements that are
fused and absorbed into a unit: father, mother, son; thesis, antithesis,
synthesis; comedy, drama, tragedy; hell, purgatory, heaven; sanguine,
muscular, and nervous constitutions; memory, will, and understand-
ing; animal, vegetable, and mineral kingdoms; aristocracy, monarchy,
and democracy. . . . This is not the place to ponder whether rhythm is
an expression of primitive social institutions, of the production sys-
tem or other "causes," or if, on the contrary, the so-called social struc-
tures are merely manifestations of this first and spontaneous attitude
of man toward reality. Such a question, perhaps the essential question
of history, possesses the same vertiginous character as the question
about man's being—because that being seems to have no support or
foundation but rather, cast out or exhaled, one would say that it rests
on its own infinity. But if we cannot provide an answer to this prob-
lem, at least it is possible to affirm that rhythm is inseparable from our
condition. I mean: it is the simplest, most permanent, and most ancient
manifestation of the decisive fact that causes us to be men: the fact
that we are temporal, mortal, and always thrown toward "something,"
toward the "other": death, God, the beloved, our fellow-men.

The constant presence of rhythmic forms in all human expressions
could not fail to provoke the temptation to construct a philosophy
founded on rhythm. But each society has a rhythm of its own. Or
more precisely: each rhythm is an attitude, a sense, and an image of
the world, distinct and particular. Just as it is impossible to reduce
rhythms to pure measure, divided into homogeneous spaces, it is also
impossible to isolate them and convert them into rational schemes.
Each rhythm implies a concrete vision of the world. Thus, the univer-
sal rhythm of which some philosophers speak is an abstraction that has
scarcely any relation with the original rhythm, creative of images,
poems, and works. Rhythm, which is image and sense, man's sponta-
neous attitude toward life, is not outside us: it is we ourselves, ex-
pressing ourselves. It is concrete temporality, unrepeatable human life.
The rhythm that Dante perceives and which moves stars and souls is
called Love; Lao-Tse and Chuang-Tzu hear another rhythm, made of
relative opposites; Heraclitus heard it as war. It is not possible to

reduce all these rhythms to unity without having each suffer a simultaneous evaporation of its particular content. Rhythm is not philosophy, but an image of the world, that is to say, the thing that philosophies lean on.

In every society there are two calendars. One governs daily life and profane activities; the other, sacred periods, rites, and festivals. The former is a division of time into equal parts: hours, days, months, years. Whatever system may be used to measure it, time is a quantitative succession of homogeneous parts. In the sacred calendar, on the contrary, the continuity is broken. The mythical date arrives if a series of circumstances combine to reproduce the event. Unlike the profane date, the sacred one is not a measure but a living reality, charged with supernatural forces, which is incarnated in determinate places. In the profane representation of time, January 1 necessarily follows December 31. In the religious one, it may very well happen that the new time will not follow the old. Every culture has felt the horror of the "end of time." That is the reason for the existence of "rites of entrance and exit." Among the ancient Mexicans the rites of fire—held at the end of each year and especially at the end of the 52-year cycle—had the sole purpose of provoking the arrival of the new time. The whole Valley of Mexico, submerged in shadows up to that moment, was illuminated as soon as the bonfires were lighted on the Hill of the Star. Once again the myth had been incarnated. Time—a time creative of life and not an empty succession—had been reengendered. Life could continue until that time, in turn, had been used up. An admirable plastic example of this idea is the Burial of Time, a small stone monument in the Anthropology Museum of Mexico: surrounded by skulls lie the signs of the old time: the new time sprouts from their remains. But its rebirth is not inevitable. Some myths, like that of the Grail, allude to the obstinacy of the old time, which insists on not dying, on not going away: sterility prevails; the fields are scorched; women do not conceive; the old people govern. The "exit rites"—which almost always include the redeeming intervention of a young hero—oblige the old time to give way to its successor.

If the mythical date is not inserted in pure succession, in what time does it occur? Stories give us the answer: "Once upon a time there was a king. . . ." The myth is not situated on a definite date, but on a "once upon a time," a knot in which space and time are intertwined. The myth is a past that is also a future. Because the temporal region where myths occur is not the irreparable and finite yesterday of every human act, but a past charged with possibilities, susceptible of being made present. The myth takes place in an archetypal time. Moreover, it is archetypal time, capable of being reincarnated. The sacred calendar is rhythmic because it is archetypal. The myth is a past that is a future ready to be realized in a present. In our quotidian conception of it, time is a present that moves toward the future but fatally issues in the past. The mythical order inverts the terms: the past is a future that issues in the present. The profane calendar blocks our access to the original time that embraces all times, past or future, in a present, in a total presence. The mythical date causes us to glimpse a present that marries the past to the future. Thus, the myth contains human life in its totality: by means of rhythm it brings immediacy to an archetypal past, that is, a past that is potentially a future ready to be incarnated in a present. Nothing could be further from our quotidian conception of time. In everyday life we persist obstinately in the chronometrical representation of time, even though we speak of "bad time" and "good time" and say goodbye to the old year and greet the arrival of the new one each December 31. None of these attitudes—relics of the ancient conception of time—keeps us from tearing off a leaf of the calendar each day, or consulting the clock for the hour. Our "good time" is not separated from succession; we can long for the past—which is thought to be better than the present—but we know that the past will not return. Our "good time" dies the same death as every time: it is succession. On the other hand, the mythical date does not die: it is repeated, incarnated. And so, what distinguishes the mythical time from every other representation of time is that it is an archetype. A past always susceptible to being today, the myth is a floating reality, always ready to be incarnated and to be again.

The function of rhythm now becomes clearer: by the action of the rhythmic repetition the myth returns. In their classic study on this subject, Hubert and Mauss observe the discontinuous character of the

sacred calendar and find the origin of this discontinuity in the rhyth-
mical magic: "The mythical representation of time is essentially
rhythmic. For religion and magic the purpose of the calendar is not to
measure, but to rhythm, time."[3] It is obviously not a case of "rhyth-
ming" time—a positivistic lapse of these authors—but of returning to
the original time. Rhythmic repetition is invocation and convocation of
the original time. And more exactly: re-creation of archetypal time.
Not all myths are poems, but every poem is a myth. As in the myth, in
the poem quotidian time undergoes a transmutation: it ceases to be
homogeneous and empty succession and becomes rhythm. Tragedy,
epic, song, the poem tends to repeat and to re-create an instant, act,
or group of acts that, in some manner, are archetypal. The time of the
poem is different from clock time. "What is done is done," people
say. To the poet what was done will be again, will be incarnated again.
The poet, says the centaur Chiron to Faust, "is not bound by time."
And Faust replies: "Achilles found Helen outside of time." Outside
of time? Rather, in the original time. Even in historical novels and in
those with a contemporary theme, the time of the story is separated
from succession. The past and the present of novels is not that of his-
tory, nor that of newspaper reporting. It is not what was, nor what is
being, but what is becoming: what is being gestated. It is a past that
is reengendered and reincarnated. And it is reincarnated in two ways;
at the moment of poetic creation, and later, as re-creation, when the
reader relives the poet's images and convokes again that past that re-
turns. The poem is archetypal time, which becomes present as soon as
some lips repeat its rhythmic phrases. Those rhythmic phrases are
what we call verses and their function is to re-create time.

In discussing the origin of poetry, Aristotle says: "In sum, the spe-
cial causes of the origin of poetry seem to have been two, both natural:
first, from childhood on it is connatural to men to reproduce imitative-
ly; and in this man differs from the other animals: in that he is much
more of an imitator than all of them and he takes his first steps in
learning by means of imitation; second, in that all take delight in imi-

[3] H. Hubert and M. Mauss, *Mélanges d'histoire des religions* (Paris, 1929).

tative reproductions."[4] And later he adds that the proper object of this imitative reproduction is contemplation by similarity or comparison: the metaphor is the principal instrument of poetry, since the image—which approximates and makes similar distant or opposite objects—permits the poet to say that this is similar to that. Aristotle's poetics has been widely criticized. But, contrary to what one would feel inclined to think instinctively, what we find inadequate is not so much the concept of imitative reproduction as his idea of the metaphor and, above all, his notion of nature.

As García Bacca explains in his introduction to the *Poetics*, "to imitate does not mean to set out to copy an original . . . but every action whose effect is to make a thing present." And the effect of such imitation, "which, literally, does not copy anything, will be an original object, never seen, or never heard, such as a symphony or a sonata." But from what place does the poet take those objects that were never seen or heard before? The poet's model is nature, a paradigm and source of inspiration for all Greeks. It is more accurate to call Greek art naturalistic than the art of Zola and his disciples. Now, one of the things that distinguishes us from the Greeks is our conception of nature. We do not know what it is like, or what its figure is, if it has one. Nature has ceased to be something animate, an organic whole possessed of a form. It is not even an object, because the very idea of object has lost its former consistency. If the notion of cause is interdicted, does it not follow that the notion of nature, with its four causes, will also be? Nor do we know where the natural ends and the human begins. For centuries now, man has ceased to be natural. Some conceive him as a bundle of impulses and reflexes, that is, as a higher animal. Others have transformed this animal into a series of responses to certain stimuli, that is, an entity whose conduct is predictable and whose reactions are not unlike those of an apparatus: for cybernetics, man behaves like a machine. At the opposite pole are those who conceive us as historical entities, with no more continuity than that of change. And that is not all. Nature and history have become incompatible terms, the opposite of what occurred with the Greeks. If man is an animal or a machine,

[4] Aristotle, *Poetics*, direct version, introduction and notes by Juan David García Bacca (Mexico City, 1945).

I do not see how he can be a political entity, except by reducing politics to a branch of biology or physics. And contrariwise: if he is historical, he is not natural or mechanical. So then, what we find strange and out-moded—as García Bacca rightly observes—is not Aristotle's poetics, but his ontology. Nature cannot be a model for us, because the term has lost all its consistency.

The Aristotelian idea of the metaphor seems equally unsatisfactory. For Aristotle, poetry is at the midpoint between history and philosophy. The former rules over events, the latter governs the world of the necessary. Between both extremes poetry presents itself "as the optative." "It is not the poet's task," says García Bacca, "to tell things as they happened, but as we would have liked them to happen." The realm of poetry is the "I wish." The poet is a "man of desires." Indeed, poetry is desire. But that desire is not articulated in the possible, or in the likely. The image is not the "likely impossible," desire for impossibles: poetry is hunger for reality. Desire always aspires to suppress distances, as is seen in the desire *par excellence*: the amorous impulse. The image is the bridge that desire places between man and reality. The world of the "I wish" is that of the image by comparison of similarities and its principal vehicle is the word "like": this is like that. But there is another metaphor that suppresses the "like" and says: this is that. In it, desire becomes active: it does not compare or show similarities but it reveals—and further, it causes—the ultimate identity of objects that seemed irreducible to us.

Then, in what sense do we find Aristotle's idea true? In the sense that poetry is an imitative reproduction, if one understands by this that the poet re-creates archetypes, in the oldest acceptance of the word: models, myths. Even the lyric poet, in re-creating his experience, convokes a past that is a future. It is not a paradox to affirm that the poet—like children, primitives and, in short, like all men when they give free rein to their deepest and most natural tendency—is an imitator by profession. That imitation is original creation: evocation, resurrection, and re-creation of something that is in the origin of times and in each man's nature, something that is confused with time itself and with us, and which, belonging to all, is also unique and singular. Poetic rhythm is the bringing immediacy to that past that is a future that is a present:

we ourselves. The poetic phrase is living, concrete time: it is rhythm, original time, perpetually re-creating itself. Continual rebirth and re-death and rebirth again. The unity of the phrase, which in prose is given by the sense or meaning, is achieved in the poem by the rhythm. Poetic coherence, therefore, must be of a different order from prose. The rhythmic phrase thus brings us to the examination of its meaning. Nevertheless, before studying how the significative unity of the poetic phrase is achieved, it is necessary to inspect the relations between verse and prose more closely.

4. Verse and Prose

RHYTHM IS NOT ONLY the most ancient and permanent element of language, but it may well precede speech itself. In a certain sense it can be said that language springs from rhythm; or, at least, that every rhythm implies or prefigures a language. Thus, all verbal expressions, not excluding the most abstract or didactic forms of prose, are rhythm. How, then, can one distinguish prose and poem? Thus: rhythm is given spontaneously in every verbal form, but only in the poem is it manifested completely. Without rhythm, there is no poem; with rhythm alone, there is no prose. Rhythm is a condition of the poem, while it is unessential for prose. By the violence of reason words separate from rhythm; that rational violence keeps prose in suspense, preventing it from falling into the mainstream of speech where the laws of attraction and repulsion, not those of discourse, prevail. But that separation is never total, because then language would be destroyed. And with it, thought itself. Language, by its own inclination, tends to be rhythm. As if they were obeying a mysterious law of gravity, words return to poetry spontaneously. At the heart of all prose, more or less attenuated by the demands of discourse, circulates the invisible rhythmic current. And thought, insofar as it is language, suffers the same fascination. To set thought free, to wander, is to return to rhythm; reasons are transformed into correspondences, syllogisms into analogies, and the intellectual march into a flow of images. But the prose writer seeks coherence and conceptual clarity. Therefore he resists the rhythmic current that, fatally, tends to manifest itself in images and not in concepts.

Prose is a tardy genre, offspring of thought's distrust of the natural tendencies of language. Poetry belongs to all epochs: it is man's natural form of expression. There are no peoples without poetry; there are some without prose. Therefore, it can be said that prose is not a form of expression inherent in society, while the existence of a society without songs, myths, or other poetic expressions is inconceivable. Poetry knows nothing of progress or evolution, and its beginnings and its end are confused with those of language. Prose, which is primordially a tool of criticism and analysis, requires a slow maturation and is only produced after a long series of efforts aimed at taming speech. Its advance is measured by the degree of the thought's dominion over the words. Prose grows in a permanent battle against the natural inclinations of language and its most perfect genres are discourse and demonstration, in which rhythm and its incessant coming and going give place to the progress of the thought.

While the poem presents itself as a closed order, prose tends to be manifested as an open and linear construction. Valéry has compared prose to the march and poetry to the dance. Narrative or discourse, history or demonstration, prose is a parade, a real theory of ideas or events. The geometric figure that symbolizes prose is the line: straight, crooked, spiral, zigzag, but always moving forward and with a precise goal. That is why the archetypes of prose are discourse and narrative, speculation and history. The poem, on the contrary, offers itself as a circle or a sphere: something that is closed on itself, a self-sufficient universe in which the end is also a beginning that returns, is repeated and re-created. And this constant repetition and re-creation is nothing but rhythm, tide that comes and goes, falls and rises. The artificial character of prose is proved each time the prose writer abandons himself to the flow of language. As soon as he turns in on himself, in the manner of the poet or the musician, and allows himself to be seduced by the forces of attraction and repulsion of language, he violates the laws of rational thought and penetrates the ambit of echoes and correspondences of the poem. This is what has happened with a large segment of the contemporary novel. The same can be said of certain Eastern novels, such as *The Tale of Genji*, by Lady Murasaki, or the famous Chinese novel, the *Dream of the Red Chamber*. The former is reminiscent of Proust, that is, of the author who has carried further than anyone else the ambiguity of the novel, always oscillating between prose and rhythm, concept and image; the latter is a vast allegory that could hardly be called a novel without causing the word to lose its usual meaning. In reality, the only Eastern works that approximate to what we call novels are books that vacillate between apologue, pornography, and genre writing, such as the *Chin P'ing Mei*.

To hold that the rhythm is the nucleus of the poem does not mean that the poem is a conglomeration of meters. The existence of a prose charged with poetry, and of many correctly versified and absolutely prosaic works, reveals the falseness of this identification. Meter and rhythm are not the same thing. The ancient rhetoricians said that rhythm is the father of meter. When a meter becomes empty of content and is converted into an inert form, a mere sonorous husk, the rhythm continues to engender new meters. The rhythm is inseparable from the phrase; it is not made of disconnected words, nor is it merely measure or syllabic quantity, accents, and pauses: it is image and meaning. Rhythm, image, and meaning are given simultaneously in an indivisible and compact unit: the poetic phrase, the verse. Meter, on the other hand, is abstract measure, independent from the image. The only exigency of meter is that each verse must have the required syllables and accents. Everything can be said in hendecasyllables: a mathematical formula, a cooking recipe, the siege of Troy, and a succession of unconnected words. One can even dispense with the word: a line of syllables or letters is enough. In itself, meter is measure divested of sense. On the other hand, rhythm is never given alone; it is not measure, but qualitative and concrete content. Every verbal rhythm already contains the image and constitutes, actually or potentially, a complete poetic phrase.

Meter is born of rhythm and returns to it. At first the boundaries between the two are imprecise. Later the meter is crystallized into fixed forms. Instant of splendor, but also of paralysis. Isolated from the flux and reflux of language, the verse is transformed into sonorous measure. The moment of accord is followed by another of immobility; then, discord supervenes and a struggle begins at the heart of the poem: the measure oppresses the image or the image breaks the prison and returns to speech to be re-created in new rhythms. Meter is measure that tends to separate from language; rhythm never separates from speech because it is speech itself. Meter is method, manner; rhythm, concrete temporality. A hendecasyllable by Garcilaso is not identical to one by Quevedo or Góngora. The measure is the same but the rhythm is different. The reason for this singularity is found, in Spanish, in the existence of rhythmic periods within each meter, after the first accented syllable and before the last. The rhythmic period forms the nucleus of the verse and does not conform to syllabic regularity but to the stress of the accents and the combination of the accents with the caesuras and slack syllables. In turn, each period is composed of at least two rhythmic clauses, also formed of tonic accents and caesuras. "The formal representation of the verse," says Tomás Navarro in his treatise *Métrica española*, "results from its metrical and grammatical components; the function of the period is essentially rhythmic; whether the movement of the verse is slow or fast, serious or light, serene or troubled depends on its composition and dimensions." Rhythm infuses meter with life and gives it individuality.[1]

[1] In *Linguistics and Poetics*, Jakobson says that "far from being an abstract, theoretical scheme, meter—or in more explicit terms, *verse design*—underlies the structure of any single line—or, in logical terminology, any single *verse instance*. . . . The verse design determines the invariant features of the verse instances and sets up the limit of variations." He then cites the example of Serbian peasants who improvise poems with fixed meters and recite them without ever making a mistake in the measure. It is possible that, indeed, meter may be unconscious measure, at least in certain cases (the Spanish octosyllable would be one of them). Nevertheless, Jakobson's observation does not annul the difference between meter and concrete verse. The reality of the former is ideal, it is a model and, therefore, it is a measure, an abstraction. The concrete verse is unique: *Resuelta en polvo ya, mas siempre hermosa* (Lope de Vega) is a hendecasyllable accented on the sixth syllable, as are *Y en uno de mis ojos te llagaste* (Saint John of the Cross) and *De ponderosa vana pesadumbre* (Góngora). It is impossible to confuse them: each has a distinct rhythm. In sum, three realities

The distinction between meter and rhythm precludes giving the name poem to a large number of correctly versified works that, out of sheer inertia, appear as such in the manuals of literature. Such works as *Les Chants de Maldoror, Alice in Wonderland* or *El Jardín de senderos que se bifurcan* are poems. In them prose denies itself; the phrases do not follow one another obeying the conceptual order or the order of the narrative, but are governed by the laws of the image and the rhythm. There is an ebb and flow of images, accents and pauses, the unequivocal mark of poetry. The same must be said of contemporary free verse: the quantitative elements of the meter have given place to the rhythmic unity. Occasionally—for example, in contemporary French poetry—the emphasis has shifted from the sonorous elements to the visual ones. But the rhythm remains: the pause, alliteration, paronomasia, the clash of sounds, the verbal tide subsist. Free verse is a rhythmic unit. D. H. Lawrence says that the unity of free verse is given by the image and not the external measure. And he cites Walt Whitman's lines, which are like the systole and diastole of a powerful heart. Free verse is a unit and is almost always uttered as a unit. The modern image is broken in the old meters: it does not fit in the traditional measure of fourteen or eleven syllables, which did not occur when meters were the natural expression of speech. The verses of Garcilaso, Herrera, Fray Luis, or any poet of the sixteenth and seventeenth centuries almost always constitute units of themselves: each verse is also an image or a complete phrase. There was a relation, which has disappeared, between those poetic forms and the language of their time. The same is true of contemporary free verse: each verse is an image and it is not necessary to take a breath in order to say it. Therefore, punctuation is often unnecessary: the poem is a rhythmic flux and reflux of words. Nevertheless, the increasing predominance of the intellectual and visual over the respiration reveals that our free verse threatens to be converted, like the alexandrine and the hendeca-

---

would have to be considered: the rhythm of the language in this or that place and at a determinate historical moment; the meters derived from the rhythm of the language or adapted from other versification systems; and each poet's rhythm. This last is the distinctive element and is what separates versified literature from poetry properly so called.

syllable, into a mechanical measure. This is particularly true of contemporary French poetry.[2]

Meters are historical, while rhythm is confused with language itself. It is not difficult to distinguish in each meter the intellectual and abstract elements and the more purely rhythmic ones. In modern languages meters are composed of a determinate number of syllables, with the duration cut by the tonic accents and pauses. The accents and pauses constitute the oldest and the purely rhythmic part of meter; they are still close to drumbeats, ritual ceremonies, and dancing heels striking the earth. The accent is dance and rite. Thanks to the accent, meter stands up and is a dancing unit. The syllabic measure implies a principle of abstraction, a rhetoric and a reflection on language. Purely linear duration, it tends to be converted into a pure mechanism. The accents, pauses, alliteration, clashes or unexpected unions of one sound with another constitute the concrete and permanent part of meter. Languages oscillate between prose and poem, rhythm and discourse. In some the predominance of rhythm is visible; in others one observes an excessive increase of the analytical and discursive elements at the expense of the rhythmic and imaginative ones. The struggle between the natural tendencies of language and the exigencies of abstract thought is expressed in the modern languages of the West by the duality of the meters: at one extreme, syllabic versification, fixed measure; at the opposite pole, the free play of accents and pauses. Latin languages and Germanic languages. Ours tend to make of rhythm a fixed measure. This inclination is not strange, because they are the offspring of Rome. The importance of syllabic versification reveals the imperialism of discourse and grammar. And this predominance of measure also explains why modern poetic creations in our languages are, likewise, rebellions against the syllabic versification system. In its attenuated forms the rebellion preserves the meter, but emphasizes the visual value of the image or introduces elements that break or alter the measure: colloquial expressions, humor, the phrase that straddles two lines, changes of accents and of pauses, and so on. In other cases the revolt presents itself as a return to the popular and spontaneous forms

[2] Concerning verbal and physiological rhythms, see Appendix II.

of poetry. And in its most extreme attempts it dispenses with meter and chooses prose or free verse as the medium of expression. With the powers of convocation and evocation of the traditional rhyme and meter exhausted, the poet doubles back in search of the original language. And he finds the primitive nucleus: rhythm.

The enthusiasm with which the French poets received German romanticism must be seen as an instinctive rebellion against syllabic versification and all that it signifies. In German, as in English, language is not a victim of rational analysis. The predominance of the rhythmic values facilitated the adventure of romantic thought. In the face of the rationalism of the century of enlightenment, romanticism brandishes a philosophy of nature and man based on the principle of analogy: "Everything," says Baudelaire in *L'Art romantique*, "in the spiritual realm as well as the natural, is significant, reciprocal, correspondent . . . everything is hieroglyphic . . . and the poet is merely the translator, the one who deciphers." Rhythmic versification and analogical thought are two sides of the same coin. Thanks to rhythm we perceive this universal correspondence; or rather, that correspondence is but the manifestation of rhythm. To return to rhythm involves a change of attitude toward reality; and vice versa: to adopt the principle of analogy means to return to rhythm. In affirming the powers of accentual versification as against the artifices of fixed meter, the romantic poet proclaims the triumph of the image over the concept, and the triumph of analogy over logical thought.

The evolution of modern poetry in French and in English is an example of the relations between verbal rhythm and poetic creation. French is a language without tonic accents; the resources of the pause and the caesura replace them. In English, what really counts is the accent. English poetry tends to be pure rhythm: dance, song. French: discourse, "poetic meditation." In French, the practice of poetry obliges one to go against the tendencies of the language. In English, to go along with the current. The former is the least poetic of modern languages, the least unexpected; the latter abounds in strange expressions loaded with verbal surprise. And thus the modern poetic revolution has different meanings in both languages.

The rhythmic richness of English leaves its stamp on the Elizabe-
than theater, the poetry of the "metaphysicals" and that of the ro-
mantics. Nevertheless, with a certain clockwork regularity there appear
reactions of a contrary sign, periods in which English poetry seeks to
insert itself again into the Latin tradition. It seems otiose to cite Mil-
ton, Dryden, and Pope. These names evoke a versification system op-
posed to what could be called the native English tradition: Milton's
blank verse, more Latin than English, and Pope's favorite medium, the
"heroic couplet." With regard to the latter, Dryden said that "it
bounds and circumscribes the Fancy." The rhyme regulates the fancy,
it is a dike against the verbal tide, a channeling of the rhythm. The first
half of our century has also been a "Latin" reaction, in an opposite di-
rection from the movement of the preceding century, from Blake to
the first Yeats. (I say "first" because this poet, like Juan Ramón Jimé-
nez, is several poets.) The renewal of modern English poetry is due
principally to two poets and a novelist: Ezra Pound, T. S. Eliot, and
James Joyce. Although their works cannot be more dissimilar, a com-
mon note unites them: they are all a reconquest of the European heri-
tage. It seems unnecessary to add that it is, above all, the Latin heri-
tage: Provençal and Italian poetry in Pound; Dante and Baudelaire in
Eliot. In Joyce the Graeco-Latin and medieval presence is even more
decisive: not for nothing was he a rebel son of the Society of Jesus.
For all three, the return to the European tradition begins, and culmi-
nates, with a verbal revolution. The most radical was that of Joyce,
creator of a language that, without ceasing to be English, is also every
European tongue. Eliot and Pound first used rhymed free verse, in the
manner of Laforgue; in their second phase, they returned to fixed
meters and stanzas and then, as Pound himself tells us, the example
of Gautier was determinative. All these changes were based on an-
other: the "poetic" language—or literary dialect of the *fin de siècle*
poets—was replaced by everyday language. Not the stylized "popular"
language, in the manner of Juan Ramón Jiménez, Antonio Machado,
García Lorca, or Alberti, in the last analysis no less artificial than the
language of "cultivated" poetry, but the speech of the city. Not the
traditional song: conversation, the language of the great urban centers
of our century. In this the French influence was decisive. But the

reasons that moved the English poets were exactly the opposite of those that had inspired their models. The irruption of prosaic expressions in verse—which begins with Victor Hugo and Baudelaire—and the adoption of free verse and the prose poem, were resources against syllabic versification and against poetry conceived as rhymed discourse. Against meter, against analytical language: an attempt to return to rhythm, key to the universal analogy or correspondence. In the English language the reform had an opposite meaning: not to yield to the rhythmic seduction, to keep alive the critical consciousness even at the moments of greatest abandonment.[3] In both languages poets sought to replace the falsity of "poetic" diction by the concrete image. But while the French rebelled against the *abstraction* of syllabic verse, the English-language poets rebelled against the *vagueness* of rhythmic poetry.

The Waste Land has been judged to be a revolutionary poem by a large segment of English and foreign criticism. Nevertheless, the significance of this poem can only be fully understood in the light of the English verse tradition. Its theme is not simply the description of the gelid modern world, but the nostalgia for a universal order whose model is the Christian order of Rome. Thus its poetic archetype is a work that is the culmination and the most complete expression of this world: *The Divine Comedy*. To the Christian order—which assumes, transmutes, and gives a sense of personal salvation to the old fertility rites of the pagans—Eliot opposes the reality of modern society, both in its brilliant Renaissance origins and in its sordid and spectral contemporary denouement. Thus, the quotations of the poem—its spiritual sources—can be divided into two parts. The references to Dante, Buddha, Saint Augustine, the Upanishads, and the myths of vegetation allude to the world of personal and cosmic health. The second part is subdivided, in turn, into two: the first corresponds to the birth of our age; the second, to its present situation. On the one hand, fragments from Shakespeare, Spenser, Webster, Marvell, in which the lu-

---

[3] This explains the slight influence of surrealism in England and the United States during that period. On the other hand, that influence is decisive in contemporary poetry and begins, generally speaking, around 1955.

minous birth of the modern world is reflected; on the other, Baude-laire, Nerval, urban folklore, the colloquial language of the suburbs. The vitality of the former is revealed in the latter as soulless life. The vision of Elizabeth of England and Lord Robert on a barge adorned with silk sails and graceful pennants, as an illustration of a painting by Titian or Veronese, dissolves into the image of the shop girl, pos-sessed by a playboy one weekend.

To this spiritual duality corresponds a duality in the language. Eliot recognizes himself the debtor of two currents: the Elizabethan and the symbolist (especially Laforgue). Both help him to express the situa-tion of the contemporary world. Indeed, modern man begins to speak through the mouth of Hamlet, Prospero, and some heroes of Marlowe and Webster. But he begins to speak like a superhuman being and not until Baudelaire does he express himself like a fallen man and a divided soul. What makes Baudelaire a modern poet is not so much the break with the Christian order as the consciousness of that break. Modernity is consciousness. And ambiguous consciousness: negation and nostalgia, prose and lyricism. Eliot's language retrieves this two-fold heritage: relics of words, fragments of truths, the splendor of the English Renaissance allied to the misery and aridity of the modern metropolis. Broken rhythms, world of asphalt and rats shot through and veined with flashes of fallen beauty. In that realm of hollow men, rhythm is followed by repetition. The Punic Wars are also World War I; confused, past and present glide toward an opening that is a mouth that masticates: history. Later, those same events and those same peo-ple reappear, attrited, without profiles, floating aimlessly on a gray water. All are that one and that one is no one. This chaos regains sig-nificance as soon as it confronts the universe of health represented by Dante. The consciousness of guilt is also nostalgia, consciousness of exile. But Dante does not need to prove his affirmations and his word tirelessly supports, as the stem the fruit, the spiritual meaning: there is no break between word and sense. Eliot, on the other hand, must re-sort to the quotation and to collage. The Florentine leans on living and shared beliefs; as the critic C. Brooks points out, the Englishman's theme is "the rehabilitation of a known but discredited system of beliefs."[4] It can now be understood in what sense Eliot's poem is also a poetic reform, and analogies between it and the reforms of Milton and Pope are not lacking. It is a restoration but it is a restoration of something against which England has rebelled since the Reformation: Rome.

Nostalgia for a spiritual order, the images and rhythms of *The Waste Land* deny the principle of analogy. Its place is occupied by the association of ideas, destructive of the unity of consciousness. The systematic utilization of this procedure is one of Eliot's greatest successes. With the disappearance of the world of Christian values—whose center is, precisely, the universal analogy or correspondence between heaven, earth, and hell—man has nothing left but the fortuitous and chance association of thoughts and images. The modern world has lost its meaning and the crudest testimony of that absence of direction is the automatism of the association of ideas, which is not governed by any cosmic or spiritual rhythm, but by chance. That whole chaos of fragments and ruins is presented as the antithesis of a theological universe, ordered in accordance with the values of the Roman church. Modern man is Eliot's protagonist. Everything is alien to him and he recognizes himself in nothing. He is the exception that belies all the analogies and correspondences. Man is not a tree, or a plant, or a bird. He is alone in the midst of creation. And when he touches a human body he does not touch a sky, as Novalis said, but rather he penetrates a gallery of echoes. There is nothing less romantic than this poem. Nothing less English. The counterpart of *The Waste Land* is the *Comedy*, and its immediate precursor, *Les Fleurs du Mal*. Is it necessary to add that the original title of Baudelaire's book was *Limbes* [Limbo], and that in Eliot's universe *The Waste Land* represents, according to the author's own declaration, not Hell but Purgatory?

Pound, "il miglior fabbro," is Eliot's teacher and to him is due the "simultaneism" of *The Waste Land*, a method that is used and abused in the *Cantos*. In the face of the modern crisis, both poets turn their eyes to the past and actualize history: every epoch is this epoch. But Eliot actually desires to return and to reinstall Christ; Pound uses

[4] See *T. S. Eliot: A Study of His Writings by Several Hands* (London, 1948).

the past as another form of the future. Having lost the center of his world, he throws himself into every adventure. Unlike Eliot, he is a reactionary, not a conservative. In fact, Pound has never ceased to be a North American and he is the legitimate descendant of Whitman, that is, he is a son of Utopia. Therefore value and future become synonyms for him: that which contains a guarantee of future has value. There is value in everything that has just been born and still shines with the humid light of that which is beyond the present. The *Shih Ching* and Arnault's poems, precisely because they are so old, are also new: they have just been disinterred, they are the unknown. For Pound history is a march, not a circle. If he embarks with Odysseus, it is not to return to Ithaca, but because of a thirst for historical space: to go farther, ever farther, toward the future. Pound's erudition is a banquet after an expedition of conquest; Eliot's, the search for a standard that will give meaning to history, stability to movement. Pound accumulates quotations with the heroic air of one who robs graves; Eliot orders them as if he were hauling in the relics of a shipwreck. Pound's work is a journey that perhaps leads us nowhere; Eliot's, a search for the ancestral home.

Pound is enamored of the great classical civilizations or, rather, of certain moments that, not without arbitrariness, he considers archetypal. The *Cantos* are an actualization in modern terms—a *presentation*—of exemplary epochs, names, and works. Our world floats on an undirected course; we live under the sway of violence, deceit, usury, and grossness because we have been severed from the past. Pound proposes a tradition: Confucius, Malatesta, Adams, Odysseus. . . . The truth is that he offers us so many and such diverse traditions because he himself has none. Therefore he goes from the Provençal poetry to the Chinese, from Sophocles to Frobenius. His whole work is a dramatic search for that tradition that he and his country have lost. But that tradition was not in the past; the real tradition of the United States, as is manifested in Whitman, *was* the future: the free society of comrades, the democratic new Jerusalem. The United States has not lost a past; it has lost its future. The great historical plan of that nation's founders was thwarted by the financial monopolies, imperialism, the cult of action for action's sake, the abhorrence of ideas. Pound turns to history and interrogates the books and the stones of great civilizations. If he loses his way in those vast cemeteries, it is because he lacks a guide: a central tradition. The Puritan heritage, as Eliot saw very well, could not be a bridge: it is itself a break, dissidence from the West.

In the face of his country's excesses, Pound seeks moderation—without realizing that he too is immoderate. The hero of the *Cantos* is not the ingenious Ulysses, always in control of himself, nor the master Kung, who knows the secret of moderation, but an exalted, tempestuous, and sarcastic being, at once an aesthete, prophet, and clown: Pound, the masked poet, incarnation of the ancient hero of the romantic tradition. It is not by accident that the work anterior to the *Cantos* is sheltered under the title of *Personae*: the Latin mask. In that book, which contains some of the most beautiful poems of the century, Pound is Bertrand de Born, Propertius, Li Po—without ever ceasing to be Ezra Pound. The same protagonist, his face covered by a no less prodigious succession of false faces, crosses the confused and brilliant pages, transparent lyricism and gibberish, of the *Cantos*. This work, as a vision of the world and of history, lacks a center of gravity; but its protagonist is a grave and central figure. He is real although he moves on an unreal stage. The theme of the *Cantos* is not the city or the collective welfare but the ancient history of the passion, condemnation, and transfiguration of the solitary poet. It is the last great romantic poem in the English language and, perhaps, in the West. Pound's poetry is not in the line of Homer, Virgil, Dante, and Goethe; perhaps not in that of Propertius, Quevedo, and Baudelaire, either. It is strange poetry, discordant and tender at the same time, like that of the great names of the English and Yankee tradition. For us, Latins, to read Pound is as surprising and stimulating as it must have been for him to read Lope de Vega or Ronsard.

The Saxons are the dissidents of the West, and their most significant creations are eccentric with respect to the central tradition of our civilization, which is Latin-Germanic. Unlike Pound and Eliot—dissidents from dissidence, heterodox individuals in search of an impossible Mediterranean orthodoxy—Yeats never rebelled against his tradition. The influence of thoughts and strange and unusual poetics does not contradict, but rather emphasizes, his essential romanticism. Irish mythology, Hindu occultism, and French symbolism are influences of similar tonalities and intentions. All these currents affirm the ultimate identity between man and nature; they all proclaim themselves heirs of a lost tradition and a lost knowledge, prior to Christ and to Rome; in them all, in short, is reflected an identical sky populated with signs that only the poet can read. Analogy is the poet's language. Analogy is rhythm. Yeats continues the line of Blake. Eliot marks time to a different beat. In the former, the rhythmic values triumph; in the latter, the conceptual ones. One invents or resuscitates myths, is a poet in the original sense of the word. The other uses ancient myths to reveal modern man's condition.

To conclude: the poetic reform of Pound, Eliot, Wallace Stevens, Cummings, and Marianne Moore can be seen as a re-Latinization of English-language poetry. It is revealing that all these poets came from the United States. The same phenomenon was produced, a little earlier, in Latin America: like the Yankee poets, who reminded English poetry of its European origin, the Spanish-American "modernists" revived the *European tradition* of poetry in the Spanish language, which had been broken or forgotten in Spain. The majority of the Anglo-American poets tried to transcend the opposition between accentual versification and metrical regularity, rhythm and discourse, analogy and analysis, either by the creation of a cosmopolitan poetic language (Pound, Eliot, Stevens) or by the Americanization of the European vanguard (Cummings and William Carlos Williams). The former looked to the European tradition for a classicism; the latter, for an anti-tradition. William Carlos Williams set out to reconquer the "American idiom," that myth that, since the time of Whitman, has reappeared again and again in Anglo-American literature. If Williams' poetry is, in some manner, a return to Whitman, one must add that this is a Whitman seen through the eyes of the European vanguard.

After what has been said, it hardly seems necessary to dwell at length on the evolution of modern French poetry. It will be enough to mention some characteristic episodes. First and foremost, the presence of German romanticism, more as a catalyst than a genuine influence. Although many of the ideas of Baudelaire and the symbolists are already

found in Novalis and in other German poets and philosophers, it is a
case of a stimulus rather than a loan. Germany was a spiritual atmos-
phere. In some cases, nevertheless, there was a transplantation. Nerval
not only translated and imitated Goethe and a number of lesser ro-
mantics; one of the *Chimères* ("Delfica") is directly inspired by *Mig-*
non: "Kennst du das Land, wo die Zitronen blühn. . . ." Goethe's
lyric song is transformed into a hermetic sonnet that is a veritable tem-
ple (in Nerval's sense a place of initiation and consecration). The
English contribution was also essential. The Germans offered France a
vision of the world and a symbolic philosophy; the English, a myth:
the figure of the poet as an exile, struggling against men and the stars.
Later Baudelaire would discover Poe. A discovery that was a re-crea-
tion. Misery creates an aesthetic in which the exception, the irregular
beauty, is the true rule. The strange poet Baudelaire-Poe thus under-
mines the ethical and metaphysical bases of classicism. On the other
hand, Italy and Spain disappear, except as illustrious ruins or pictur-
esque landscapes. Spain's influence, determinate in the sixteenth and
seventeenth centuries, is nonexistent in the nineteenth: in *Poésies*, Lau-
tréamont casually cites Zorrilla (did he read him?) and Hugo pro-
claims his love for our Romancero. This indifference does not cease to
be noteworthy, if one thinks that Spanish literature—especially Calde-
rón—profoundly impressed the German and English romantics. I sus-
pect that the reason for these divergent attitudes is this: while the
Germans and English see in the Spanish of the baroque period a justi-
fication for their own singularity, the French poets seek something that
Germany but not Spain could give them: a poetic principle contrary to
their tradition.

The German contagion, with its emphasis on the correspondence be-
tween dream and reality and its insistence on seeing nature as a book
of symbols, could not be limited to the sphere of ideas. If the word is
the double of the cosmos, the realm of spiritual experience is language.
Hugo is the first to attack prosody. In making the alexandrine more
flexible, he prepares the way for free verse. Nevertheless, owing to the
nature of language, poetic reform could not consist in a change of the
versification system. That change, moreover, was and is impossible.
The caesuras within the line can be multiplied and enjambment prac-

ticed: the rhythmic supports of the accentual versification will always
be lacking. French free verse is distinguished from that of other lan-
guages in being a combination of different syllabic measures and not
of different rhythmic units. Therefore Claudel resorts to assonance and
Saint-John Perse to internal rhyme and alliteration. And thus the re-
form has consisted in the intercommunication between prose and verse.
Modern French poetry is born with romantic prose and its precursors
are Rousseau and Chateaubriand. Prose ceases to be the servant of rea-
son and becomes the confidant of sensibility. Its rhythm obeys the effu-
sions of the heart and the soaring of the fancy. It is soon converted into
a poem. Analogy rules the universe of *Aurélia*; the prose poems of Al-
oysius Bertrand and Baudelaire lead to the vertiginous succession of
visions of *Les Illuminations*. The image causes prose to crack as de-
scription or narrative. Lautréamont consummates the downfall of dis-
course and demonstration. Poetry's vengeance has never been so com-
plete. The way was opened for such books as *Nadja, Le Paysan de
Paris, Un Certain Plume.* . . . Verse is benefited in a different way. The
first to accept prosaic elements is Hugo; later, with greater lucidity and
sense, Baudelaire. It was not a rhythmic reform but rather the insertion
of a foreign body—humor, irony, reflective pause—intended to in-
terrupt the tripping of the syllables. The advent of prosaism is a halt,
a mental caesura; a suspension of thought, its function is to provoke an
irregularity. Aesthetic of passion, philosophy of exception. The next
step was popular poetry and, above all, free verse. But, as I stated
before, the possibilities of free verse were limited; Eliot observes that
in Laforgue's hands it was merely a contraction or distortion of the tra-
ditional alexandrine. For a time it seemed that it was impossible to go
beyond the prose poem and free verse. The process had reached its
end. But in 1897, a year before his death, Mallarmé published in a
review *Un Coup de dés jamais n'abolira le hasard.*

What is surprising, first of all, is the typographical arrangement of
the poem. Printed in type of different sizes and thicknesses—capitals,
boldface, and italics—the words are united or dispersed in a manner
that is far from arbitrary but that is not usual for prose or for poetry.
One has the sensation of looking at a poster or an advertisement. Mal-
larmé compares this distribution to a musical score: "La différence de

caractères d'imprimerie . . . dicte son importance à l'émission orale."
At the same time, he points out that these are not properly verses—
"traits sonores réguliers"—but rather "subdivisions prismatiques de
l'Idée." Music for the understanding and not for the ear: but an un-
derstanding that hears and sees with the inner senses. The Idea is not
an object of reason but a reality that the poem reveals to us in a series
of fleeting forms, that is, in a temporal order. The Idea, always equal
to itself, cannot be contemplated in its totality because man is time,
perpetual movement: what we see and hear are the "subdivisions" of
the Idea through the prism of the poem. Our apprehension is partial
and successive. Moreover, it is simultaneous: visual (images stimulated
by the text), sonorous (typography: mental recitation), and spiritual
(intuitive, conceptual, and emotive meanings). Later, in the same note
that precedes the poem, the poet confides that the music heard in the
concert was not alien to his inspiration. And to make his affirmation
more complete, he adds that his text inaugurates a genre that will be to
the old verse what the symphony is to vocal music. The new form, he
insinuates, will serve for themes of pure imagination and for those of
the intellect, while the traditional verse will continue to be the domain
of passion and fantasy. Finally, he gives us a capital observation: his
poem is an attempt to unite "de poursuites particulières et chères à
notre temps, le vers libre et le poème en prose."

Although Mallarmé's influence has been central to the history of
modern poetry, in and out of France, I do not believe that all of the
ways that this text opens up to poetry have been fully explored. Per-
haps in this second half of the century, thanks to the invention of ever
better instruments for reproducing the sound of the word, the poetic
form initiated by Mallarmé will unfold in all its richness. Western
poetry was born allied to music; later, the two arts separated and each
attempt to unite them has resulted in a quarrel or the absorption of
the word by the sound. Thus, I am not thinking of an alliance be-
tween the two. Poetry has its own music: the word. And this music, as
Mallarmé shows, is more vast than that of the traditional verse and
prose. In a rather summary fashion, but one that is a testimony of his
lucidity, Apollinaire affirms that the days of the book are numbered:
"La typographie termine brillamment sa carrière, à l'aurore des

moyens nouveaux de reproduction que sont le cinéma et le phono-
graphe." I do not believe in the end of writing; I believe that the
poem will tend more and more to be a musical score. Poetry will again
be spoken word.

Un Coup de dés closes one period, that of properly symbolist poe-
try, and opens another: that of contemporary poetry. Two paths lead
from *Un Coup de dés*: one goes from Apollinaire to the surrealists;
the other from Claudel to Saint-John Perse. The cycle is not yet closed,
and in one way or another the poetry of René Char, Francis Ponge,
and Yves Bonnefoy is nourished from the tension, union and separa-
tion, between prose and verse, reflection and song. Despite its rhyth-
mic poverty, thanks to Mallarmé the French language in this half cen-
tury has unfolded the possibilities that German romanticism virtually
held in check. At the same time, by a path different from that of Eng-
lish poetry, but with similar intensity, it is word that reflects on itself,
consciousness of its song. In short, French poetry has destroyed the il-
lusory architecture of prose and has shown us that syntax leans on an
abyss. Devastation of that which traditionally is called "French spirit":
analysis, discourse, moral meditation, irony, psychology, and all the
rest. The most profound poetic rebellion of the century occurred in
the place where the discursive spirit had taken possession almost totally
of the language, to the degree that it seemed devoid of rhythmic
powers. At the core of a reasoning people a forest of images sprang
up, a new order of chivalry, armed cap-a-pie with poisoned arms. A
hundred years away from German romanticism, poetry fought again
on the same frontiers. And that rebellion was primordially a rebellion
against French verse: against syllabic versification and poetic discourse.

Spanish verse combines accentual and syllabic versification more
completely than French and English verse. Thus it appears to be equi-
distant from the extremes of these languages. Pedro Henríquez Ureña
divides Spanish verse into two main currents: regular versification—
based on fixed metrical and strophic schemes, in which each verse is
composed of a determinate number of syllables—and irregular versi-
fication, in which the measure is not as important as the rhythmic beat

of the accents. Now, the tonic accents are decisive even in the case of the purest syllabic versification, and without them there is no verse in Spanish. The rhythmic freedom is increased by virtue of the fact that Spanish meters in reality do not require fixed accentuation; even the strictest, the hendecasyllable, tolerates a great variety of rhythmic beats: on the fourth and eighth syllables; on the sixth; on the fourth and seventh; on the fourth; on the fifth. Add to this the variable syllabic value of antepenultimate and acute accents, the dissolution of the diphthongs, synaloepha, and other resources that permit a modification of the syllable count. Indeed, they are not properly two independent systems, but a single current in which syllabic and accentual versifications combat and separate, alternate and fuse.

The struggle waged at the heart of Spanish by regular and rhythmic versifications is not expressed as opposition between the image and the concept. Among us the duality is shown as a tendency toward story and an inclination for song. Spanish verse, whatever its length may be, consists of a combination of accents—dance steps—and syllabic measure. It is a unit in which two opposites embrace: one that is dance and another that is linear narrative, a march in the military sense of the word. Our traditional verse, the octosyllable, is a verse on horseback, made for trotting and fighting, but also for dancing. The same duality is observed in the major meters, hendecasyllables and alexandrines, which served Berceo and Ercilla for narration and Saint John and Darío for song. Our meters oscillate between the dance and the gallop and our poetry moves between two poles: the Romancero and the *Spiritual Canticle*. Spanish verse possesses a natural facility for relating heroic or commonplace events with objectivity, precision, and sobriety. When one says that the distinctive quality of our epic poetry is realism, does one perceive that this realism, which is ingenuous and, therefore, of a very different nature from the modern, always intellectual and ideological realism, coincides with the character of Spanish rhythm? Virile verses, octosyllables and alexandrines, show an irresistible vocation for the chronicle and the narrative. The ballad always induces us to relate. At the very apogee of the so-called "pure poetry," García Lorca, lured by the rhythm of the octosyllable, turned to the anecdote and was not afraid to indulge in descriptive detail. Those episodes and those images would lose their value in more irregular metrical combinations. When Alfonso Reyes translated the *Iliad*, he had no choice but to return to the alexandrine. On the other hand, our poets failed when they attempted the narrative in free verse, as is seen in the long and unbound passages of Pablo Neruda's *Canto general*. (In other cases he was completely successful, as in *Alturas de Macchu Picchu*; but that poem is not description or narrative, but song.) Darío also failed when he tried to create a kind of hexameter for his epic attempts. This modality does not cease to be surprising if one thinks that our medieval epic poetry is irregular and that syllabic versification begins in the lyric, in the fifteenth century. Be that as it may, tonic accents express our love for elegance, grace, and, more profoundly, for the frenzy of the dance. Spanish accents lead us to conceive man as an extreme being and, at the same time, as the meeting place of the lower and higher worlds. Words stressed on the ultima, the penultima, the antepenultima—beats on the leather drumhead, hands clapping, shouts of "Ay!", bugle calls: poetry in the Spanish language is revelry and funereal dance, erotic dancing and mystical flight. Almost all our poems, not excluding the mystic ones, can be sung and danced, as the pre-Socratic philosophers are said to have danced theirs.

This duality explains the antitheses and contrasts in which our poetry abounds. If the baroque is a dynamic game, chiaroscuro, violent opposition between this and that, we are baroque by a fatality of the language. Already in the language, in the germ, are all our contrasts, the realism of the mystics and the mysticism of the *pícaros*. But it has become tiresome to allude to those two veins, identical and opposite, of our tradition. And what is there to say of Góngora? A visual poet, there is nothing more plastic than his images; and, simultaneously, nothing less seemly for our eyes: there are lights that blind. This double tendency battles unceasingly in each poem and spurs the poet on to risk the whole poem for one image clenched like a fist. Thus the tension, the rotund character, the valor of our classics. Thus, too, the lapses into the prolix, the striving for an effect, the rigidity, and that constant getting lost in the galleries of the castle of escape if you can

from the ingenious. But sometimes the struggle ceases and transparent
verses appear in which all is harmony and rhythm:

> Corrientes aguas, puras, cristalinas,
> árboles que os estáis mirando en ellas . . .

miraculous combination of vowel and consonant clarity and accents.
The language is clothed in "beauty and unaccustomed light." All is
transfigured, all glides, dances, or soars, moved by a few accents.
Spanish verse wears spurs on its old shoes, but also wings. And the
expressive power of the rhythm is such that at times the sonorous
elements alone are enough for poetic illumination to be produced, as
in the obsessive and oft-quoted "un no sé *qué que que*dan balbucien-
do" of Saint John of the Cross. Ecstasy is not manifested as image, nor
as idea or concept. It is, in truth, the ineffable expressing itself ineffa-
bly. The language has arrived, effortlessly, at its extreme tension. The
verse expresses the inexpressible. It is a stammering that says it all
without saying anything, ardent repetition of a poor sound: pure
rhythm. Compare this verse with one of Eliot's in *The Waste Land*
that endeavors to express the same rapture, at once stuffed with and
empty of words: the English poet resorts to a quotation in the San-
skrit language. The sacred—or, at least, a certain familiarity with the
divine, tender and fulminating at the same time—seems to be incar-
nated in our language with greater naturalness than in others. And in
the same way: Blake's "Auguries of Innocence" says things that never
have been said in Spanish and, perhaps, never will be.

Prose suffers more than verse from this continuous tension. And it
is understandable: the struggle is resolved in the poem with the tri-
umph of the image, which embraces the opposites without annihilating
them. The concept, on the other hand, has to grapple with two hostile
forces. Therefore Spanish prose triumphs in the narrative and prefers
description to reasoning. Our phrase is drawn out between commas
and parentheses; if we cut it with periods, the paragraph is converted
into a succession of blasts, a puffing and blowing of fitful affirmations
and the fragments of the serpent explode in all directions. Occasional-
ly, to keep the march from becoming monotonous, we resort to images.
Then discourse vacillates and the words begin to dance. We touch the

limits of the poetic or, more frequently, of oratory. Only the return to the concrete, to the palpable with the eyes of the body and soul, restores its equilibrium to prose. Novelists, chroniclers, theologians, or mystics, all great Spanish prose writers relate, tell, describe, abandon ideas for images, chisel concepts. Even such a philosopher as Ortega y Gasset has created a prose that does not reject the plasticity of the image. Solar prose, the ideas parade under a noonday light, beautiful bodies in a transparent and resonant air, air of a high plateau made for the eyes and sculpture. Never before had ideas moved more gracefully: "There are styles of thinking that are styles of dancing." The nature of the language favors the birth of extreme, solitary, and eccentric talents. Unlike what happens in France, among us the majority write badly and sing well. Even among the great writers the boundaries between prose and poetry are hazy. In Spanish there is a prose in the artistic sense of the word, that is, in the sense in which the prose writer Valle-Inclán is a great poet but there is not a prose in the true sense of the word: discourse, intellectual theory.

Each time a great prose writer appears, the language is born again. And with him a new tradition begins. Thus, prose tends to be confused with poetry, to be itself poetry. The poem, on the contrary, cannot lean on Spanish prose. A situation unique in the modern era. Contemporary European poetry is inconceivable without the critical studies that precede, accompany, and prolong it. An exception would be that of Antonio Machado. But there is a break between his poetics —at least between what I consider the center of his thought—and his poetry. Machado showed the same reticence toward the symbolism of the "modernist" poets and the images of the vanguard; and with respect to the experiments of this latter movement his judgments were rigid and uncomprehending. His opposition to these tendencies caused him to return to the forms of the traditional song. On the other hand, his reflections on poetry are completely modern and even ahead of his time. To the prose writer, not to the poet, we owe this capital intuition: poetry, if it is anything, is a revelation of the "essential heterogeneity of being," eroticism, "otherness." It would be useless to seek in his poems the revelation of that "otherness" or the vision of our estrangement. His discovery appears in his poetic work as idea, not as reality. I mean: it was not translated into the creation of a language that would body forth our "otherness." Thus, it had no effect on his poetry.

For many years the prestige of neoclassic precepts prevented an honest appraisal of our medieval poetry. The irregular versification appeared to be the floundering and uncertainty of apprentices. The presence of meters of different lengths in our epic poems was the fruit of the poet's ineptitude, although scholars perceived a certain tendency toward metrical regularity. I suspect that this tendency toward "regularity" is a modern invention. Neither the poet nor the listeners heard the metrical "irregularities," and they were very sensitive indeed to their profound rhythmic and imaginative unity. I do not believe, moreover, that we know how those verses were said. One frequently forgets that we not only think and live differently from our ancestors, but we also hear and see differently. Around the end of the Middle Ages the apogee of regular versification begins. But the adoption of regular meters did not cause accentual versification to disappear because, as has already been said, it is not a case of different systems but of two tendencies within the same current. Since the triumph of Italian versification in the sixteenth century, the balance has swung toward ametrical versification only twice: in the romantic period and in the modern. In the former, timidly; in the latter, openly. The modern period is divided into two moments: the "modernist," apogee of the Parnassian and symbolist influences of France; and the contemporary. In both, Spanish-American poets were the initiators of the reform; and on both occasions peninsular criticism denounced the "mental Gallicism" of the Spanish Americans—to recognize later that those importations and innovations were also, and above all, a rediscovery of the verbal powers of Castilian.

The "modernist" movement begins around 1885 and comes to an end, in America, in the years of the First World War. In Spain it begins and ends later. The French influence was predominant. Also influential, to a lesser degree, were two North American poets (Poe and Whitman) and a Portuguese (Eugenio de Castro). Hugo and Verlaine, especially the latter, were Rubén Darío's principal gods. He had others. In his book *Los raros* (1896) he offers a series of portraits and

studies of the poets he admired or who interested him: Baudelaire, Le-
conte de Lisle, Moréas, Villiers de l'Isle Adam, Castro, Poe, and the
Cuban José Martí, as the only Spanish-language writer. . . . Darío
speaks of Rimbaud, Mallarmé, and, a greater novelty, of Lautréamont.
The study on Ducasse was perhaps the first to appear outside France;
and even there it was only preceded, if I remember rightly, by the ar-
ticles of Léon Bloy and Remy de Gourmont. The poetics of modern-
ism, stripped of the dross of the period, oscillates between Gautier's
sculptural ideal and symbolist music: *I pursue a form that my style
does not find*, says Darío, *and all I encounter is the word that flees . . .
and the neck of the great white swan that interrogates me*. The "celes-
tial unity" of the universe is in the rhythm. In the sea shell the poet
hears *a deep surge and a mysterious wind: the shell is shaped like a
heart*. The "modernists' " method of poetic association, sometimes a
veritable mania, is synesthesia. Correspondences between music and
colors, rhythm and ideas, a world of sensations that rhyme with in-
visible realities. In the center, woman: *the sexual rose* [that] *moves
everything in existence as it unfolds*. To hear the rhythm of creation—
but also to see it, and touch it—in order to build a bridge between the
world, the senses, and the soul: the poet's mission.

Nothing more natural than for the core of his preoccupations to be
the music of the verse. The theory accompanied the practice. Apart
from the numerous statements of Darío, Díaz Mirón, Valencia, and
the other coryphaei of the movement, two poets devoted whole books
to the subject: the Peruvian Manuel González Prada and the Bolivian
Ricardo Jaimes Freyre. Both maintain that the nucleus of the verse is
rhythmic unity and not syllabic measure. Their studies amplify and
confirm the doctrine of the Venezuelan Andrés Bello, who as early as
1835 had indicated the basic function of the tonic accent in the forma-
tion of the clauses (or feet) that compose rhythmic periods. The
"modernists" invented meters, some even of twenty syllables; they
adopted others from French, English, and German; and they resusci-
tated many that had been forgotten in Spain. With them, semifree and
free verse appears in Spanish. The French influence on the attempts at
ametrical versification was minor; more decisive, it seems to me, was
the example of Poe, Whitman, and Castro. At the turn of the century

Spanish poets gave a favorable reception to these novelties. The ma-
jority were sensitive to the "modernist" rhetoric but few perceived the
real significance of the movement. And two great poets showed their
reserve: Unamuno with a certain impatience, Antonio Machado with
amicable aloofness. Both, nevertheless, used many of the metrical in-
novations. Juan Ramón Jiménez, in his first period, adopted the most
external manner of the school; later, like the Rubén Darío of *Cantos
de vida y esperanza*, although with a more certain instinct for the in-
ternal word, he stripped the poem of useless trappings and attempted
a poetry that has been called "bare" and that I prefer to call essential.

Jiménez does not deny "modernism": he assumes its profound con-
sciousness. In his second and third periods he uses short traditional
meters and the free and semifree verse of the "modernists." His poetic
evolution resembles that of Yeats. Both were influenced by the French
symbolists and their disciples (English and Spanish-American); both
utilized the lesson of their followers (Yeats, more generous, confessed
his debt to Pound; Jiménez denigrated Guillén, García Lorca, and
Cernuda); the starting point of both is a heavily charged poetry that
slowly grows lighter and becomes transparent; both reach old age to
write their best poems. Their race toward death was a race toward
poetic youth. In all his changes Jiménez was faithful to himself. There
was not an evolution but a maturation, growth. His coherence is like
that of the tree that changes but is not displaced. He was not a sym-
bolist poet: he is symbolism in the Spanish language. To say this is not
to make any discovery; he himself said it many times. Criticism insists
on seeing in the second and third Jiménez a repudiator of "modern-
ism": how could he be that if he carries it to its most extreme and, let
me add, *natural* consequences: the symbolic expression of the world?
A few years before his death he writes *Espacio*, a long poem that is a
recapitulation and a criticism of his poetic life. He is in the tropical
landscape of Florida (and in all the landscapes he has seen or intuit-
ed): is he talking to himself or conversing with the birds? Jiménez
perceives for the first time, and perhaps for the last, the *in-significant*
silence of nature. Or is it the human words that are only air and noise?
The poet's mission, he tells us, is not to save man but to save the
world: to name it. *Espacio* is one moment of the modern poetic con-

sciousness, and that capital text crowns and terminates the great swan's interrogation of Darío in his youth.

"Modernism" also opens the way for the interpenetration between prose and verse. The spoken language, and also the technical word and that of science, the expression in French or in English and, in short, all that constitutes urban speech. Humor, monologue, conversation, verbal collage appear. As always, Darío is the first. But the real master is Leopoldo Lugones, one of the greatest poets in our language (or perhaps one would have to say: one of our greatest writers). In 1909 he published *Lunario sentimental.* He is Laforgue but an immoderate Laforgue, with less heart and more eyes, and in whom the irony has increased to the point of becoming grotesque and monstrous vision. The world seen through a telescope from a sordid window in Buenos Aires. The vacant lot is a lunar valley. The vast South American plain comes in through the roof and is spread out on the poet's table like a wrinkled tablecloth. The Mexican López Velarde adopts and transforms Lugones' inhuman aesthetic. He is the first to really hear people talking and to perceive in that confused murmur the surge of rhythm, the music of time. López Velarde's monologue is disquieting because it is made of two voices: the "other," our double and our stranger, appears in the poem at last. Around the same years Jiménez and Machado proclaim the return to the "popular language."

López Velarde leads us to the doors of contemporary poetry. It will not be he who will open them but Vicente Huidobro. With Huidobro, the "magnificent bird," come Apollinaire and Reverdy. The image recovers its wings. The Chilean poet's influence was very great in America and Spain; great and controversial. This latter quality has hurt the appreciation of his work; his legend obscures his poetry. Nothing could be more unjust: *Altazor* is a poem, a great poem in which the poetic aviation is transformed into a fall toward "one's innermost self," vertiginous immersion in the void. Vicente Huidobro, the "citizen of oblivion": *he contemplates from such heights that everything turns into air.* He is everywhere and nowhere: he is the invisible oxygen of our poetry. Opposite the aviator, the miner: César Vallejo. The word, plucked with difficulty from insomnia, blackens and reddens, is stone and is red-hot coal, carbon, and ash: *it is so hot it is cold.*

The language turns in upon itself. Not the language of books, that of the street; not the language of the street, that of the hotel room with no one inside. Fusion of the word and physiology: *The day is coming, put on your coat. The day is coming; hold fast to your large intestine. . . . The day is coming, put on your soul. . . . tonight you dreamed that you lived on nothing and died of everything. . . .* Not the poetry of the city: the poet in the city. Hunger not as a dissertation topic but speaking directly, with a faint and delirious voice. A voice more powerful than that of the dream. And that hunger becomes an infinite desire to give and be given: *his corpse was full of world.*

As in the epoch of "modernism," the two centers of the vanguard were Buenos Aires (Borges, Girondo, Molinari) and Mexico (Pellicer, Villaurrutia, Gorostiza). Mulatto poetry appears in Cuba: to sing, dance, and curse (Nicolás Guillén, Emilio Ballagas); in Ecuador, Jorge Carrera Andrade begins a "world register," an inventory of American images. . . . But the poet who incarnates this period best is Pablo Neruda. Of course, he is the most prolific and uneven, and this causes him to be misunderstood; it is also true that he is almost always the richest and densest of our poets. The vanguard has two periods: the first, Huidobro's, around 1920, volatilization of the word and the image; and the second, Neruda's, ten years later, rapt penetration into the heart of things. Not the return to the land: immersion in an ocean of deep and sluggish waters. The history of "modernism" is repeated. The two Chilean poets influenced the whole ambit of the language and were recognized in Spain, as Darío had been in his time. And it could be added that the pair Huidobro-Neruda is like the unfolding of a mythical vanguardist Darío, and would correspond to the two epochs of the real Darío: *Prosas profanas*, Huidobro; *Cantos de vida y esperanza*, Neruda. In Spain the break with the earlier poetry is less violent. The first to realize the fusion between spoken language and image is not a poet in verse but in prose: the great Ramón Gómez de la Serna. In 1930 the anthology of Gerardo Diego appears, which introduces the richest and most singular group of poets that Spain has had since the seventeenth century: Jorge Guillén, Federico García Lorca, Rafael Alberti, Luis Cernuda, Aleixandre. . . . But I must stop. I am not writing a literary survey. And the next chapter has almost overtaken me.

The modern poetry in our language is one more example of the relations between prose and verse, rhythm and meter. The description could be extended to the Italian, which possesses a structure similar to Spanish, or to the German, a mine of rhythms. With regard to the Spanish, it is worth repeating that the apogee of rhythmic versification, a consequence of the reform carried out by the Spanish-American poets, is in reality a return to the traditional Spanish verse. But this return would not have been possible without the influence of foreign poetic currents, the French in particular, which showed us the correspondence between rhythm and poetic image. Once again: rhythm and image are inseparable. This long digression brings us to the starting point: only the image will be able to tell us how the verse, which is rhythmic phrase, is also phrase possessed of meaning.

5. The Image

Like all words, the word *image* has a number of different meanings. For example: a representation, statue, as when we speak of a picture or sculpture of Apollo or the Virgin. Or a real or unreal figure we evoke or produce with our imagination. In this sense, the word has a psychological value: images are products of the imagination. These are not its only meanings, or those that concern us here. It is fitting to note, then, that we use the word image to designate every verbal form, phrase, or group of phrases that the poet says and that together compose a poem.[1] These verbal expressions have been classified by rhetoric and are called comparison, simile, metaphor, play on words, paronomasia, symbol, allegory, myth, fable, and so on. No matter what differences separate them, it is their common function to preserve the word's plurality of meanings without destroying the syntactical unity of the phrase or group of phrases. Each image—or each poem made of images—contains many opposite or disparate meanings, which it embraces or reconciles without suppressing. Thus, Saint John speaks of

[1] To avoid confusion, Roberto Vernengo proposes the expression "poetic mention."

"silent music," a phrase in which two apparently irreconcilable terms are allied. In this sense, the tragic hero is also an image. For example: the figure of Antigone, torn between divine piety and human laws. Nor is Achilles' anger simple, for in it opposites are united: love for Patroclus and pity for Priam, fascination with a glorious death and desire for a long life. Sleep and waking are bound together in Segismundo in an indissoluble, mysterious way. In Oedipus, liberty and destiny. . . . The image is the key to the human condition.

Epic, dramatic, or lyric, condensed in a phrase or spread out over a thousand pages, every image approximates or unites realities that are opposite, indifferent, or far apart. That is, it subjects the plurality of the real to unity. Concepts and scientific laws attempt nothing else. Thanks to the same rational reduction, individuals and objects—light feathers and heavy stones—become homogeneous unities. Not without righteous amazement do children discover one day that a pound of stones weighs the same as a pound of feathers. It is difficult for them to reduce stones and feathers to the abstraction pound. They realize that stones and feathers have abandoned their proper nature and, by a sleight-of-hand trick, lost all their qualities and their autonomy. The unifying operation of science mutilates and impoverishes them. But this is not the case with poetry. The poet names things: these are feathers, those are stones. And suddenly he affirms: stones are feathers, this is that. The elements of the image do not lose their concrete and singular character: stones continue to be stones, rough, hard, impenetrable, yellow with sun or green with moss: heavy stones. And feathers, feathers: light. The image shocks because it defies the principle of contradiction: the heavy is the light. When it enunciates the identity of opposites, it attacks the foundations of our thinking. Therefore, the poetic reality of the image cannot aspire to truth. The poem does not say what is, but what could be. Its realm is not the realm of being, but that of Aristotle's "likely impossible."

In spite of this adverse judgment, poets persist in affirming that the image reveals what is and not what could be. Moreover: they say that the image re-creates being. In their desire to restore the philosophical dignity of the image, some do not hesitate to seek the aid of dialectical logic. In fact, many images conform to the three stages of the process:

stone is one moment of reality; feather another; and from their forci-
ble encounter springs the image, the new reality. One does not have to
resort to an impossible enumeration of images in order to realize that
dialectic does not encompass them all. Sometimes the first term de-
vours the second. Other times, the second neutralizes the first. Or the
third term is not produced and the two elements appear face to face,
irreducible, hostile. The images of humor generally belong to this last
group: the contradiction merely serves to indicate the irreparably
absurd character of reality or of language. Finally, despite the fact
that many images develop according to the Hegelian order, it is almost
always a case of a similarity rather than a true identity. In the dia-
lectical process stones and feathers disappear in favor of a third reality,
which is no longer stones or feathers but something else. But in some
images—precisely the best ones—stones and feathers continue to be
what they are: this is this and that is that; and at the same time, this is
that: stones are feathers, without ceasing to be stones. The heavy is the
light. There is not the qualitative transmutation demanded by Hegel's
logic, as there was not the quantitative reduction of science. In short,
the image is also a shock and a challenge to dialectic, it also violates
the laws of thought. The reason for this insufficiency—because it is an
insufficiency for something that is there, before our eyes, as real as the
rest of so-called reality, not to have an explanation—perhaps consists
in the fact that dialectic is an attempt to preserve logical principles—
especially the principle of contradiction—threatened by their in-
creasingly visible incapacity to digest the contradictory nature of reali-
ty. The thesis is not produced at the same time as the antithesis; and
both disappear to give place to a new affirmation that, in engulfing
them, transmutes them. In each of the three moments the principle of
contradiction holds sway. Affirmation and negation are never given as
simultaneous realities, for that would imply the suppression of the
very idea of process. In leaving the principle of contradiction intact,
dialectical logic condemns the image, which dispenses with that prin-
ciple.

The principle of complementary contradiction absolves some
images, but not all. The same, perhaps, must be said of other logical
systems. Now, the poem not only proclaims the dynamic and necessary

coexistence of opposites, but also their ultimate identity. And this reconciliation, which does not imply a reduction or transmutation of the singularity of each term, is a wall that Western thought has refused to leap over or to perforate as yet. Since Parmenides our world has been the world of the clear and trenchant distinction between what is and what is not. Being is not nonbeing. This first extirpation—because it was an uprooting of being from the primordial chaos—constitutes the basis of our thinking. On this conception was built the edifice of "clear and distinct ideas," which, if it has made Western history possible, has also condemned to a kind of illegality every attempt to lay hold upon being by any means other than those of these principles. Mysticism and poetry have thus lived a subsidiary, clandestine and diminished life. The split has been inexpressible and constant. The consequences of that banishment of poetry are more evident and frightening each day: man is an exile from the cosmic flux and from himself. Because now no one is unaware that Western metaphysics ends in a solipsism. To destroy it, Hegel went back to Heraclitus. His attempt has not given us back our health. The rock-crystal castle of dialectic is revealed to us at last as a labyrinth of mirrors. Husserl restates all the problems and proclaims the need "to get back to the facts." But Husserl's idealism also seems to lead to a solipsism. Heidegger goes back to the pre-Socratics to ask himself the same question that Parmenides asked and to find an answer that will not immobilize being. We have not yet heard Heidegger's last word, but we know that his attempt to find being in existence ran up against a stone wall. Now, as some of his writings show, he has turned to poetry. Whatever may be the outcome of his adventure, the fact is that, from this angle, Western history can be seen as the history of an error, a going astray, in both senses of the word: in losing our way in the world we have become estranged from ourselves. We have to begin again.

Eastern thought has not suffered this horror of the "other," of what is and is not at the same time. The Western world is the world of "this or that"; the Eastern, of "this and that" and even of "this is that." In the most ancient Upanishad the principle of the identity of opposites is plainly stated: "Thou art woman. Thou art man. Thou art

the youth and also the maiden. Thou, like an old man, leanest on a
staff. . . . Thou art the dark blue bird and the green bird with red eyes.
. . . Thou art the seasons and the seas."[2] And these affirmations are
condensed by the Chandogya Upanishad in the famous formula: "That
art thou." The whole history of Eastern thought begins with this very
ancient assertion, in the same way that the history of Western
thought originates with Parmenides. This is the perennial theme of
speculation of the great Buddhist philosophers and the exegetes of
Hinduism. Taoism reveals the same tendencies. All these doctrines
reiterate that the opposition between this and that is, simultaneously,
relative and necessary, but that there comes a time when the enmity
ceases between terms we thought were mutually exclusive.

As if he were making an advance commentary on certain contempo-
rary speculations, Chuang-Tzu explains the functional and relative
character of opposites thus: "There is nothing that is not this; there is
nothing that is not that. This lives in relation to that. Such is the doc-
trine of the interdependence of this and that. Life is life in rela-
tion to death. And vice versa. Affirmation is affirmation in relation to
negation. And vice versa. Therefore, if one leans on this, it would
have to deny that. But this possesses its affirmation and its negation
and also engenders its this and its that. Therefore, the true sage rejects
the this and the that and takes refuge in Tao. . . ." There is a point at
which this and that, stones and feathers, fuse. And that moment is not
before or after, at the beginning or at the end of the times. It is neither
a natal or prenatal paradise nor an ultraterrestrial heaven. It does not
dwell in the realm of succession, which is precisely the realm of rela-
tive opposites, but it is in each moment. It is each moment. It is time it-
self engendering itself, flowing itself, opening itself to an ending that
is a continuous beginning. A water-jet, fountain. There, at the heart of
existence—or rather, of existing oneself—stones and feathers, the
light and the heavy, being born and dying, being oneself, are one and
the same.

The knowledge that Eastern doctrines propose to us is not transmis-

---

[2] *Svetasvatara Upanishad. The Thirteen Principal Upanishads, translated from the Sanskrit by R. E. Hume* (Oxford: Oxford University Press, 1951).

sible in formulas or reasonings. Truth is an experience and each one
must attempt it on his own. Doctrine shows us the way, but no one can
travel it for us. That is why meditation techniques are so important.
Learning is not the accumulation of knowledge, but the attuning of
body and spirit. Meditation does not teach us anything, except to for-
get everything we have been taught and to renounce all knowledge.
After these trials, we know less but we are lighter; we can begin our
journey and face the vertiginous and empty look of truth. Vertiginous
in its immobility; empty in its plenitude. Many centuries before Hegel
affirmed the final equivalence between absolute nothing and com-
plete being, the Upanishads had defined states of emptiness as instants
of communion with being: "The highest state is reached when the five
instruments of knowing remain quiet and joined together in the mind
and the mind does not move."[3] To think is to breathe. To hold one's
breath, to stop the circulation of the idea: to make the void so that
being may appear. To think is to breathe because thought and life are
not separate universes but communicating vessels: this is that. The ul-
timate identity between man and the world, consciousness and being,
being and existence, is man's most ancient belief and the root of sci-
ence and religion, magic and poetry. All our endeavors are aimed at
finding the old path, the forgotten way of communication between
both worlds. Our search tends to rediscover or to verify the universal
correspondence of opposites, reflection of their original identity. In-
spired by this principle, the Tantric systems conceive the body as a
metaphor or image of the cosmos. Sense centers are knots of energy,
confluences of stellar, sanguineous, nervous currents. Each one of the
postures of embracing bodies is the sign of a zodiac ruled by the triple
rhythm of sap, blood, and light. The temple of Konarak is covered
with a delirious jungle of interlocking bodies: stone burns, enamored
substances intertwine. Alchemical weddings are not unlike human
ones. In an autobiographical poem Po-Chü-i tells us that

> *In the middle of the night I stole a furtive glance.*
> *The two ingredients were in affable embrace;*
> *Their attitude was most unexpected,*

[3] *Katha Upanishad*, see note 2, above.

They were locked together in the posture of man and wife,
Intertwined as dragons, coil on coil.[4]

In Eastern tradition truth is a personal experience, and strictly speaking, it cannot be communicated. Sometimes the "being in the know" is expressed by a hearty laugh, a smile, or a paradox. But this smile can also indicate that the adept has not found anything. All knowledge would then be reduced to knowing that knowledge is impossible. Again and again the texts delight in ambiguities of this kind. Doctrine is resolved into silence. Chuang-Tzu affirms that language, by its very nature, cannot express the absolute, a difficulty that is not so different from the one that vexes the creators of symbolic logic. "Tao cannot be defined. . . . The one who knows does not speak. And the one who speaks does not know. Therefore, the Sage preaches the doctrine without words." The condemnation of words stems from the incapacity of language to transcend the world of relative and interdependent opposites, of the *this* in relation to the *that*. "When people speak of apprehending truth, they are thinking of books. But books are made of words. Of course, words have some value. The value of words lies in the meaning they conceal. Now, this meaning is merely an effort to overtake something that cannot truly be overtaken by words."[5] Indeed, the meaning points to things, indicates them, but never overtakes them. Objects are beyond the reach of words.

Despite his criticism of language, Chuang-Tzu did not renounce the word. The same is true of Zen Buddhism, a doctrine that is resolved into paradoxes and silence but to which we owe two of man's highest verbal creations: the Nō theater and Basho's haiku. How can we explain this contradiction? Chuang-Tzu affirms that the sage "preaches the doctrine without words." Now, Taoism—unlike Christianity—does not believe in good works. Or in bad ones: it simply does not believe in works. The wordless preaching to which the Chinese philosopher alludes is not that of example, but of a language that is something more than language: a word that expresses the inexpressible. Although Chuang-Tzu never thought of poetry as a language capable of

4 Arthur Waley, *The Life and Times of Po Chü-i* (London, 1949).
5 Arthur Waley, *The Way and Its Power: A Study of the Tao Te Ching and Its Place in Chinese Thought* (London, 1949).

transcending the meaning of this and that and saying the unsayable, his reasoning cannot be separated from the image, the play on words and other poetic forms. Poetry and thought are interwoven in Chuang-Tzu to form a single fabric, a single uncommon matter. The same must be said of other doctrines. By means of poetic images Taoist, Hindu, and Buddhist thought becomes comprehensible. When Chuang-Tzu explains that the experience of Tao involves a turning back to a kind of elemental or original consciousness where the relative meanings of language are inoperative, he resorts to a play on words that is a poetic enigma. He says that this experience of returning to what we are originally is "to enter the bird cage without making the birds sing." *Fan* is cage and return; *ming* is song and names.[6] Thus, the phrase also means: "to return to the place where names are superfluous," to silence, realm of the evident. Or to the place where names and things fuse and are the same: to poetry, the realm where naming is being. The image expresses the inexpressible: light feathers are heavy stones. We must return to language in order to see how the image can say that which language, by its very nature, seems incapable of saying.

Language is meaning: sense of this or that. Feathers are light; stones, heavy. The light is light in relation to the heavy, the dark is dark in relation to the bright, and so on. All communications systems live in the world of references and of relative meanings. Thus they constitute groups of signs endowed with a certain mobility. For example, in the case of numbers, a zero on the left is not the same a zero on the right: numbers change their meaning according to their position. The same occurs with language, but its range of mobility is much greater than that of other methods of signification and communication. Each word has a number of meanings, which are more or less interrelated. Those meanings are ordered and made precise in accordance with the word's place in the sentence. All the words that compose the phrase —and with them, their diverse meanings—suddenly acquire one sense: that of the sentence. The others disappear or weaken. Or in other words: of itself language is an infinite possibility of meanings;

[6] Ibid.

when it is actualized in a phrase, when it truly becomes language, that possibility is fixed in a single direction. In prose, the unity of the phrase is achieved by the sense, which is something like an arrow that forces all the words that compose it to aim at the same object or in the same direction. Now, the image is a phrase in which the plurality of meanings does not disappear. The image receives and exalts all the values of the words, without excluding the primary and secondary meanings. How can the image, containing two or more meanings, be one and resist the tension of so many opposing forces, without turning into sheer nonsense? There are many propositions, perfectly correct with regard to what we would call the grammatical and logical syntax, that are resolved into a meaning opposite to that which was intended. Others end in nonsense, like those cited by García Bacca in his *Introduction to Modern Logic* ("the number two is two stones"). But the image is neither countersense nor nonsense. Thus, the unity of the image must be something more than the merely formal unity that is given in the countersense and, in general, in all those propositions that mean nothing or that constitute mere incoherence. What can be the sense of the image if a number of disparate meanings struggle within it?

The poet's images possess meaning on different levels. In the first place, they have authenticity: the poet has seen or heard them, they are the genuine expression of his vision and experience of the world. This is a truth of a psychological order, which obviously has nothing to do with the problem that concerns us. In the second place, those images constitute an objective reality, valid per se: they are works. A landscape by Góngora is not the same as a natural landscape, but both possess reality and consistency, although they live in different spheres. They are two orders of parallel and autonomous realities. In this case, the poet does something more than tell the truth; he creates realities possessed of a truth: the realities of his own existence. Poetic images have their own logic and no one is shocked because the poet says that water is crystal or "the pepper tree is cousin to the willow" (Carlos Pellicer). But this aesthetic truth of the image is only valid within its own universe. Finally, the poet affirms that his images tell us something about the world and about ourselves and that this something, although it seems absurd, really reveals to us what we are. Does this pretension of poetic images possess any objective foundation, does the apparent countersense or nonsense of the poetic utterance have any meaning?

When we perceive any object, it presents itself to us as a plurality of qualities, sensations, and meanings. This plurality is unified, instantaneously, at the moment of perception. The unifying element of that whole contradictory cluster of qualities and forms is the meaning. Things have a meaning. Even in the case of the simplest, most casual and distracted perception there is a certain intentionality, as phenomenological analyses have shown. Thus, the meaning is not only the foundation of language, but also of every laying hold upon the real. Our experience of the plurality and ambiguity of reality seems to be redeemed in the sense. Like ordinary perception, the poetic image reproduces the plurality of reality and, at the same time, gives it unity. Up to this point the poet merely does what all men do. Now let us see in what the unifying operation of the image consists, in order to differentiate it from the other modes of expressing reality.

All our versions of the real—syllogisms, descriptions, scientific formulas, commentaries of a practical order, and so on—do not re-create that which they try to express. They limit themselves to representing or describing it. If we see a chair, for example, we perceive instantaneously its color, its shape, the materials of which it is constructed, and the rest. The apprehension of all these scattered and contradictory notes is no obstacle to our being given, simultaneously, the meaning of the chair: being a piece of furniture, a tool. But if we wish to describe our perception of the chair, we shall have to proceed with care, and one part at a time: first its form, then its color and so on successively until we arrive at the meaning. In the course of the descriptive process the totality of the object has gradually been lost. At first the chair was only form, then a certain kind of wood and finally pure abstract meaning: the chair is an object that is used for sitting. In the poem the chair is an instantaneous and total presence, which strikes our attention all at once. The poet does not describe the chair: he puts it before us. As at the moment of perception, the chair is given to us with all its contrary qualities and, crowning all, the meaning. Thus, the image re-

produces the moment of perception and compels the reader to sum-
mon within himself the object perceived one day. The verse, the
rhythm-phrase, evokes, resuscitates, awakens, re-creates. Or as Macha-
do said: it does not represent, it presents. It re-creates, relives our ex-
perience of the real. It seems useless to point out that such resurrec-
tions are not only those of our everyday experience, but also those of
our most obscure and remote life. The poem makes us remember that
which we have forgotten: this that we really are.

The chair is many things at the same time: it is to sit in, but it can
also have other uses. And the same is true of words. As soon as they
reconquer their plenitude, they reacquire their lost meanings and val-
ues. The ambiguity of the image is no different from that of reality, as
we apprehend it at the moment of perception: immediate, contradic-
tory, plural, and, nevertheless, possessed of a recondite meaning.
Thanks to the image there is produced the instantaneous reconcilia-
tion between the name and the object, between the representation and
the reality. Therefore, the agreement between the subject and the ob-
ject is given with a certain plenitude. That agreement would be im-
possible if the poet did not make use of language and if that language,
by virtue of the image, did not recover its original richness. But this
return of words to their original nature—that is, to their plurality of
meanings—is merely the first act of the poetic operation. We have still
not fully grasped the meaning of the poetic image.

Every phrase has a reference to another, is susceptible to being ex-
plained by another. Thanks to the mobility of signs, words can be
explained by words. When we encounter an obscure sentence we say:
"What these words are trying to say is this or that." And in order to
say "this or that" we resort to other words. Every phrase means some-
thing that can be expressed or explained by another phrase. Conse-
quently, the sense or meaning is a *trying to say*. Or rather: an utterance
that can be said in another way. On the contrary, the meaning of the
image is the image itself: it cannot be said with other words. *The
image explains itself*. Nothing, except it, can say what it tries to say.
Meaning and image are the same thing. A poem has no meaning other
than its images. When we see the chair, we instantaneously apprehend
its meaning: with no need to resort to the word, we sit down in it. The

same occurs with the poem: its images do not lead us to something else, as happens with prose, but bring us face to face with a concrete reality. When Quevedo says of the lips of his beloved: "With disdain they utter sonorous ice," he does not make a symbol of whiteness or of pride. He confronts us with a fact without recourse to demonstration: teeth, words, ice, lips, disparate realities, appear at once before our eyes. Goya does not describe for us the horrors of war: he offers us, starkly, war's image. Commentaries, references, and explanations are superfluous. The poet does not try to say: *he says*. Sentences and phrases are means. The image is not a means; sustained by itself, it is its meaning. The sense begins and ends in the image. The sense of the poem is the poem itself. Images cannot be reduced to any explanation and interpretation. So then words—which had recovered their original ambiguity—now undergo another disconcerting and more radical transformation. In what does it consist?

Words, derived from the expressive nature of language, are distinguished by two attributes: first, their mobility or interchangeability; second, by virtue of their mobility, the capacity of one word to be explained by another. We can express the simplest idea in many ways. Or change the words of a text or a phrase without seriously altering the meaning. Or explain one sentence by another. None of this is possible with the image. There are many ways to say the same thing in prose; there is only one in poetry. It is not the same to say "of its very nakedness shines the star" as "the star shines because it is naked." In the second version the meaning has been debased: it has changed from an affirmation to an abject explanation. The tension of the poetic current has been relaxed. The image causes words to lose their mobility and interchangeability. They become irreplaceable, irreparable. They have ceased to be instruments. Language is no longer a tool. The return of language to its original nature, which seemed to be the ultimate purpose of the image, is thus only the preliminary step for an even more radical operation: language, touched by poetry, suddenly ceases to be language. Or rather: a cluster of mobile and expressive signs. The poem transcends language. Now what I said at the beginning of this book has been explained: the poem is language—and language before being subjected to the mutilation of prose or conversation—but it is also something more. And that something more cannot be explained by language, although it can only be reached by means of it. Born of the word, the poem issues in something that surpasses it.

The poetic experience cannot be reduced to the word and, nevertheless, only the word expresses it. The image reconciles opposites, but this reconciliation cannot be explained by words—except by those of the image, which have now ceased to be what they were. Thus, the image is a desperate measure against the silence that invades us each time we try to express the terrible experience of that which surrounds us and of our selves. The poem is language in tension: in the extreme of being and in being to the extreme. Extremes of the word and extreme words, turned in upon their own entrails, showing the reverse of speech: silence and non-meaning. On this side of the image lies the world of language, of explanations and history. On the other side open the doors to the real: meaning and non-meaning become equivalent terms. This is the ultimate sense of the image: the image itself.

Of course, opposites are not reconciled in all images without being destroyed. Some images reveal similarities between the terms or elements of which reality is made: they are the comparisons, as Aristotle defined them. Others approximate "contrary realities" and thus produce a "new reality," as Reverdy says. Others provoke an insuperable contradiction or an absolute absurdity, which betrays the ridiculous nature of the world, of language, or of man (to this class belong flashes of wit and, outside the ambit of poetry, jokes). Still others show us the plurality and interdependence of the real. There are, in short, images that achieve what seems to be a logical as well as a linguistic impossibility: the marriage of opposites. In them all—scarcely visible or fully realized—is observed the same process: the plurality of the real is manifested or expressed as ultimate unity, while each element retains its essential singularity. Feathers are stones, without ceasing to be feathers. Language, turned in on itself, says that which by nature seemed to elude it. Poetic expression expresses the inexpressible.

The reproach that Chuang-Tzu made to words does not apply to the image, because it no longer is, strictly speaking, a verbal function. Indeed, language is the meaning of this or that. Meaning is the nexus between the name and the thing we name. Thus, it implies a distance between the two. When we enunciate a certain kind of proposition ("the telephone is to eat," "Mary is a triangle," etc.) the result is non-sense because the distance between the word and the thing, the sign and the object, cannot be traversed: the bridge, the sense, has been broken. Man is left to himself, shut up in his language. And, in fact, he is also left without a language, because the words he utters are pure sounds that no longer mean anything. The opposite occurs with the image. Far from increasing, the distance between the word and the thing decreases or disappears completely: the name and the named are now the same. The sense—insofar as it is a nexus or bridge—also disappears: now there is nothing to grasp, nothing to indicate. But what is produced is not nonsense or countersense, it is something that is inexpressible and inexplicable except by means of itself. Again: the sense of the image is the image itself. Language goes beyond the circle of relative meanings, the *this* and the *that*, and says the unsayable: stones are feathers, this is that. Language indicates, represents; the poem does not explain or represent: it presents. It does not allude to reality; it tries to re-create it—and sometimes succeeds.

The truth of the poem leans on the poetic experience, which does not differ essentially from the experience of identification with the "reality of reality," as it has been described by Eastern thought and a part of Western. This experience, reputed to be unutterable, is expressed and communicated in the image. And here we confront another troubling property of the poem, which will be examined in a later chapter: because it cannot be explained, except by itself, the image's proper form of communication is not conceptual transmission. The image does not explain: it invites one to re-create and, literally, to relive it. The poet's utterance is incarnated in poetic communion. The image transmutes man and converts him in turn into an image, that is, into a space where opposites fuse. And man himself, split asunder since birth, is reconciled with himself when he becomes an image, when *he becomes another*. Poetry is metamorphosis, change, an alchemical operation, and therefore it borders on magic, religion, and other attempts to transform man and make of "this one" and "that one" that "other one" who is he himself. The universe ceases to be a vast storehouse of heterogeneous things. Stars, shoes, tears, locomotives, willow trees, women, dictionaries, all is an immense family, all is in mutual communication and is unceasingly transformed, the same blood flows through all the forms and man can at last be his desire: he himself. Poetry puts man outside himself and, simultaneously, makes him return to his original being: returns him to himself. Man is his image: he himself and that other one. By the phrase that is rhythm, that is image, man—that perpetual becoming—is. Poetry is entry into being.

The Poetic Revelation

6. The Other Shore

MAN REVEALS HIMSELF in rhythm, the emblem of his temporality; rhythm, in turn, declares itself in the image; and the image returns to man as soon as two lips repeat the poem. By means of rhythm, creative repetition, the image—a bundle of meanings that rebel at explanation —is opened to participation. The recitation of poetry is a festival: a communion. And what is shared and re-created in it is the image. The poem is realized in participation, which is nothing but the re-creation of the original instant. Thus, the examination of the poem leads us to the examination of the poetic experience. Poetic rhythm does not fail to offer analogies to mythical time; the image, to mystical utterance; participation, to magical alchemy and religious communion. Everything leads us to insert the poetic act into the realm of the sacred. But all things, from the primitive mentality to fashion, political fanaticism, and even crime, are susceptible to being regarded as a form of the sacred. The fertility of this notion—which has been abused as much as psychoanalysis and historicism—can bring us to the utmost confusion. And therefore these pages do not propose to explain poetry in terms of the sacred as much as to trace the limits between the two and to show that poetry constitutes an irreducible act, which can only be totally understood in and of itself.

Modern man has discovered modes of thinking and feeling that are not far from what we call the nocturnal part of our being. All that reason, morality, or modern customs cause us to hide or despise constitutes the only possible attitude toward reality for the so-called primitive. Freud revealed that merely to ignore the unconscious life was not enough to make it disappear. And anthropology demonstrates that one can live in a world governed by dreams and the imagination without being abnormal or neurotic. The world of the divine never ceases to fascinate us because, beyond intellectual curiosity, there is in modern man a nostalgia. The popularity of studies about myths and magical and religious institutions has the same roots as other contemporary enthusiasms, such as primitive art, the psychology of the unconscious, or occult tradition. These preferences are not accidental. They are the testimony of an absence, the intellectual forms of a nostalgia. And so, as I reflect on this theme, I cannot fail to be aware of its ambiguity. On the one hand, I believe that poetry and religion spring from the same source and that it is not possible to dissociate the poem from its pretension to change man without the risk of turning the poem into an inoffensive form of literature. On the other hand, I believe that the Promethean thrust of modern poetry consists in its belligerence toward religion, the source of its deliberate will to create a new "sacred," in contradistinction to the one that churches offer us today.

In studying the institutions of the aborigines of Australia and Africa, or examining the folklore and mythology of historical peoples, anthropologists found patterns of thought and conduct that seemed to defy reason. Constrained to find an explanation, some thought that mistaken applications of the principle of causality were responsible. Frazer believed that magic was "man's most ancient attitude toward reality," from which science, religion, and poetry had developed. A fallacious science, magic was "an erroneous interpretation of the laws that govern nature." Lévy-Bruhl entertained the notion of a prelogical mentality, grounded on participation: "The primitive does not associate logically, causally, the objects of his experience. He neither sees them as a chain of causes and effects, nor regards them as different phenomena, but rather experiences a reciprocal participation of such objects, so that one of them cannot be moved without affecting the other. That is, one cannot be touched without influencing the other and without causing a change in man himself." Freud, with limited success, applied his ideas to the study of certain primitive institutions. C. G. Jung has also attempted a psychological explanation based on the collective unconscious and on universal mythical archetypes. Lévi-Strauss seeks the origin of incest, perhaps the first "no" that man has set against nature. Dumézil reflects on Aryan myths and finds in the springtime communion—or as he calls it poetically in one of his books: *The Feast of Immortality*—the origin of Indo-European mythology and poetry. Cassirer conceives myth, magic, art, and religion as man's symbolic expressions. Malinowski . . . but the field is vast and it changes constantly as new ideas and discoveries appear.

In the face of this enormous mass of facts and hypotheses, the first question we must ask ourselves is whether there really is such a thing as a primitive society. Nothing is more debatable. The Lacandons, for example, can be regarded as a group of people who live under really archaic conditions. But they are the direct descendants of the Mayas, whose civilization was the richest and most complex that flourished in the Americas. The institutions of the Lacandons do not represent the genesis of a culture, but its last residuum. Their mentality is not pre-logical, nor do their magic practices represent a prereligious state, since Lacandon society does not precede anything except death. And thus, those forms seem to show us how certain cultures die, rather than how they are born. In other cases—as Toynbee indicates—there are societies whose civilization has been petrified, like the Eskimo. Whether decadent or petrified, it is doubtful that any of the societies studied by the specialists really deserve to be called primitive.

The idea of a "primitive mentality"—in the sense of something ancient, anterior, and now surpassed or in the process of being surpassed—is merely one of many manifestations of a linear conception of history. From this standpoint it is an excrescence of the notion of "progress." Moreover, both proceed from the quantitative conception of time. And that is not all. In the first of his great works, Lévy-Bruhl affirms that "the need for participation is surely more compelling and intense, even among ourselves, than the need for knowing or for adapting oneself to logical exigencies. It is more profound and its origin is more remote." Psychiatrists have found certain analogies between the genesis of neurosis and that of myths; schizophrenia reveals a similarity to magic thought. For children, the psychologist Piaget says, true reality is constituted of what we call fantasy: given two explanations of a phenomenon, one rational and the other miraculous, they inevitably choose the latter because they find it more convincing. Frazer has pointed out the persistence of magical beliefs in modern man. But it is not necessary to resort to more testimonies. We all know that not only poets, madmen, savages, and children apprehend the world in an act of participation that cannot be reduced to logical reasoning; but each time they dream, fall in love, or take part in their professional, civic, or political ceremonies, other human beings "participate," return, form part of that vast "society of life" that Cassirer regards as the source of magical beliefs. And I do not exclude teachers, psychiatrists, and politicians. The "primitive mentality" is everywhere, covered by a layer of rationality or out in the open. But it does not seem legitimate to classify all these attitudes as "primitive," because they do not constitute ancient, infantile, or regressive forms of the psyche, but a present possibility that is common to all men.

If for many the protagonist of rites and ceremonies is a man radically different from us—a primitive or a neurotic—for others not man but institutions are the essence of the sacred. An aggregation of social forms, the sacred is an object. Rites, myths, festivals, legends—what are revealingly called the "material"—are there, before us: they are objects, things. Hubert and Mauss maintain that the believer's feelings and emotions vis-à-vis the sacred do not constitute specific experiences or special categories. Man does not change and human nature is always the same: love, hate, dread, fear, hunger, thirst. Social institutions change. But I do not agree with this opinion. Man is inseparable from his creations and his objects; if all the institutions that form the universe of the sacred really constitute something closed and unique, a real universe, the one who participates in a festival or a ceremony is also a different being from the one who, a few hours before, hunted in the woods or drove a car. Man is never identical to himself. His mode of being, the thing that distinguishes him from other living beings, is change. Or as Ortega y Gasset says: man is an insubstantial being: he lacks substance. And precisely what characterizes the religious experience is the abrupt leap, the fulminating change of nature. Therefore it is not true that our feelings are the same before the real tiger and the tiger-god, before an erotic print and the Tantric images of Tibet.

Social institutions are not the sacred, but the "primitive mentality" or neurosis is not, either. Both methods reveal the same insufficiency. Both change the sacred into an object. Consequently, one must flee from these extremes and embrace the phenomenon as a totality of which we ourselves form part. Neither the institutions separated from their protagonist, nor the protagonist isolated from the institutions. A description of the experience of the divine as something outside us would also be inadequate. That experience includes us, and its description will be our own description.[1]

The starting point of some sociologists is the division of society into two opposite worlds: the sacred and the profane. The taboo could be the dividing line between the two. Certain things may be done in one area that are forbidden in the other. Notions like purity and pollution would stem from this division. But, as I stated before, a mere description in which we ourselves were not included would give us only a series of external data. Moreover, every society is divided into different spheres, and each sphere is governed by a system of rules and prohibitions that are not applicable to the others. Legislation on inheritance has no function in penal law (although it did have, in remote epochs); acts like the giving of gifts, required by the laws of etiquette, would be scandalous if performed by the public administration; norms governing the political relations between nations are not applicable to the family, nor are those of the family to international trade. In each

[1] All this was written ten years before *La pensée sauvage* came out in 1962. In this capital work, Lévi-Strauss shows that the "primitive mentality" is no less rational than our own.

sphere things happen in a "certain way," which is always privative. Thus, we must penetrate the world of the sacred to see concretely how "things happen" and, above all, what happens to us.

If the sacred is a world apart, how can we penetrate it? By means of what Kierkegaard calls the "leap" and we, in the Spanish way, call the "mortal leap." Hui-neng, the seventh-century Chinese patriarch, explains the central experience of Buddhism as follows: "Mahaprajnaparamita is a Sanskrit term of the western country; in the T'ang language it means: great-wisdom-other-shore-reached.... What is Maha? Maha is great.... What is Prajna? Prajna is wisdom.... What is Paramita? The other shore reached. . . . To be attached to the objective world is to be attached to the cycle of living and dying, which is like the waves that rise in the sea; this is called: this shore. . . . When we detach ourselves from the objective world, there is neither death nor life and one is like water flowing incessantly; this is called: the other shore."[2]

At the end of many sutras, Prajnaparamita, the idea of the journey or leap, is expressed imperiously: "Oh, gone, gone, gone to the other shore, fallen on the other shore." Few attain the experience of the leap, in spite of the fact that baptism, communion, the sacraments, and other rites of initiation or passage are intended to prepare us for that experience. They all aim to change us, to make us "others." Thus we are given a new name, to indicate that now we are others: we have just been born or reborn. The rite reproduces the mystical experience of the "other shore" as well as the capital event of human life: our birth, which requires the previous death of the fetus. And perhaps our deepest and most meaningful acts are merely the repetition of this death of the fetus that is reborn as an infant. In short, the "mortal leap," the experience of the "other shore," implies a change of nature: it is a dying and a being born. But the "other shore" is within ourselves. Motionless, still, we feel ourselves being drawn, stirred by a great wind that casts us out of ourselves. It casts us out and, at the same time, pushes us into ourselves. The metaphor of the gust of wind

[2] D. T. Suzuki, *Manual of Zen Buddhism: From the Chinese Zen Masters* (London, 1950).

presents itself again and again in the great religious texts of all cultures: man is uprooted like a tree and thrown beyond, to the other shore, to the encounter of himself. And here another extraordinary note presents itself: the will intervenes little or participates in a paradoxical way. If he has been chosen by the great wind, it is useless for man to try to resist it. And vice versa: whatever the value of the works or the fervor of the supplication, the act is not produced if the strange power does not intervene. The will is inextricably mingled with other forces, exactly as at the moment of poetic creation. Freedom and fatality rendezvous in man. The Spanish theater offers a number of illustrations of this conflict.

In *El condenado por desconfiado*, Tirso de Molina—or whoever the author of this work may be—introduces us to Paulo, a hermit who has spent ten years in the austerity of a cave seeking salvation. One day he dreams that he is dead; he appears before God and learns the truth: he will go to hell. On awakening, he doubts. The devil appears to him in the form of an angel and tells him that God orders him to go to Naples: there he will find the answer to the doubt that torments him, in the figure of Enrico. In him he will find his destiny "because the end that Enrico will have will also be your end." Enrico is "the most evil man in the world," although he has two virtues: filial love and faith. Before the mirror of Enrico, Paulo recoils in horror; then, not without a certain logic, he decides to imitate him. But Paulo sees only one part of his model, the part that is most external, and does not know that this criminal is also a man of faith who surrenders himself to God at decisive moments. At the end of the work, Enrico repents and yields uncompromisingly to the divine will: he takes the mortal leap and is saved. The stubborn Paulo takes another leap: to the infernal void. In some manner he sinks into himself, because doubt has drained him inwardly. What is Paulo's crime? To Tirso, the theologian, it is distrust, doubt. And more deeply, pride. Paulo never abandons himself to God. His lack of confidence in the divinity is transformed into an excess of confidence in himself: in the devil. Paulo is guilty of not being able to hear. But God expresses Himself as silence; the devil, as voice. Surrender frees Enrico from the weight of sin and gives him eternal freedom; the affirmation of himself causes Paulo to be lost.

Freedom is a mystery, because it is a divine grace and God's will is inscrutable.

Over and beyond the theological problems raised by *El condenado por desconfiado*, the instantaneous transition, the fulminating change of nature in the protagonists is noteworthy. Enrico is a monster; suddenly he becomes "another" and dies repentant. Paulo, also in an instant, turns from an ascetic into a libertine. In another work, *El esclavo del demonio* by Mira de Mescua, the psychic revolution is equally vertiginous and total. One of the first scenes of the drama shows Don Gil, a pious priest, as he surprises a gallant in the act of climbing up to the balcony of Lisarda, his beloved. The religious manages to dissuade him and the youth leaves. When the priest is alone, the surge of pride for his good deed opens up the doors to sin. In a scintillating monologue, Don Gil takes the mortal leap: from joy he proceeds to pride and thence to lust. In the twinkling of an eye he becomes "another": he climbs the ladder the young man has left and, under cover of night and desire, sleeps with the maiden. The next morning Lisarda learns the priest's identity. For her too one world closes and another opens. From love she proceeds to the affirmation of herself, a negative affirmation, as it were: since love is denied her, she has no choice but to embrace evil. Vertigo takes possession of them both. From this point on the action, literally, plunges downward. The two stop at nothing: robbery, murder, parricide. But their acts, like those of Paulo and Enrico, do not tolerate a psychological explanation. It is useless to seek reasons for this somber fervor. Free, but also driven, drawn by an abyss that beckons, in one instant that is every instant, they throw themselves over the precipice. Although their acts are the fruit of a decision at once instantaneous and irrevocable, the poet shows them to us inhabited by other forces, violent, excessive. They are possessed: they are "others." And this being others consists in throwing themselves downward into themselves. Like Enrico and Paulo, they have taken a leap. Leaps: acts that wrench us from this world and cause us to penetrate the other shore without knowing for certain if it is we ourselves or the supernatural that casts us there.

The "world of here and now" is made of relative opposites. It is the realm of explanations, reasons, and motives. The great wind blows and the chain of cause and effect breaks. And the first consequence of this catastrophe is the abolition of the laws of gravity, both natural and moral. Man loses weight, he is a feather. The heroes of Tirso and Mira de Mescua do not meet any resistance: they sink or rise vertically, and nothing can stop them. At the same time, the shape of the world is transposed: what was above is below; what was below is above. The leap is to the void or to absolute being. Good and evil are notions that acquire another meaning as soon as we enter the realm of the sacred. Criminals are saved, the just are lost. Human acts are ambiguous. We do evil, we listen to the devil when we think we are acting with righteousness, and vice versa. Morality is alien to the sacred. We are in a world that is, actually, another world.

The same ambiguity distinguishes our feelings and sensations vis-à-vis the divine. Before the gods and their images we feel simultaneously loathing and longing, terror and love, repulsion and fascination. We flee from that which we seek, as do the mystics; our delight is in suffering, say the martyrs. In one of Quevedo's sonnets, which bears a quotation by San Juan Crisólogo (*Plus ordebat, quam urebat*) as its epigraph, the poet describes the joys of martyrdom:

> Arde Lorenzo y goza en las parrillas;
> el tirano en Lorenzo arde y padece,
> viendo que su valor constante crece
> cuanto crecen las llamas amarillas.
>
> Las brasas multiplica en maravillas
> y Sol entre carbones amanece
> y en alimento a su verdugo ofrece
> guisadas del martirio sus costillas.
>
> A Cristo imita en darse en alimento
> a su enemigo, esfuerzo soberano
> y ardiente imitación del Sacramento.
>
> Mírale el cielo eternizar lo humano,
> y viendo victorioso el vencimiento
> menos abrasa que arde el vil tirano.

As he burns, Lawrence delights in his martyrdom; the tyrant suffers and is burned in his enemy. In order to perceive the distance that separates this sacred martyrdom from profane tortures, we have only to think of the Marquis de Sade's world. There the relation between victims and executioner is nonexistent; nothing destroys the libertine's loneliness because his victims turn into objects. The pleasure of his executioners is pure and solitary. It is not really pleasure, but cold fury. The desire of Sade's characters is infinite because it can never be satisfied. His world is the world of incommunication: each person is alone in his hell. In Quevedo's sonnet, the ambiguity of communion is brought to its ultimate consequences. The gridiron is an instrument of torture and a cooking utensil, and Lawrence's transfiguration is two-sided: he becomes a roast and a sun. The duality is repeated on the moral plane: the tyrant's triumph is defeat; Lawrence's defeat is victory. And not only do their feelings intermingle to such a degree that it is impossible to know where suffering ends and pleasure begins, but Lawrence, by the action of communion, is also his executioner and the latter is his victim.

The divine affects the notions of space and time, the foundations and limits of our thinking, perhaps even more decisively. The experience of the sacred affirms: here is there; bodies are ubiquitous; space is not an extension, but a quality; yesterday is today; the past returns; the future has already happened. If one examines closely the way time passes and things happen, one perceives the presence of a center that attracts or separates, elevates or plunges, moves or immobilizes. Sacred dates return according to a certain rhythm, which is not different from the one that joins or separates bodies, reverses feelings, turns joy into pain, suffering into pleasure, good into evil. The universe is magnetized. A kind of rhythm weaves together time and space, thoughts and feelings, acts and judgments and makes a single fabric of yesterday and tomorrow, here and there, disgust and delight. All is today. All is present. All is, all exists here. But also all is in another place and another time. Outside of itself and filled with itself. And the feeling that all is arbitrary and capricious is transformed into the intimation that things are governed by something radically strange and different from us. The mortal leap puts us face to face with the supernatural. The sensation of being in the presence of the supernatural is the starting point of every religious experience.

The supernatural manifests itself, first of all, as a sensation of radical strangeness. And that strangeness interdicts reality and existence itself, at the very moment when it affirms them in their most commonplace and palpable expressions. Lawrence becomes a sun, but also an atrocious piece of burned flesh. Everything is real and unreal. Rites and religious ceremonies emphasize this ambiguity. I recall that one evening in Mathura, sacred city of Hinduism, I had occasion to attend a little ceremony on the banks of the Jumna. The rite is very simple: at the twilight hour a Brahman lights the sacred fire in a little niche and feeds the turtles that live along the river's edge; then he intones a hymn as the devout ring bells, sing, and burn incense. That day about twenty-five or thirty followers of Krishna, whose great shrine is located a few miles away, were present at the ceremony. When the Brahman lighted the fire (and how faint was that light in comparison with the vast night that began to rise before us!), the pious shouted, sang, and jumped about. Their shouts and contortions caused me to feel contempt and sorrow. Nothing less solemn, nothing more sordid, than that decadent fervor. While the wretched shouting grew louder, a few naked children laughed and played; others fished or swam. Standing motionless, a peasant urinated in the opaque water. Some women washed clothes. The river flowed on. Everything went on with its usual life and only the turtles, craning their necks to capture their food, seemed exalted. Finally, all was still. The beggars returned to the market, the pilgrims to their inns, the turtles to the water. Was the cult of Krishna nothing more than this?

Every rite is a performance. The one who participates in a ceremony is like an actor who plays a part: at the same time he is and is not in his character. The stage also plays a part: that mountain is a serpent's palace, that river flowing carelessly is a divinity. And yet mountain and river do not cease to be what they are on that account. Everything is and is not. Those followers of Krishna were acting a part, but by this I do not mean to say that they were the actors in a farce; I simply wish to emphasize the ambiguous nature of their act. Everything happens in a common, ordinary way, frequently in a way that wounds us by its aggressive vulgarity; and at the same time, everything is anointed. The believer is and is not in this world. This world is and is not real.

Sometimes the ambiguity is manifested as humor. The adept of Zen, by means of exercises that do not exclude the grotesque and a kind of circular nihilism, which ends by refuting itself, attains to sudden enlightenment. A disciple asks, "Could you play any music on a harp without strings?" The master does not answer for a time and then says, "Did you hear it?" "No," the other replies. Whereupon the master says, "Why didn't you ask me to play louder?"[3]

Strangeness is wonder at a commonplace reality that is suddenly revealed as that which was never seen before. Alice's doubts show us to what extent the ground of so-called certainties can sink beneath our feet: "*I'm sure I'm not Ada, for her hair goes in such long ringlets and mine doesn't go in ringlets at all, and I'm sure I can't be Mabel. . . . Besides, she's she, and I'm I, and—oh dear, how puzzling it all is!*" Alice's doubts are not very different from those of the poets and mystics. Like them, Alice is astonished. But what is she astonished at? At herself, her own reality, yes, but also at something that casts doubt on her reality, the identity of her very being. This thing that is before us —tree, mountain, image of stone or of wood, I myself who contemplate myself—is not a natural presence. It is another. It is inhabited by the Other. The experience of the supernatural is the experience of the Other.

For Rudolf Otto the presence of the Other—and we could add, the sensation of "otherness"—manifests itself "as a *tremendum mysterium*, a mystery that causes one to tremble."[4] In analyzing the content of the tremendous, the German thinker finds three elements. First, sacred terror, that is, "a special terror," which cannot be compared to the fear a known danger produces in us. Sacred terror is inexpressible dread, precisely because it is the experience of the inexpressible. The second element is the majesty of the Presence or Apparition: "tremendous majesty." Finally, to the majestic power is allied the notion of "energy of the numinous" and thus the idea of a living, active, omnipotent God is the third element. Now, the last two notes are attributes of the divine presence and seem to be derived from the experience rather

[3] D. T. Suzuki, *Essays on Zen Buddhism*, first series (London, 1927).
[4] Rudolf Otto, *The Idea of the Holy*, translated as *Lo santo* by Fernando Vela (Madrid, 1928).

than to constitute its original nucleus. Therefore, we can exclude them and still retain the essential mark: "a mystery that causes one to tremble." But as soon as we consider this terrible mystery, we perceive that what we feel toward the unknown is not always terror or dread. We may well experience just the opposite: joy, fascination. In its purest and most primitive form the experience of "otherness" is strangeness, stupefaction, paralysis of the mind: astonishment. The same German philosopher acknowledges this when he says that the term "mysterium" must be understood as the "capital notion" of the experience. Mystery—that is, "absolute inaccessibility"—is nothing but the expression of "otherness," of this Other that presents itself as something by definition alien or strange to us. The Other is something that is not like us, a being that is also nonbeing. And the first thing its presence evokes is stupefaction. Now, stupefaction vis-à-vis the supernatural is not manifested as terror or dread, as joy or love, but as horror. Included in the horror is terror—the drawing back—and the fascination that makes us want to fuse with the presence. The horror paralyzes us. And not because the Presence is in itself a threat, but because its apparition is unbearable and fascinating at the same time. And that presence is horrible because in it all has been externalized. It is a face into which all depths flow, a presence that shows the obverse and reverse of being.

Baudelaire has devoted unforgettable pages to horrible, irregular beauty. That beauty is not of this world: the supernatural has consecrated it and it is an incarnation of the Other. The fascination it causes us to feel is the fascination of vertigo. But before falling into it, we experience a kind of paralysis. Not in vain does the theme of petrifaction appear again and again in myths and legends. Horror "takes our breath away," "freezes our blood," petrifies us. Stupefaction before the strange Presence is above all a state of suspended animation, that is, an interruption of the breathing, which is the flow of life. Horror interdicts existence. An invisible hand keeps us in suspense: we are nothing and that which surrounds us is nothing. The universe becomes an abyss and there is nothing before us but that motionless Presence, which does not talk, or move, or affirm this or that, but is only present. And that just being present engenders the horror.

The central moment of the *Bhagavad Gita* is the epiphany of Krishna. The god has assumed the form of the driver of Arjuna's war chariot. Before battle Arjuna and Krishna engage in a dialogue. The hero vacillates. It is not cowardice that troubles his spirit, but piety: victory means the slaying of people of his own blood, since the leaders of the enemy army are his cousins, his teachers, and his half brother. The destruction of the caste, Arjuna says, brings about "the destruction of the laws of the caste." And with them, the very foundations of the world, the destruction of the whole universe. At first Krishna attacks these reasons with earthly arguments: the warrior must fight because struggle is his "dharma." To withdraw from combat is to betray his destiny and that which he himself is: a fighter. None of this convinces Arjuna: to kill is a crime. And an inexpiable crime, because it will produce an endless karma. Krishna replies with reasons that are equally powerful: to abstain will not prevent bloodshed, but it will lead the Pandavas to defeat and death. Arjuna's situation reminds us a little of Antigone's, but the conflict of the *Gita* is more radical. Antigone wavers between the sacred law and the law of the city: to inter an enemy of the state is an unjust act; not to bury a brother is impiety. The act that Krishna proposes to Arjuna is not inspired by piety or by justice. Nothing justifies it. Thus, when reasons have been exhausted, Krishna manifests himself. It is not by accident that the god presents himself as a horrible form, because this is a true Apparition, I mean, a Presence in which all the forms of existence and, above all, the hidden and concealed forms, become apparent—visible, external, palpable. Arjuna, petrified, stupefied, describes his vision thus:

> Looking upon thy mighty form of many mouths and eyes, of
> many arms and thighs and feet, of many bellies, and grim with
> many teeth, O mighty-armed one, the worlds and I quake.
> For as I behold thee touching the heavens, glittering,
> many-hued, with yawning mouths, with wide eyes agleam, my
> inward soul trembles . . .

Vishnu is the "house of the universe" and his appearance is horrible because he manifests himself as a variegated presence, made of all forms: those of life as well as those of death. Horror is wonder at a fully packed and inaccessible whole. Before this Presence, which comprises all presences, good and evil cease to be contrary and discernible worlds and our acts lose weight, become inscrutable. Measures are different. Krishna sums up the situation in a phrase: *Thou art my tool.* Arjuna is merely a tool in the hands of the god. The axe does not know what animates the hand that grasps it. There are acts that cannot be judged by the morality of men: sacred acts.

In Aztec sculpture the sacred is also expressed as the replete, the too full. But the horrible does not consist in the mere accumulation of forms and symbols; rather it is the showing, on the same plane and at the same instant, of the two sides of existence. The horrible shows the entrails of being. Coatlicue is covered with ears of corn and skulls, flowers and claws. His being is every being. That which is within is outside. The entrails of life are visible at last. But those entrails are death. Life is death. And death, life. The organs of gestation are also those of destruction. Through the mouth of Krishna flows the river of creation. Through it the universe hurtles toward its ruin. All is present. And this *all is present* is the equivalent of *all is vacuous.* Indeed, the horror is not only manifested as total presence, but also as absence: the ground sinks, forms decay, the universe bleeds. All is rushing toward the void. There is an open mouth, a pit. Baudelaire felt this like no one else:

> Pascal avait son gouffre, avec lui se mouvant.
> —Hélas! tout est abîme—action, désir, rêve,
> Parole! et sur mon poil qui tout droit se relève
> Mainte fois de la Peur je sens passer le vent.
>
> En haut, en bas, partout, la profondeur, la grève,
> Le silence, l'espace affreux et captivant . . .
> Sur le fond de mes nuits Dieu de son doigt savant
> Dessine un cauchemar multiforme et sans trêve.
>
> J'ai peur du sommeil comme on a peur d'un grand trou,
> Tout plein de vague horreur, menant on ne sait où;
> Je ne vois qu'infini par toutes les fenêtres,

Et mon esprit, toujours du vertige hanté,
Jalouse du néant l'insensibilité.
—Ah! ne jamais sortir des Nombres et des Êtres!

Wonder, stupefaction, joy, the gamut of sensations vis-à-vis the Other is very rich. But they all have this in common: the spirit's first impulse is to draw back. The Other repels us: abyss, serpent, delight, beautiful and atrocious monster. And this repulsion is followed by the opposite impulse: we cannot take our eyes away from the presence, we lean toward the bottom of the precipice. Repulsion and fascination. And then, vertigo: to fall, to lose oneself, to be one with the Other. To empty oneself. To be nothing: to be everything: to be. Force of gravity of death, forgetting of self, abdication, and, simultaneously, instantaneous realization that this strange presence is also we. This thing that repels me, attracts me. That Other is also I. The fascination would be inexplicable if the horror at "otherness" were not, from its origin, tinged by the suspicion of our final identity with that which seems so strange and alien to us. Immobility is also a fall; the fall, ascension; presence, absence; fear, profound and invincible attraction. The experience of the Other culminates in the experience of Unity. The two opposite movements are intermingled. In the drawing back the leap forward is already latent. The downward plunge into the Other presents itself as a return to something from which we were previously uprooted. Duality ceases, we are on the other shore. We have taken the mortal leap. We have become reconciled with ourselves.

Sometimes, without an apparent cause—or as we say in Spanish: *porque sí* [just because]—we truly see that which surrounds us. And that vision is, in its own way, a kind of theophany or apparition, because the world is revealed to us in its plicatures and abysses as Krishna revealed himself to Arjuna. Every day we cross the same street or the same garden; every evening our eyes encounter the same reddish wall, made of bricks and urban time. Suddenly, any day, the street leads to another world, the garden has just been born, the weary wall is covered with signs. We never saw them before, and now it astonishes us that they are like this: such and so oppressively real. Their very compact reality causes us to doubt: are things thus or are they otherwise? No, what we are seeing for the first time we had already seen before. In a certain place, where we have perhaps never been, were the wall, the street, the garden. And the strangeness is followed by nostalgia. We seem to remember and we would like to go back there, to that place where things are always thus, bathed in a very ancient light and, at the same time, newly born. We too are from there. A puff of wind touches our forehead. We are enchanted, suspended in the midst of the motionless evening. We feel that we are from another world. It is the "former life," which returns.

States of strangeness and recognition, of repulsion and fascination, separation from and union with the Other, are also states of loneliness and communion with ourselves. The one who is truly alone with himself, the one who is sufficient unto himself in his own solitude, is not alone. Real loneliness consists in being separated from one's being, in being two. All of us are alone, because all of us are two. The strange one, the other, is our double. Again and again we try to lay hold upon him. Again and again he eludes us. He has no face or name, but he is always there, hiding. Each night for a few hours he fuses with us again. Each morning he breaks away. Are we his hollow, the trace of his absence? Is he an image? Yet it is not the mirror, but time, that multiplies him. And it is useless to flee, to be disconcerted, to get caught in the web of occupations, tasks, pleasures. The other is always absent. Absent and present. There is a hole, a pit at our feet. Man is violent, anguished, searching for that other who is he himself. And nothing can bring him back to himself, except the mortal leap: love, the image, the Apparition.

In the presence of the Apparition, because it is a real apparition, we waver between advancing and retreating. The contradictory character of our emotions paralyzes us. That body, those eyes, that voice hurt us and at the same time they fascinate us. We had never seen that face before, and already it is confused with our most remote past. It is total strangeness and the return to something that can only be qualified by the word intimate. To touch that body is to lose oneself in the unknown; but, also, it is to reach solid ground. Nothing is more alien and

118 THE POETIC REVELATION

nothing more our own. Love suspends us, draws us out of ourselves and throws us into the strange *par excellence*: another body, other eyes, another being. And only in that body that is not ours and in that irremediably alien life can we be ourselves. There is no longer another, there are no longer two. The instant of the most complete alienation is that of the absolute reconquest of our being. Here too all makes itself present and we see the other side, the dark and hidden side, of existence. Again being opens up its entrails.

The similarities between love and the experience of the sacred are something more than coincidences. These are acts that issue from the same source. On different levels of existence one takes the leap and tries to reach the other shore. Communion, to cite a very common example, operates a kind of change in the believer's nature. The sacred food transmutes us. And that being "others" is simply the recovery of our original nature or condition. "Woman," Novalis said, "is the highest corporal food." Thanks to erotic cannibalism man changes, that is, returns to his former state. The idea of the return—present in all religious acts, in all myths, and even in utopias—is the force of gravity of love. Woman exalts us, makes us come out of ourselves, and, simultaneously, makes us return. To fall: to be again. Hunger for life: hunger for death. Leap of energy, explosion, expansion of being: laziness, cosmic inertia, fall into the infinite. Strangeness before the Other: return to oneself. Experience of the unity and final identity of being.

The first to perceive that love, religion, and poetry have a common origin were the poets. Modern thinking has appropriated this discovery for its own purposes. For contemporary nihilism, poetry and religion are merely forms of sexuality: religion is a neurosis, poetry a sublimation. It is not necessary to dwell at length on these explanations. Nor on those that attempt to explain one phenomenon by means of another—economic, social, or psychological—which in turn requires another explanation. All those hypotheses, as has been said many times, betray the ascendancy of the particular, characteristic of the conceptions of the last century. The truth is that in the experience of the supernatural, as in that of love and in that of poetry, man feels uprooted or separated from himself. And this initial sensation of rupture is followed by another of total identification with that which seemed alien to us and with which we have become so closely entwined that it is now indistinguishable and inseparable from our own being. Why, then, should we not think that the common center of all these experiences is something more ancient than sexuality, economic or social organization, or any other "cause"?

The sacred transcends sexuality and the social institutions in which it is crystallized. It is eroticism, but it is something that goes beyond the sexual impulse; it is a social phenomenon, but it is something else. The sacred eludes us. When we try to lay hold upon it, we find that it has its origin in something preexistent, something that is confused with our being. The same is true of love and poetry. The three experiences are manifestations of something that is the very root of man. Latent in all three is the nostalgia for a former state. And that state of primordial unity, from which we were previously separated, from which we are constantly being separated, constitutes our original condition, to which we return again and again. We scarcely know what it is that calls to us from the depths of our being. We glimpse its dialectic and we know that the antagonistic movements in which it expresses itself—strangeness and recognition, rise and fall, horror and devotion, repulsion and fascination—tend to be resolved into unity. Is this how we escape our condition? Do we truly return to that which we are? A return to what we were and foretaste of what we shall be. Nostalgia for the former life is presentiment of the future life. But a former life and a future life that are here and now and are resolved in a lightning flash. That nostalgia and that presentiment are the substance of all great human endeavors, whether poems or religious myths, social utopias or heroic undertakings. And perhaps man's real name, the emblem of his being, is Desire. For what is Heidegger's temporality or Machado's "otherness," what is man's continuous casting himself toward that which is not he himself, if not Desire? If man is a being who is not, but who is being himself, a being who never finishes being himself, is he not a being of desires as much as a desire for being? In the amorous encounter, in the poetic image and in theophany, thirst and satisfaction are joined together: we are at once fruit and mouth, in indivisible unity. Man, the moderns say, is temporality. But that temporality wishes to quiet itself, to satiate itself, to contemplate itself. It pours out in order to satisfy itself. Man imagines himself; and in imagining himself, reveals himself. But what is it that poetry reveals to us?

7. The Poetic Revelation

RELIGION AND POETRY tend to fulfill, once and for all, that possibility of being that we are and that constitutes our own mode of being; both are attempts to embrace that "otherness" that Machado called the "essential heterogeneity of being." The poetic experience, like the religious one, is a mortal leap: a change of nature that is also a return to our original nature. Hidden by the profane or prosaic life, our being suddenly remembers its lost identity; and then that "other" that we are appears, emerges. Poetry and religion are a revelation. But the poetic word dispenses with divine authority. The image is sustained by itself, without the need to appeal to rational demonstration or to the protection of a supernatural power: it is the revelation of himself that man makes to himself. The religious word, on the contrary, aims to reveal a mystery that is, by definition, alien to us. This diversity does not fail to make the similarities between religion and poetry more disturbing. How, if they seem to issue from the same source and to obey the same dialectic, do they branch apart until they crystallize into irreconcilable forms: on the one hand, rhythms and images; on the other, theophanies and rites? Is poetry a kind of excrescence of religion or a sort of dark and shadowy prefiguration of the sacred? Is religion poetry changed into dogma? The description in the previous chapter does not give us sufficient elements to answer these questions with certainty.

For Rudolf Otto the sacred is an *a priori* category, composed of two elements: some rational and others irrational. The rational elements are constituted of the ideas "of absolute, perfection, necessity and entity—and even that of the good as an objective and objectively obligatory value—which do not proceed from any sense perception. . . . These ideas oblige us to abandon the sphere of sense experience and lead us to that which, independently of all perception, exists in pure reason and constitutes an original disposition of the spirit itself."[1] I confess that the *a priori* existence of ideas such as perfection, necessity, or good is not so obvious to me. Nor do I see how they can constitute an original disposition of our reason. It is true that it could be affirmed that such ideas are rather like constitutive aspirations of consciousness. But each time they are crystallized in an ethical judgment, they deny other ethical judgments that also seek to body forth, with the same rigor and absolutism, that aspiration to the good. Each ethical judgment denies the others and, in some manner, denies that *a priori* idea on which they are based and by which the judgment itself is sustained. But it is not necessary to dwell at length on this question, which exceeds the scope of this essay (not to mention the still narrower scope of my competence). Because even if those ideas actually constitute a domain anterior to perception, or anterior to the interpretations of perception, how can we know if they really are a native element of the category of the sacred? There is no trace of their presence in the experience of the supernatural, nor does their mark appear in many religious conceptions. The idea of perfection, conceived as an *a priori* rationale, should be reflected automatically in the notion of divinity. Facts seem to disprove that presumption. The Aztec religion shows us a god that surrenders and sins: Quetzalcóatl; the Greek religion and other faiths can provide similar examples. Likewise, the ideas of good and of necessity require the complementary notion of omnipotence. The same Aztec religion offers us a disconcerting interpretation of sac-

---

[1] Rudolf Otto, *The Idea of the Holy* [*Lo santo*] (Madrid, 1928).

rifice: the gods are not all-powerful, since they need human blood in order to assure the maintenance of the cosmic order. The gods move the world, but blood moves the gods. It seems useless to give a catalogue of examples, since Otto himself is careful to limit his affirmation: "Rational predicates do not exhaust the essence of the divine ... they are essential but synthetic predicates. One will not understand exactly what they are unless they are regarded as attributes of an object that in some manner serves them as a support and is inaccessible to them."

The experience of the sacred is a repulsive experience. Or more accurately: revulsive. It is a casting out of the inner and secret, a showing of the entrails. The demoniacal, all myths tell us, springs from the center of the earth. It is a revelation of the hidden. At the same time, every apparition involves a break in time or space: the earth opens, time splits; through the wound or opening we see "the other side" of being. Vertigo gushes from this breaking in two of the world, this showing us that creation is grounded upon an abyss. But as soon as man tries to systematize his experience and to conceptualize the original horror, he tends to introduce a kind of hierarchy into his visions. It is not implausible to see this operation as the source of dualism and, therefore, of the so-called rational elements. Certain components of the experience are changed into attributes of the nocturnal or sinister manifestation of the god (the destructive aspect of Shiva, the wrath of Jehovah, the drunkenness of Quetzalcóatl, the north side of Tezcatlipoca, and so on). Other elements are transformed into expressions of the god's luminous form, the solar or saving aspect. In other religions the dualism becomes more radical, and the god with two faces or manifestations gives place to autonomous divinities, to the prince of light and the prince of darkness. In short, by means of a purge or purification the atrocious elements of the experience are separated from the figure of the god and prepare for the advent of the religious ethic. Whatever moral value religious precepts may have, there is no doubt that they do not constitute the ultimate essence of the sacred, nor do they proceed from a pure ethical intuition. They are the result of a rationalization or purification of the original experience, which is produced on deeper levels of being.

Otto grounds the anteriority and originality of the irrational elements as follows: "The ideas of the numinous and their correlative feelings are, like rational ideas, absolutely pure ideas and feelings, to which are applied with complete accuracy the signs that Kant specifies as inherent in *pure* concept and feeling." That is, ideas and feelings prior to the experience, although they may only be given in it and we may only be able to apprehend them through it. Side by side with theoretical reason and practical reason, Otto postulates the existence of a third domain "which constitutes something higher or, if you will, deeper." This third domain is the divine, the holy, or the sacred, and all religious conceptions lean on it. Therefore, the sacred is merely the expression of a divinizing disposition, innate in man. We are thus in the presence of a kind of "religious instinct," which tends to have consciousness of itself and of its objects "thanks to the development of the obscure content of that *a priori* idea from which it has sprung." The content of the representations of that original disposition is irrational, like the same *a priori* on which it rests, because it cannot be reduced to reasons or to concepts: "Religion is a *terra incognita* for the reason." The numinous object is that which is radically strange to us, precisely because the human reason cannot lay hold upon it. When we wish to express it we have no choice but to resort to images and paradoxes. The Nirvana of Buddhism and the Nothing of the Christian mystic are negative and positive notions at the same time, veritable "numinous ideograms of the Other." Antinomy, "which is the most subtle form of the paradox," thus constitutes the natural element of mystic theology, for Christians as well as for Moslems, Hindus, and Buddhists.

Otto's conception brings to mind the statement of Novalis: "When the heart listens to itself and, free of every particular and real object, becomes its own ideal object, then religion is born." The experience of the sacred is not so much the revelation of an object external to us— god, demon, alien presence—as an opening of our heart or our entrails so that that hidden "Other" may emerge. Revelation, in the sense of a gift or grace that comes from without, is transformed into an opening of man to himself. The least that can be said of this idea is that the notion of transcendence—the foundation of religion—is seriously weakened. Man is not "suspended by the hand of God," but rather God lies hidden in the heart of man. The numinous object is always internal and is given as the other face, the positive one, of the void with which every mystical experience begins. How can we reconcile this emerging of God in man with the idea of a Presence absolutely strange to us? How can we accept the fact that we see God thanks to a divinizing disposition without at the same time undermining His very existence, making it depend on human subjectivity?

Moreover, how can we distinguish the religious or divinizing disposition from other "dispositions," among which is, precisely, that of poetizing? Because we can alter the phrase of Novalis and say, with the same right and without shocking anyone: "When the heart listens to itself . . . then poetry is born." Otto himself recognizes that "the notion of the sublime is closely associated with that of the numinous" and that the same thing occurs with poetic and musical feelings. But, he says, the apparition of the feeling of the sublime is subsequent to that of the numinous. Thus, the distinctive essence of the sacred would be its antiquity.

The anteriority of the sacred cannot be of a historical order. We do not know, nor shall we ever know, what man first felt or thought at the moment when he appeared on the earth. The antiquity that Otto claims must be understood differently: the sacred is the original feeling, from which the sublime and the poetic stem. Nothing is more difficult to prove. In every experience of the sacred an element is given that could safely be called "sublime," in the Kantian sense of the word. And vice versa: in the sublime there is always a tremor, an uneasiness, a spasm, and a choking sensation, which betray the presence of the unknown and incommensurable, traits of the divine horror. The same can be said of love: sexuality manifests itself in the experience of the sacred with terrible force; and the sacred, in the erotic life: every love is a revelation, a jolt that causes the foundations of the ego to tremble and leads us to utter words that are not very different from those used by the mystic. In poetic creation something similar happens: absence and presence, silence and word, emptiness and plenitude are poetic states as well as religious and amorous ones. In each of them the rational elements are given at the same time as the irrational ones, with no possibility of their being separated until a subsequent purification or interpretation has taken place. All this leads us to presume that it is impossible to affirm that the sacred constitutes an *a priori* category, irreducible and original, from which the others arise. Each time we try to lay hold upon it we find that what seemed to distinguish it is also present in other experiences. Man is a being who is capable of wonder; when filled with wonder, he poetizes, loves, divinizes. In love there is wonder, poetization, divinization, and fetishism. Poetizing also springs from wonder, and the poet divinizes like the mystic and loves like the lover. None of these experiences is pure; the same elements appear in them all, and it cannot be said that one precedes the others.

The sense, and not the composition of the elements that form them, could distinguish each one of these experiences. The special coloration that distinguishes the mystic's words from those of the poet is the object to which they relate. A text by Saint John acquires a religious tonality because the numinous object bathes them in a particular light. Thus, the really privative in each experience would be its object. But here the difficulty begins to appear really insurmountable. We move in a circle. Because external objects can only "arouse or awaken the divinizing disposition." It is not they, but that elusive disposition, that inscribes them within the sacred. But that disposition is not pure, as we have seen. In short: nothing permits us to isolate the category of the sacred from other analogous categories, except its object or reference; and yet the object is not given outside, but rather inside, in the experience itself. All means of access are closed. The only recourse is to abandon *a priori* ideas and categories and to lay hold upon the sacred at the moment of its birth in man.

Sacred horror springs from radical strangeness. Wonder produces a kind of diminution of the ego. Man feels small, lost in the immensity, as soon as he sees he is alone. The sensation of smallness can even reach the affirmation of misery: man is nothing but "dust and ashes." Schleiermacher calls this state the "feeling of dependence." A qualitative difference separates this "dependence" from other kinds. Our dependence on a superior or on any circumstance is relative and ceases as soon as its agent disappears; our dependence on God is absolute and permanent: it is born with our birth and never ends, not even after death. This dependence is something "original and fundamental of the spirit, something that is not definable except by itself." The sacred is thus obtained by inference: from the feeling of me myself, from feeling myself dependent on something, springs the notion of divinity. Otto embraces the romantic philosopher's idea, but reproaches him for his rationalism. Indeed, for Schleiermacher the sacred or numinous does not really constitute an idea that is prior to all ideas, but rather it is a consequence of this feeling ourselves dependent on something unknown. That unknown something, always present and never quite visible, is called God. To avoid any ambiguity, Otto calls the original feeling the "creature state." The center of gravity changes. What is really characteristic lies in the fact "of being nothing but creatures." By which he does not mean that our original feeling stems from the obscure consciousness of our finitude and smallness, but that we feel we are creatures because we find ourselves before the face of a creator. The immediate apprehension of the creator thus constitutes the first and distinctive element of the original feeling. Unlike Schleiermacher, Otto regards the creature state as a consequence of this sudden encounter with the creator. We feel we are unimportant or nothing because we are in the presence of the all. We are creatures and we have consciousness of ourselves because we have glimpsed the creator.

It is difficult to accept this interpretation. Every mystical and religious text seems instead to affirm the opposite: negative states precede positive ones, the creature state is prior to the notion or vision of a creator. At birth, the child does not feel he is a son, nor does he have any notion of fatherhood or motherhood. He feels uprooted, cast out into a strange world and nothing more. Strictly speaking, the feeling of orphanhood is anterior to the notion of maternity or paternity. Thus, Otto merely reproduces—in the opposite direction—the operation he criticizes in Schleiermacher. One makes the idea of God spring from the feeling of dependence; the other makes of the numinous the source of the creature state. In both cases there is an interpretation of a given situation. And what is that situation? Here Otto hits the mark exactly. Because it involves precisely man's original and determinate situation: having been born. Man has been cast out, thrown into the world. And throughout our existence the situation of the newborn is repeated: each minute throws us into the world; each minute engenders us naked and helpless; the unknown and alien surrounds us on all sides. Stripped of its theological interpretation, Otto's creature state is merely what Heidegger calls "the abrupt feeling of being (or finding oneself) there." And as Waelhens says in his commentary on *Being and Time*: "The feeling of the original situation affectively expresses our fundamental condition."[2] The category of the sacred is not an affective revelation of that fundamental condition—being creatures, having been born, and being born at each moment—but it is an interpretation of that condition. The radical fact of "being there," of finding ourselves always thrown, finite and defenseless, into the strange, is transformed into a having been created by an all-powerful will to whose midst we are to return.

In the Heideggerian analysis of the matter, anguish and fear are the two inimical and parallel paths that open and close, respectively, our means of access to our original condition. Thanks to the experience of the sacred—which has as its starting point the vertigo before his own hollow—man succeeds in laying hold upon himself as that which he is: contingency and finitude. But a moment later this fulgurant revelation is obscured by the interpretation of our condition in terms of elements external to it: a creator, a divinity. Indeed, "many authors have discerned very clearly the nothing that is revealed in anguish. But they have immediately turned askew the sense of this revelation, proclaiming the sinner's nothingness before God. By the Redemption and the pardon He grants to our sins, it seems that our misery is erased; and the regained prospect of an eternal salvation restores the value of our existence and permits us to overcome the nothing we glimpsed for a moment. Once again the real significance of anguish is disguised, as occurs in Saint Augustine, Luther, and Kierkegaard himself."[3] We can add other names: Miguel de Unamuno and, especially, Quevedo (in his poems "Lágrimas de un penitente" and "Heráclito cristiano," thus far ignored by our critics). It can be concluded that

2 Alphonse de Waelhens, *La philosophie de Martin Heidegger* (Louvain, 1948).
3 Ibid.

the experience of the sacred is a revelation of our original condition, but that it is also an interpretation that tends to conceal the meaning of that revelation from us. A reaction to the fundamental fact that defines us as men: being mortal and knowing it and feeling it, religion is an answer to that condemnation to live his mortality that every man is. But it is an answer that hides from us the very thing that, in its first movement, it reveals to us. And this is seen more clearly as soon as the notions of sin and expiation are examined.

In contradistinction to our primordial wretchedness, the divine concentrates in its numinous form the plenitude of being. The numinous is "the august," a notion that transcends the ideas of good and morality. "The august inspires respect," requires veneration, demands obedience. "Independently of every moral systematization, religion is an intimate obligation that is imposed on the consciousness and that binds. . . ."[4] The notions of sin, propitiation, and expiation spring from this feeling of obedience that the august inspires in the creature. It is useless to seek in the idea of sin an echo of a concrete fault or any other ethical resonance. In the same way that we feel orphanhood before we have consciousness of our sonship, sin is anterior to our faults and crimes. Anterior to morality. "In the properly moral sphere appear neither the need for redemption, nor the ideas of propitiation and expiation." These ideas, Otto concludes, "are authentic and necessary in the sphere of mysticism, but apocryphal in that of ethics." The need to expiate, like the no less compelling need to be redeemed, spring from a *fault*, not in the moral sense of the word, but in its literal acceptance. We are at fault, because something in us is indeed faulty: we are little or nothing in relation to the being that is all. Our fault is not moral: it is original insufficiency. Sin is littleness of being.

In order to be, man must propitiate the divinity, that is, appropriate it: by means of consecration, man has access to the sacred, to the plenitude of being. This is the meaning of the sacraments, especially that of communion. And this is also the ultimate object of sacrifice: a propitiation that culminates in a consecration. But the sacrifice of others does not suffice. Man is "unworthy of approaching the sacred," by virtue of

4 R. Otto, *The Idea of the Holy.*

his original fault. Redemption—the God that through sacrifice returns to us the possibility of being—and expiation—the sacrifice that purifies us—are born of this feeling of original unworthiness. Religion thus affirms that guilt and mortality are equivalent terms. We are guilty because we are mortal. Now, guilt requires expiation; death, eternity. Guilt and expiation, death and eternal life form pairs that complete each other, especially for the Christian religions. The oriental religions, at least in their highest forms, do not promise us that salvation in spite of all that so moved Unamuno and that constitutes one of the most disquieting and sickly aspects of their character.

Strictly speaking, nothing permits us to infer that "fault" and "littleness of being" are the same as original sin: the analysis of the "debtor being does not prove anything either for or against the possibility of sin."[5] Catholic theology differs from the Protestant in this. For Saint Augustine human nature—and, in general, the natural world—is not bad in itself, so that he does not identify man's "littleness of being" with guilt. Before God, the perfect being, all beings—not excluding angels and men—are defective. Their "defect" lies precisely in not being God, that is, in being contingent. Contingency is given in angels and in men as freedom: moving, being able to ascend to Being or fall to Nothing, implies freedom. Contingency, on the one hand, engenders freedom; on the other, freedom is a possibility of redeeming or attenuating that contingency or original "defect." Thus, man is a perpetual possibility of fall or salvation. Saint Augustine conceives man as possibility, an idea that the Spanish theater develops with the brilliance with which we are acquainted and which seems valid to me even if one does not accept the Catholic point of view. Thus, original sin is not the equivalent of "littleness of being" but of a concrete fault: man's preferring himself and turning his back on God. But we live in a fallen world, in which man by himself alone cannot choose. Grace—even when it is manifested, as Sor Juana wrote in a famous letter, as a "negative favor"—is indispensable for salvation. Man's freedom, therefore, is subordinated to grace; his "littleness of being" is really littleness, slightness, insufficiency. By this it is not

[5] Martin Heidegger, *Being and Time*, translated by José Gaos as *El ser y el tiempo*, second edition (Mexico City: Fondo de Cultura Económica, 1962).

meant that grace replaces freedom, but that it reestablishes it: "With grace we do not have our free will plus the power of grace, but rather our free will, by grace, recovers its power and its freedom."[6] Catholic thought is richer, freer, and more coherent than Protestant thought; but, in my opinion, it does not succeed in destroying completely this causal connection that is established between man's "littleness of being" and sin: how could freedom, before the fall, have chosen evil? What freedom is this that denies itself and does not choose being but rather nothing?

In opposing man's "littleness of being" to God's totality of being, religion posits an eternal life. It thus redeems us from death, but it makes of the earthly life a long punishment and an expiation of the original fault. In killing death, religion de-lifes life. Eternity depopulates the instant. Because life and death are inseparable. Death is present in life: we live dying. And each minute that we die, we live. In taking away our death, religion takes away our life. In the name of eternal life, religion affirms the death of this life.

The starting point of poetry, like that of religion, is the original human situation—being there, knowing we have been thrown into that *there* that is the hostile or indifferent world—and the fact that makes it precarious among all others: its temporality, its finitude. By a path that, in its own way, is also negative, the poet comes to the brink of language. And that brink is called silence, blank page. A silence that is like a lake, a smooth and compact surface. Down below, submerged, the words are waiting. And one must descend, go to the bottom, be silent, wait. Sterility precedes inspiration, as emptiness precedes plenitude. The poetic word crops out after periods of drought. But whatever its express content may be, whatever its concrete meaning, the poetic word affirms the life of this life. I mean: the poetic act, poetizing, the poet's utterance—independently of the particular content of that utterance—is an act that, originally at least, does not constitute an interpretation, but rather a revelation of our condition. Speak of this or that, of Achilles or the rose, of dying or being born,

6 Etienne Gilson, *L'esprit de la philosophie médiévale* (Paris, 1944).

of the lightning flash or the wave, of sin or of innocence, the poetic word is rhythm, temporality gushing out and being reengendered unceasingly. And being rhythm it is an image that embraces opposites, life and death in a single utterance. Like existence itself, like the life that even at its moments of greatest exaltation carries within it the image of death, the poetic utterance, stream of time, is the simultaneous affirmation of death and life.

Poetry is not a judgment or an interpretation of human existence. The image-rhythm spout simply expresses that which we are; it is a revelation of our original condition, whatever the immediate and concrete sense of the poem's words may be. Without prejudice to a reconsideration of this problem, it is worth repeating that the meanings of the poem and the sense of the poetizing are two different things: here we are concerned with the significance of the poetic act—the poet's creating poems and the reader's re-creating them—and not what this or that poem says. Now, how can poetizing not be a judgment about our original fault or defect, if it has been agreed precisely that poetry is a revelation of our fundamental condition? This condition is essentially defective, for it consists in contingency and finitude. We are astonished at the world because it presents itself to us as the strange, the "inhospitable"; the world's indifference to us stems from the fact that in its totality it has no meaning other than that which our possibility of being gives it; and this possibility is death, because "as soon as a man enters life he is already old enough to die."[7] From birth on, our living is a permanent being in the strange and inhospitable, a radical malaise. We get along badly because we throw ourselves into the nothing, into nonbeing. Our fault or debt is original: it does not proceed from an event subsequent to our birth and it constitutes our own mode of being: lack is our original condition because originally we are lack of being. And here Heidegger seems to coincide with Otto: "Being nothing but creatures" is the same as saying that our being is reduced to a "present, permanent possibility of nonbeing, or dying."[8] Of course, the notion of God is dispensed with and thus the fault is

---

[7] José Gaos, Introduction to *El ser y el tiempo* (Mexico City: Fondo de Cultura Económica, 1951).
[8] Ibid.

left without a reference and the debt without redemption. But it is affirmed that, since birth, we have been in debt or at fault. Unpayable debt, indelible stain. Calderón and Buddhism are right: our worst crime is to be born, since every being born includes dying. Heidegger's analysis, which had served us to reveal the function of the religious interpretation, in the end seems to belie us. If poetizing really discloses our original and permanent condition, it affirms the lack.

It does not fail to be revealing that throughout *Being and Time*— and more markedly in other works, especially *What is Metaphysics?*— Heidegger himself strives to show that this "nonbeing," this negativity in which our being culminates, does not constitute a deficiency. Man is not an incomplete being or a being to whom something is lacking. Because it has already been seen that this something that he could be lacking would be death. Now, death is not outside man, it is not an extraneous event that comes to him from without. If one regards death as an event that does not form part of ourselves, the stoic attitude is the only one possible: while we are alive, death does not exist for us; as soon as it enters us, we cease to exist: then why should we fear it and make it the center of our thinking? But death is inseparable from us. It is not outside: it is we ourselves. To live is to die. And precisely because death is not something external, but is included in life, so that all living is also dying, it is not something negative. Death is not a lack of human life; on the contrary, it completes it. To live is to go forward, to advance toward the strange, and this advancing is to go to the encounter of ourselves. Therefore, to live is to face death. Nothing is more affirmative than this facing, this continuous coming out of ourselves to the encounter of the strange. Death is the void, the open space, that permits the passage forward. Living consists in having been thrown into dying, but that dying is only accomplished in and through living. If being born implies dying, dying also implies being born; if being born is bathed in negativity, dying acquires a positive tonality because being born determines it. It is said that we are surrounded by death; can it not also be said that we are surrounded by life?

Life and death, being or nothing, do not constitute separate substances or things. Negation and affirmation, lack and plenitude, coexist in us. They are what we are. Being implies nonbeing; and vice versa. This is, no doubt, what Heidegger meant when he affirmed that being emerges or springs from the experience of nothing. Indeed, as soon as man contemplates himself, he observes that he is submerged in a totality of things and objects without significance; and he himself is seen as one more object, all toppling over one another, all tumbling aimlessly. The absence of significance proceeds from the fact that man, being he who gives meaning to things and to the world, suddenly realizes that he has no meaning other than dying. The experience of the fall into chaos is inexpressible: we can say nothing about ourselves, nothing about the world, because we are nothing. But if we name the nothing—as in fact we do—it will be illuminated by the light of being. For in the same way: to live in the presence of death is to insert death into life. Because being is the previous condition of nothing, because death is born of life, we can name it and thus reintegrate them. We can approach nothing through being. And being, through nothing. We are the "foundation of a negativity," but also the transcendence of that negativity. The negative and the positive intersect and form a single indissoluble nucleus. The phrase "because we are a possibility of being, we are a possibility of nonbeing" can be transposed without losing its truth.

Anguish is not the only path that leads to the encounter of ourselves. Baudelaire has referred to the revelations of boredom: the universe flows, aimlessly, like a gray and dirty sea, while the stranded consciousness reflects nothing but the monotonous pounding of the surf. "Nothing happens," says the one who is bored and, indeed, nothing is the only thing that shines on the dead sea of consciousness. Loneliness in a crowd—a very prevalent situation in the contemporary world—can also be propitious for revelations of this kind. At first, man feels himself separated from the multitude. As he sees people grimacing and throwing themselves into meaningless, mechanical acts, he takes refuge in his consciousness. But consciousness opens and shows him an abyss. He too throws himself, he too drifts, toward death. Nevertheless, in all these states there is a kind of rhythmic tide: the revelation of man's nothingness is transformed into that of his being. To die, to live: by living we die, we die living.

The amorous experience gives us fulgurantly the possibility of glimpsing, if only for an instant, the indissoluble unity of opposites. That unity is being. Heidegger himself has pointed out that the joy in the presence of the beloved is a means of access to the revelation of ourselves. Although he has never developed his affirmation, it is noteworthy that the German philosopher confirms what we all know with an obscure and prior knowledge: love, the joy of love, is a revelation of being. Like man's every movement, love is a "going to the encounter." In the wait our whole being leans forward. It is a yearning, a reaching out toward something that is still not present and is a possibility that *can* not be produced: the apparition of woman. The waiting keeps us up in the air, that is, suspended, outside ourselves. A minute ago we were settled in our world, and we moved about so naturally and easily among things and beings that we did not perceive their distance. Now, as impatience and yearning increase, the landscape recedes, the wall and the things before us draw back and turn inward, the clock moves more slowly. Everything has begun to live a separate, impenetrable life. The world becomes alien. Now we are alone. The very waiting turns into despair, because the hope for the presence has been exchanged for the certainty of loneliness. The loved one will not come. There will be no one. There is no one. I myself am no one. The nothing opens at our feet. And at that instant the unexpected, that which we no longer hoped for, supervenes. The joy in the irruption of the beloved presence is expressed as suspended animation: we lack support, we are speechless, the rapture takes our breath away. Everything is motionless, at the midpoint of the leap into the void. The impenetrable, unintelligible, and unnamable world, falling heavily on itself, suddenly rises, stands erect, rushes to the encounter of the presence. It is magnetized by some eyes, suspended in a mysterious equilibrium. Everything had lost its meaning, and we were on the brink of the precipice of brute existence. Now everything is illuminated and acquires significance. The presence redeems being. Or rather, it wrests it from the chaos in which it was sinking, re-creates it. Being is born of nothing. But you have only to cease to look at me to make everything collapse again and cause me to sink in the chaos. Tension, a walk on the abyss, a walk on the cutting edge of a sword. You are here, before me, the emblem of the world, emblem of myself, emblem of being.

Like the outpouring of a deep water, like the ocean covering the sand, the presences return to the surface. Everything can be seen, touched, felt. Being and appearance are one and the same. Nothing is hidden, all is present, radiant, stuffed with itself. Tidal wave of being. And borne by the wave of being, I draw near, I touch your breasts, I graze your skin, I look deep into your eyes. The world disappears. Now there is nothing and no one: things and their names and their numbers and their signs fall at our feet. Now we are denuded of words. We have forgotten our names and our pronouns are confused and entwined: I is you, you is I. We ascend, blasted violently upward. We fall, clinging to one another, while names and forms flow out and are lost. Down river, up river, your face slips away. The presence is out of its depth, drowned in itself. The body loses body. Being plunges downward into nothing. Being is nothing. Nothing is being. I open my eyes: an alien body. Being has hidden itself again and appearances surround me. At that moment the question may erupt, sadism, torture to know what is there behind that irremediably alien presence. That question contains the whole despair of love. Because behind that presence there is nothing. And, at the same time, from the nothing of that presence, being arises.

Love issues in death, but we left that death in being born. It is a dying and a being born. "Woman," Machado says, "is the obverse of being." Pure presence, being crops out and makes itself present in her. And in her it sinks and is hidden. Thus, love is simultaneous revelation of being and of nothing. Not a passive revelation, something that is done and undone before our eyes, like a theatrical performance, but something in which we participate, something we make for ourselves: love is the creation of being. And that being is ours. We ourselves annihilate ourselves in creating ourselves, and we create ourselves in annihilating ourselves.

Our attitude toward the natural world has an analogous dialectic.

By the sea or before a mountain, lost among the trees of a forest or at the entrance to a valley that spreads out at our feet, our first sensation is strangeness or separation. We feel different. The natural world presents itself as something alien, possessing an existence of its own. This estrangement soon turns into hostility. Each branch of the tree speaks a language we do not understand; from each thicket a pair of eyes spies on us; unknown creatures threaten or mock us. And the opposite may occur: nature turns inward and the sea heaves and plunges before us, indifferently; the rocks become even more dense and impenetrable; the desert, more vacuous and inaccessible. We are nothing in relation to so much existence turned in on itself. And from this feeling that we are nothing we proceed, if contemplation is prolonged and panic does not overtake us, to the opposite state: the rhythm of the sea keeps time with that of our blood; the silence of the rocks is our own silence; to walk among the sands is to walk through the span of our consciousness, as boundless as they; the forest murmurs allude to us. We are all part of all. Being emerges from nothing. The same rhythm moves us, the same silence surrounds us. The very objects are animated, and as the Japanese poet Buson so happily puts it:

> Before the white chrysanthemums
> the scissors hesitate
> for an instant.

That instant reveals the unity of being. All is still and all is in motion. Death is not a thing apart: it is, in an inexpressible way, life. The revelation of our nothingness leads us to the creation of being. Thrown into the nothing, man creates himself in the face of it.

The poetic experience is a revelation of our original condition. And that revelation is always resolved into a creation: the creation of our selves. The revelation does not uncover something external, which was there, alien, but rather the act of uncovering involves the creation of that which is going to be uncovered: our own being. And in this sense it can indeed be said, without the fear of incurring any inconsistency, that the poet creates being. Because being is not something given, on which our existing leans, but something that is made. Being can lean on nothing, because the nothing is its foundation. Thus, it has no re-course but to lay hold upon itself, to create itself at each instant. Our being consists only in a possibility of being. All that is left to being is being oneself. Its original fault—being the foundation of a negativity —obliges it to create for itself its abundance or plenitude. Man is lack of being, but also conquest of being. Man is thrown to name and to create being. That is his condition: being able to be. And the power of his condition consists in this. In sum, our original condition is not only lack, nor is it abundance, but possibility. Man's freedom is rooted and grounded on being nothing but possibility. To realize that possi-bility is to be, to create one's self. The poet reveals man by creating him. Between being born and dying there is our existing, throughout which we perceive that if our original condition is helplessness and abandonment, it is also the possibility of a conquest: that of our own being. By virtue of our birth, we can all accede to that vision and thus transcend our condition. Because our condition demands to be tran-scended and we only live by transcending ourselves. The poetic act shows that being mortal is merely one side of our condition. The other is: being alive. Being born contains dying. But being born ceases to be a synonym for lack and condemnation as soon as we stop perceiving death and life as opposites. This is the ultimate meaning of all poet-izing.

Between being born and dying poetry opens up to us a possibility, which is not the eternal life of religions or the eternal death of philos-ophies, but rather a living that implies and contains dying, a being this that is also a being that. The poetic antinomy, the image, does not conceal our condition from us: it reveals it and invites us to realize it completely. The possibility of being is given to all men. Poetic creation is one form of that possibility. Poetry affirms that human life is not re-duced to the "preparing oneself to die" of Montaigne, nor is man re-duced to the "being for death" of existential analysis. Human exis-tence includes a possibility of transcending our condition: life and death, reconciliation of opposites. Nietzsche said that the Greeks in-vented the tragedy because of an excess of health. And so it is: only a people who live life with total exaltation can be tragic, because to live completely means also to live death. That state Breton speaks of in which "life and death, the real and the imaginary, the past and the future, the communicable and the incommunicable, the high and the low cease to be perceived contradictorily" is not called eternal life, nor is it there, outside of time. It is time and it is here. It is man thrown to be all the opposites that constitute him. And he can become them all because at birth he has them in him already, he already is these opposites. In being he himself, he is another. Others. To manifest them, to realize them, is the task of the man and the poet. Poetry does not give us eternal life, but it causes us to glimpse that which Nietzsche called "the incomparable vivacity of life." The poetic experience is an opening up of the wellsprings of being. An instant and never. An instant and forever. Instant in which we are that which we were and shall be. Being born and dying: an instant. In that instant we are life and death, this and that.

The poetic word and the religious word are confused throughout history. But the religious revelation does not constitute—at least insofar as it is word—the original act but rather its interpretation. On the other hand, poetry is the revelation of our condition and, for that very reason, the creation of man by means of the image. The revelation is creation. Poetic language reveals man's paradoxical condition, his "otherness" and thus leads him to realize that which he is. It is not the sacred writings of religions that establish man, because they lean on the poetic word. The act by which man grounds and reveals himself is poetry. In sum, the religious experience and the poetic one have a common origin; their historical expressions—poems, myths, prayers, exorcisms, hymns, theatrical performances, rites, and so on—are sometimes indistinguishable; in short, both are experiences of our constitutive "otherness." But religion interprets, channels, and systematizes inspiration within a theology, at the same time that churches confiscate its products. Poetry opens up to us the possibility of being that is intrinsic in every birth; it re-creates man and makes him assume his true condition, which is not the dilemma: life or death, but a totality: life and death in a single instant of incandescence.

8. Inspiration

THE REVELATION of our condition is, likewise, the creation of our selves. As we have seen, that revelation can be given in many ways and can even exist in the absence of any verbal formulation whatever. But even then it implies a creation of the very thing it reveals: man. Our original condition is, by its very nature, something that is always making itself. Now, when the revelation assumes the particular form of the poetic experience, the act is inseparable from its expression. Poetry is not felt: it is said. I mean: it is not an experience that words translate later, but rather the words themselves constitute the nucleus of the experience. The experience is given as a naming of that which, until it is named, properly lacks existence. Therefore, the analysis of the experience includes the analysis of its expression. The two are one and the same. In the preceding chapter I tried to dredge up and isolate the meaning of the poetic revelation. Now it is necessary to see how it is actually given. Or rather: how are poems written?

The first difficulty our question confronts lies in the ambiguity of the testimonies we possess concerning poetic creation. If one is to believe the poets, at the moment of expression there is always a fatal and unexpected collaboration. This collaboration can be given with our will or without it, but it always assumes the form of an intrusion. The poet's voice is and is not his own. What is his name, who is it that interrupts my discourse and makes me say things that I did not intend to say? Some call it demon, muse, spirit, genius; others name it work, chance, the unconscious, reason. Some affirm that poetry comes from without; others, that the poet is sufficient unto himself. But all are obliged to admit of exceptions. And these exceptions are so frequent that only out of laziness can one call them thus. To prove this, let us imagine two poets as ideal types of these opposite conceptions of creation.

Bending over his desk, his eyes fixed in a vacant stare, the-poet-who-does-not-believe-in-inspiration has just finished his first stanza in accordance with the prearranged plan. Nothing has been left to chance. Each rhyme and each image possess the rigorous necessity of an axiom, as well as the gratuitousness and lightness of a geometric game. But one word is needed to complete the final hendecasyllable. The poet consults the dictionary, searching for the rebel rhyme. He does not find it. He smokes, stands up, sits down, stands up again. Nothing: emptiness, sterility. And suddenly, the rhyme appears. Not the expected one, but another—always another—that completes the stanza in an unforeseen way, perhaps contrary to the original plan. How can we explain this strange collaboration? It is not enough to say: the poet had a flash of wit, which exalted him and took him out of himself for a moment. Nothing comes from nothing. That word—where was it? And above all, how do these poetic "flashes of wit" occur to us?

Something similar happens in the opposite case. Abandoned to "the inexhaustible flow of the murmur," his eyes closed to the outside world, the poet writes without pause. At first, the words come too fast or too slowly, but gradually the rhythm of the hand that writes conforms to that of the thought that dictates. Now the fusion has been achieved, there is no longer any distance between thought and utterance. The poet has lost consciousness of the act he performs: he does not know if he is writing or not, or what it is that he is writing. Everything flows with felicity until the interruption comes: there is a word —or the reverse of a word: a silence—that blocks his way. The poet tries again and again to elude the obstacle, to go around it, to avoid it somehow and continue. But it is useless: every path leads back to the same stone wall. The spring has dried up. The poet rereads what he has just written and confirms, not without wonder, that this snarled text is possessed of a secret coherence. The poem has an undeniable unity of tone, rhythm, and temperature. It is a whole. Or the fragments, still living, still coruscating, of a whole. But the poem's unity is not of a physical or material order: the tone, temperature, rhythm, and images possess unity because the poem is a work. And the work, every work, is the fruit of a will that transforms and subjects raw material to its own designs. In that text, in the writing of which the critical consciousness has scarcely participated, there are words that are repeated, images that give birth to others in accordance with certain tendencies, phrases that seem to stretch out their arms in search of an elusive word. The poem flows, marches. And that flowing is what gives it unity. Now, to flow not only means to move but to move toward something; the tension that inhabits words and hurtles them forward is a going to the encounter of something. Words seek a word that will give meaning to their march, stability to their mobility. The poem is illuminated by and in relation to that last word. It is an aiming at that unsaid and perhaps unsayable word. In short, the poem's unity, like that of every work, is given by its direction or meaning. But who stamps a meaning on the poem's zigzagging course?

In the case of the reflective poet we discover a mysterious alien collaboration, with the uninvoked apparition of another voice. In that of the romantic poet, we face the no less inexplicable presence of a will that makes of the murmur a concerted whole possessed of an obscure premeditation. Manifested in both cases is what, at the risk of inaccuracy, must be provisionally called the "irruption of an alien will." But it is obvious that we give this name to something that has scarcely any relation with the phenomenon called will. Something, perhaps, more ancient than the will and on which the will leans. Indeed, in the usual meaning of the word, the will is that faculty that makes plans and subjects our acts to certain norms in order to carry them out. The will that concerns us here does not involve reflection, calculation, or foresight; it is anterior to every intellectual operation and it is manifested at the precise moment of creation. What is the true name of that will? Is it really ours?

The act of writing poems looms up before us like a knot of opposing forces, in which our voice and the other voice are entwined and confused. The contours grow dim: our thinking is imperceptibly transformed into something that we cannot control completely; and our ego gives place to an unnamed pronoun, which is not totally a *you* or a *he*. The mystery of inspiration consists in this ambiguity. Mystery or problem? Both: for the ancients inspiration was a mystery; for us, a problem that contradicts our psychological conceptions and our very idea of the world. Now, this conversion of the mystery of inspiration into a psychological problem is the root of our inability to understand correctly the nature of poetic creation.

Unlike what happens in Hindu thought, which from the beginning raised the problem of the existence of the external world, Western thought long accepted the world's reality with confidence and did not question what our eyes see. The poetic act, in which "otherness" intervenes as a decisive trait, was always regarded as something inexplicable and obscure without constituting a problem that jeopardized the conception of the world. On the contrary, it was a phenomenon that could be inserted quite naturally into the world and that, far from contradicting its existence, affirmed it. It can even be asserted that it was a proof of the world's objectivity, reality, and dynamism. For Plato the poet is a person possessed, whose delirium and enthusiasm are signs of the demonic possession. In the *Ion*, Socrates defines the poet as "a winged being, light and sacred, incapable of producing unless enthusiasm draws him and makes him come out of himself. . . . It is not the poets who say such marvelous things, but rather they are the organs of the divinity that speaks to us through their mouth." Aristotle conceives poetic creation as an imitation of nature. But, as we have already seen, it cannot be clearly understood what this imitation means if one forgets that for Aristotle nature is an animate whole, an organism, and a living model. In his Introduction to Aristotle's *Poetics*, García Bacca pertinently emphasizes that the Aristotelian conception of nature is animated by a more or less hidden hylozoism. Thus, poetic originality does not spring from nothing, nor does the poet extract it from himself: it is the fruit of the encounter between that animated nature, possessing an existence of its own, and the poet's soul.

Greek hylozoism is transformed later into Christian transcendence. But external reality did not lose consistency on that account. Whether nature was inhabited by gods or created by God, the external world is there, before us, visible or invisible, always our necessary horizon. Angel, stone, animal, demon, plant, the "other" exists, has a life of its own and sometimes takes possession of us and speaks through our mouth. In a society where external reality, far from being questioned, is the source from which ideas and archetypes spring, it is not difficult to identify inspiration. The "other voice," the "strange will," are the "other," that is, God or nature with its gods and demons. Inspiration is a revelation because it is a manifestation of the divine powers. A numen speaks and supplants man. Sacred or profane, epic or lyric, poetry is a grace, something external that descends on the poet. Poetic creation is a mystery because it consists in the gods' speaking through a human mouth. But that mystery does not provoke any problem, nor does it contradict commonly accepted beliefs. Nothing more natural than for the supernatural to be incarnated in men and to speak their language.

Since Descartes, our idea of external reality has been radically transformed. Modern subjectivism affirms the existence of the external world only as a derivation of consciousness. Again and again that consciousness is postulated as a transcendental consciousness and again and again it opposes solipsism. Consciousness cannot come out of itself and found the world. Meanwhile, nature has been changed for us into a cluster of objects and relations. God has disappeared from our vital perspectives, and the notions of object, substance, and cause have reached a crisis. Where idealism has not destroyed external reality— in the sphere of science, for example—it has changed it into an object, into a "field of experiences" and thus has stripped it of its former attributes.

Nature has ceased to be a living and animate whole, a power possessed of obscure or clear designs. But the disappearance of the former idea of the world has not done away with inspiration. The "alien voice," the "strange will," continue to defy us. Thus, a wall has come between our idea of inspiration and our idea of the world. Inspiration has become a problem for us. Its existence denies our most deeply rooted intellectual beliefs. It is not strange, therefore, that throughout the nineteenth century there were numerous attempts to attenuate or put an end to the scandal of a notion that tends to return to external reality its former sacred power.

One way to solve problems is to deny them. If inspiration is incompatible with our idea of the world, nothing is easier than to deny its existence. From the sixteenth century on, inspiration begins to be conceived as a rhetorical phrase or a literary figure. No one speaks through the mouth of the poet, except his own consciousness; the true poet does not hear another voice, nor does he write from dictation: he is wideawake and in control of himself. The impossibility of finding an answer that would really explain poetic creation is gradually transformed into a condemnation of a moral and aesthetic order. At one time the excesses resulting from the belief in inspiration were denounced. Their true names were laziness, negligence, love for improvisation, ease. Delirium and inspiration were transformed into synonyms for madness and disease. The poetic act was work and discipline; to write: "to struggle against the current." It is not an exaggeration to see in these ideas an abusive transfer of certain notions of bourgeois morality into the sphere of aesthetics. One of the major merits of surrealism is its having denounced the moral core of this mercantilist aesthetic. Indeed, inspiration has no relation whatever to such base notions as those of ease and difficulty, laziness and work, negligence and expertise, which are contained in the notion of reward and punishment: the "hard cash payment" by which the bourgeoisie, according to Marx, has replaced the human relations of old. The value of a creative work is not measured by the labor it has cost its author.

Moreover, it must be said that poetic creation requires a complete rearranging of our everyday perspectives: the happy facility of inspiration springs from an abyss. The poet's utterance begins as silence, sterility, and drought. It is a lack and a thirst before it is a plenitude and a harmony; and afterward, it is an even greater lack, because the poem separates from the poet and ceases to belong to him. Before and after the poem there is nothing and no one around; we are alone with ourselves; and as soon as we begin to write, that "we," that I, also disappears and sinks. Bending over the paper, the poet throws himself into himself. Thus, poetic creation is irreducible to ideas of gain and loss, effort and reward. All is gain in poetry. All is loss. But the pressure of bourgeois morality often caused poets to pretend to stop up their ears to the numen's ancient voice. Even Baudelaire insinuates the praise of work—he who wrote so much about the barren wastes of sterility and the paradises of laziness! But the displeasure of critics and creators did not stop the outpouring of inspiration. And the poetic voice continued to be a challenge and a problem.

One of the attributes of the modern age consists in the creation of abstract divinities. The prophets reproached the Jews for their falls into idolatry. The moderns could be reproached for doing the opposite: everything tends to be discarnated. Modern idols have no body or form: they are ideas, concepts, forces. The place of God and of the old nature populated by gods and demons is now occupied by faceless beings: Race, Class, the Unconscious (individual or collective), the Genius of Peoples, Heredity. Inspiration can easily be explained by appealing to any of these ideas. The poet is a medium through whom Sex, Climate, History, or some other succedaneum of the ancient gods and demons is expressed in code. I do not mean to deny the value of these ideas. But they are inadequate; conspicuous in them all is a limitation that permits us to reject them totally: their exclusivism, their attempting to explain the whole by the part. Moreover, in them all is evident their incapacity to grasp and explain the essential and decisive fact: how are those determinate forces or realities transformed into words; how does the libido, race, class, or historical moment become word, rhythm, and image? For psychoanalysts, poetic creation is a sublimation; then, why does that sublimation become a poem in some cases and not in others? Freud confesses his ignorance and speaks of a mysterious "artistic faculty." He is obviously dodging the issue, because he merely gives a new name to an enigmatic reality, whose essence is unknown to us. To explain the difference between the poet's words and those of the simple neurotic, one would have to resort to a classification of the subconscious: that of the average mortal and that

of the artist. But there is more to it than that: in undirected thought—
or rather, in dream or fantasy—the flow of images and words does not
lack meaning: "It has been demonstrated that it is untrue that we sur-
render ourselves to a succession of representations lacking in purpose
. . . when the notions of purpose that we know cease, others that are
unknown immediately assert themselves—unconscious ones, as we say
incorrectly—which maintain determinate the progress of representa-
tions alien to our will. A thought cannot be formulated without a
notion of purpose. . . ."[1] Here Freud hits the mark exactly. The notion
of purpose is indispensable even in unconscious processes. But, having
divided the human being into different layers: consciousness, subcon-
sciousness, etc., he conceives two different purposes: one rational, in
which our will participates; the other, alien to us, "unconscious" or
unknown to man, purely instinctive. In reality, Freud transfers the
notion of purpose to the libido and the instinct, but omits the funda-
mental and decisive explanation: what is the meaning of that instinc-
tive purpose? The "unconscious" purpose is not such a purpose, be-
cause it lacks an object and a meaning: it is pure appetite, a natural
mechanism. And this is not all. The notion of purpose implies a cer-
tain awareness and a knowledge, no matter how obscure, of what one
is trying to achieve. The notion of purpose requires that of conscious-
ness. Psychoanalysis, in all its branches, has hitherto been powerless
to answer these questions in a satisfactory way. And even to state them
correctly.

Something similar can be said of the conception of the poet as
"spokesman " or "expression" of history: how are "historical forces"
transformed into images and how do they "dictate" the poet's words to
him? No one denies the interrelation that is presupposed by every his-
torical existence: man is a cluster of interpersonal forces. The poet's
voice is always social and common, even when it is most hermetic. But,
as is the case with psychoanalysis, it is not clear how that "march of his-
tory" or of "economics," those "historical purposes"—alien to the hu-
man will like the "purposes" of the libido—can really be purposes with-
out passing through consciousness. Moreover, no one "is in history," as

[1] S. Freud, *The Interpretation of Dreams.*

if history were one "thing" and we, before it, another: we are all history and we all make it together. The poem is not the echo of society, but rather it is, at the same time, its offspring and its maker, as occurs with every other human activity. In short, neither Sex, nor the Unconscious, nor History is a merely external reality, object, power, or substance that works on us. The world is not outside us; nor, in reality, is it within. If inspiration is a "voice" that man hears in his own consciousness, will it not be better to interrogate that consciousness, which alone has heard it and which constitutes its own ambit?

For the intellectual—and, also, for the common man—inspiration is a problem, a superstition or a fact that resists the explanations of modern science. In either case, he may shrug his shoulders and slough the matter from his mind, like one who flicks a speck of dust from his clothing. On the other hand poets must face up to it and live the conflict. The history of modern poetry is that of the continuous dichotomy of the poet, torn between the modern conception of the world and the sometimes intolerable presence of inspiration. The first to suffer this conflict were the German romantics. They were also those who faced it with the greatest lucidity and plenitude, and the only ones—until the surrealist movement—who did not merely suffer it but who tried to transcend it. Descendants, on the one side, of the Enlightenment and, on the other, of the Sturm und Drang, they lived between the sword of the Napoleonic Empire and the reaction of the Holy Alliance, lost on a dead-end street, as it were. In them, opposites waged an unending battle.

Inspiration, tenaciously defended by these poets and thinkers, is irreconcilable with the subjectivism and idealism that, no less vehemently, is preached by romanticism. The very violence of the dilemma provokes the audacity and temerity of the endeavors that aim to resolve it. When Novalis proclaims that "to destroy the principle of contradiction is perhaps the loftiest task of higher logic," is he not alluding, in his most general way, to the need to suppress the duality between subject and object that divides modern man and thus to resolve once and for all the problem of inspiration? But the suppression of the principle of contradiction—for example, by a "return to unity"—also implies the destruction of inspiration, that is, of that duality of the poet who receives and the power that dictates. Therefore, Novalis affirms that the unity is broken as soon as it is won. Contradiction springs from identity, in an endless process. Man is plurality and dialogue, ceaselessly agreeing and uniting with himself, but also splitting apart ceaselessly. Our voice is many voices. Our voices are a single voice. The poet is, at the same time, the object and the subject of poetic creation: he is the ear that listens and the hand that writes what his own voice dictates. "To dream and not to dream simultaneously: the operation of genius." And similarly: the poet's receptive passivity requires an activity by which that passivity is sustained. Novalis expresses this paradox in a memorable phrase: "Activity is the faculty of receiving." The poet's dream requires, on a more profound level, wakefulness; and wakefulness, in turn, involves abandoning oneself to the dream. In what, then, does poetic creation consist? The poet, Novalis tells us, "does not make, but makes it possible for one to make." The sentence is scintillating, and aptly describes the phenomenon. But who is that "one"? Whom does the poet empower "to make"? Novalis does not say clearly. Sometimes, the one who "makes" is Spirit, People, Idea, or any other power with a capital letter. Then again, it is the poet himself. We must pause at this second explanation.

For the romantics, man is a poetic being. In human nature there is a kind of innate faculty—the poet, Baudelaire said, "is born with experience"—that leads us to poetize. This faculty is analogous to the divinizing disposition that permits us to perceive the holy: the poetizing faculty is an *a priori* category. The explanation is not unlike the one that appeals to the "feeling of dependence" to ground the divinity upon the subjectivity of the believer. The analogy with Protestant theological thought is not accidental. None of these poets completely separated the poetic from the religious, and many of the German romantics owed their conversions to their poetic conception of religion as much as to their religious conception of poetry. Again and again Novalis affirms that poetry is something like religion in a wild state and that religion is merely practical poetry, poetry lived and made act. Therefore, the category of the poetic is merely one of the names of the sacred. It is not necessary to repeat here what I said in the foregoing chapter: the really distinctive essence of the religious experience does not consist so much in the revelation of our original condition as in the interpretation of that revelation. Moreover, the poetic operation is inseparable from the word. Poetizing consists, primarily, in naming. The word distinguishes poetic activity from any other. To poetize is to create with words: to make poems. The poetic is not something given, which is in man since his birth, but something that man makes and that, reciprocally, makes man. The poetic is a possibility, not an *a priori* category or an innate faculty. But it is a possibility that we ourselves create for ourselves. In naming, in creating with words, we create that which we name and which did not exist before except as threat, void, and chaos. When the poet affirms that he does not know "what it is that he is going to write" he means that he does not yet know what is the name of that which his poem is going to name and which, until it is named, only presents itself in the guise of unintelligible silence. Reader and poet create themselves in creating that poem that only exists because of them and so that they may truly exist. Thus there are no poetic states, as there are no poetic words. The essence of poetry consists in its being a continuous creation and thus driving us out of ourselves, dislodging us, and leading us to the limits of our possibilities.

Neither anguish, nor amorous exaltation, nor joy or enthusiasm is a poetic state in itself, because the poetic in itself does not exist. They are situations that, because of their extreme character, cause the world and everything that surrounds us, including the dead everyday language, to crumble. Then all that is left for us is silence or image. And that image is a creation, something that was not in the original feeling, something that we have created in order to name the unnamable and to say the unsayable. For that reason every poem lives at the expense of its creator. Once the poem has been written, that which he was prior to the poem and which led him to creation—that, inexpressible: love, joy, anguish, boredom, nostalgia for another condition, loneliness, anger—has been resolved into an image: it has been named and it is a poem, transparent word. After creation, the poet is alone; now it is others, the readers, who are going to create themselves in re-creating the poem. The experience is repeated, but in reverse: the image opens up to the reader and shows him its translucent abyss. The reader leans forward and plunges. And as he falls—or as he ascends, as he penetrates the chambers of the image and abandons himself to the flow of the poem—he breaks away from himself to enter "another himself" previously unknown or ignored. The reader, like the poet, becomes an image: something that is projected and separates from itself and goes to the encounter of the unnamable. In both cases the poetic is not something that is outside, in the poem, or inside, in us, but something that we make and that makes us. Novalis' sentence could then be modified: the poem does not make, but makes it possible for one to make. And the one who makes is man, the creator. The poetic is not in man like something given, nor does poetizing consist in taking the poetic out of us, as if it were a matter of "something" that "someone" had deposited inside us or with which we were born. The poet's consciousness is not a cave where the poetic lies like a hidden treasure. In the presence of the future poem the poet is naked and empty of words. Anterior to creation, the poet as such does not exist. Nor after it. He is a poet because of the poem. The poet is a creation of the poem as much as the poem is a creation of the poet.

The conflict is prolonged throughout the nineteenth century. It is prolonged, aggravated, and, at the same time, veiled and confused. The contradiction is keener and the consciousness of the split is enhanced; the lucidity to face it and the courage to resolve it, diminished. Victims, witnesses, and accomplices of inspiration, none of the great poets of the nineteenth century possess the clarity of Novalis. They all struggle in a contradiction with no exit. To renounce inspiration was to renounce poetry itself, that is, the only thing that justified their presence on earth; to affirm its existence was an act incompatible with the idea they had of themselves and of the world. Thus these poets frequently reject and condemn the world. There is no doubt that, from a moral standpoint, Baudelaire's attacks, Mallarmé's disdain, Poe's criticism are completely justified: the world they had to live in was abominable. (We know this only too well, because those times immediately foreshadow the unparalleled horror of our own.) But it is not enough to deny or condemn the world; no one can escape from his world and that denial and condemnation are also ways of living it without transcending it, that is, of suffering it passively. Nothing more penetrating, nothing more illuminative of the mysteries of the poetic operation, its barren wastes and its paradises, than the descriptions of Baudelaire, Coleridge, or Mallarmé. And at the same time, nothing less clear than the explanations and hypotheses with which they try to reconcile the notion of inspiration with the modern idea of the world. Read any of the capital texts of modern poetics (Poe's *Philosophy of Composition*, for example), to verify their disconcerting and contradictory lucidity and blindness. The contrast to the ancient texts is revealing. For the poets of the past inspiration was a natural thing, precisely because the supernatural formed part of their world.

A spirit as self-possessed as Dante relates with simplicity and candor that during sleep Love dictates and inspires his poems, and he adds that that revelation occurs at certain hours and under circumstances that make the intervention of higher powers unequivocal and absolutely certain: "On saying those words, it disappeared and my dream was interrupted. And later, reflecting on this Vision, I discovered that I had experienced it at the ninth hour of the day; and therefore, even before leaving my chamber, I resolved to compose that ballad in which I would carry out the mandate of my Lord (Love); and then I made the ballad that begins as follows. . . ."[2] The number nine has for Dante the same importance that seven has for Nerval. But for Dante the repetition of nine has a clear, although mysterious and sacred meaning, which merely illumines with a purer light the exceptional character of his love and the redemptive significance of Beatrice. For Nerval seven is an ambiguous number, sometimes disastrous, sometimes beneficent, whose true meaning is impossible to determine. Dante accepts the revelation and uses it to show us the arcana of heaven and hell; Nerval recoils fascinated, and does not try to communicate his visions to us as much as to learn what the revelation is: "I decided to examine my dream and discover its secret. I told myself, why not force these mystical doors at last, armed with all my will to dominate my sensations instead of tolerating them? Is it not possible to conquer this attractive and dreadful chimera, to impose order on the spirits that mock our

2 *Vita Nuova*, XII.

reason?" For Dante, inspiration is a supernatural mystery that the poet accepts with reflection, humility, and veneration. For Nerval, it is a catastrophe and a mystery that provokes and challenges us. A mystery that must be unveiled. The transition between "mystery to be deciphered" and "problem to be solved" is gradual and will be made by Nerval's successors.

The need to reflect and meditate on poetic creation, to root out its secret, can only be explained as a consequence of the modern age. Or rather, modernity consists in that attitude. And the vexation of poets stems from their inability to explain, as modern men and in terms of our conception of the world, that strange phenomenon that seems to deny us and to deny the foundations of the modern age: there, at the heart of consciousness, in the ego, pillar of the world, the only rock that does not disintegrate, suddenly appears a strange element, one that destroys the identity of consciousness. Our conception of the world had to be shaken, that is, the modern age had to reach a crisis, before the problem of inspiration could be properly formulated. In the history of poetry that moment is called surrealism.

Surrealism presents itself as a radical attempt to suppress the duel between subject and object, the form assumed for us by that which we call reality. For the ancients the world existed with the same plenitude as consciousness, and its relations were clear and natural. For us its existence takes on the form of a bitter controversy: on the one hand, the world evaporates and changes into an image of consciousness; on the other, consciousness is a reflection of the world. The surrealist adventure is an attack on the modern world because it tries to suppress the quarrel between subject and object. Heir of romanticism, it sets out to accomplish the task that Novalis assigned to "higher logic": to destroy the "old antinomy" that divides us. The romantics deny reality —the spectral husk of a world replete with life yesterday—in favor of the subject. Surrealism also attacks the object. The same acid that dissolves the object disintegrates the subject. There is no self, there is no creator, but rather a kind of poetic force that blows where it will and produces gratuitous and inexplicable images.

We can all make poetry together because the poetic act is, by nature, involuntary and it is always produced as a negation of the subject. The poet's mission consists in attracting that poetic force and converting himself into a high-tension wire that will permit the discharge of images. Subject and object dissolve in favor of inspiration. The "surrealist object" turns to vapor: it is a bed that is an ocean that is a cave that is a mousehole that is a mirror that is the mouth of Kali. The subject also disappears: the poet is transformed into a poem, meeting place of two words or two realities. In this way surrealism tries to break, at its two extremes, contradiction and solipsism. Bent on drastic measures, it closes all the exits: neither world nor consciousness. Neither consciousness of the world nor world in consciousness. There is no escape, except the upward flight: the imagination. Inspiration is manifested or actualized in images. By means of inspiration, we imagine. And as we imagine, we dissolve subject and object, we dissolve our selves and suppress contradiction.

Unlike the previous poets, who merely suffer it, surrealists brandish inspiration like a sword, transforming it into idea and theory. Surrealism is not a poetry but a poetics and even more, and more decisively, a vision of the world. External revelation, inspiration breaks the subjectivistic labyrinth: it is something that assaults us as soon as consciousness dozes, something that irrupts through a door that only opens when the doors of wakefulness close. Internal revelation, it causes our belief in the unity and identity of that same consciousness to waver: there is no self, and within each one of us diverse voices are in conflict. The surrealist idea of inspiration presents itself as a destruction of our vision of the world, since it denounces as mere phantoms the two terms that constitute it. At the same time, it postulates a new vision of the world, in which it is precisely inspiration that occupies the central place. The surrealist vision of the world is grounded on the activity, which both dissociates and re-creates, of inspiration. Surrealism proposes to make a poetic world, to establish a society in which the central place of God or reason will be occupied by inspiration. Thus, the true originality of surrealism consists not only in having made of inspiration an idea but, more radically, an *idea of the world*. Thanks to this transmutation, inspiration ceases to be an indecipherable mystery, a vain superstition or an anomaly and becomes an idea that is not contradictory to our fundamental conceptions. This does not mean that inspiration has changed its nature, but that for the first time our idea of inspiration does not clash with the rest of our beliefs.

All great poets prior to surrealism had meditated on inspiration, trying to fathom its secret—and this trait distinguishes them from baroque, renaissance, and medieval poets—but none was able to insert inspiration fully into the image that modern man makes for himself of the world and of himself. In them all there were remnants of former ages. And what is more: for them all, inspiration was to return to the past: to become medieval, Greek, savage. The gothicism of the romantics, the general archaism of modern poetry and, in short, the figure of the poet as an exile in the heart of the city stem from the fact that it is impossible to acclimatize inspiration. Surrealism causes the opposition and the exile to cease as it affirms inspiration as an idea of the world, without positing its dependence on an external factor: God, Nature, History, Race, etc. Inspiration is something that is given in man, is confused with his very being and can only be explained by man. That is the point of departure of the *First Manifesto*. And the originality, hitherto little mentioned, of the attitude of Breton and his friends, is rooted in this.

During the movement's "research period"—the epoch of automatism, autohypnosis, induced dreams, and collective games—poets adopted a twofold attitude toward inspiration: they suffered it, but they also observed it. The most valiant did not hesitate to break away to go and seek it in those places from which few return. Surrealist activity denounced the penury of many of our conceptions—notably that which consists in seeing in every human creative work a fruit of the "will"—and showed the suspicious frequency with which "distraction," "chance," and "negligence" intervene in great discoveries. With a fascination that did not exclude lucidity, Breton tried to unearth the mysterious mechanism of that which he called "objective chance," meeting place of man and the "other," field of choice of "otherness." Woman, image, mathematical or biological law, all those Americas sprout in the middle of the ocean, when we look for something else or when we have ceased to look. How and why are those meetings produced? We know that there is a magnetic field, a point of intersection and that is all. We know that the "other voice" filters through the holes that the vigilance of attention leaves unattended, but—where does it come from and why does it leave us as suddenly as it comes? Despite the experimental work of surrealism, Breton confessed that "we continue to be as little informed as ever about the origin of this voice." Let us say, in passing, that we do indeed know something: each time we hear the "voice," each time the unexpected encounter is produced, it seems that we hear our selves and see that which we had already seen. It seems that we return, hear again, remember. Although we shall come back to this sensation of already known, already heard, and already recognized that the irruption of "otherness" gives us, let us emphasize that Breton's confession of ignorance is of utmost value: it reveals the intimate resistance of the author of *Nadja* to the purely psychological interpretation of inspiration. And this leads us to treat more concretely the theme of the surrealists' idea of inspiration.

Since romanticism, the poet's ego had grown in direct proportion to the contraction of the poetic world. The poet felt himself the master of his poem with the same naturalness—and the same absence of legality—felt by the landowner or factory proprietor toward the products of his land or his factory. In answer to the individualism and rationalism that precede them, the surrealists accentuate the unconscious, involuntary, and collective character of all creation. Inspiration and the dictation of the unconscious become synonyms: that which is properly poetic lies in the unconscious elements that, without the poet's willing it, are revealed in his poem. Poetry is undirected thought. To destroy the dualism of subject and object, Breton appeals to Freud: the poetic is the revelation of the unconscious and, therefore, it is never deliberate. But the problem that torments Breton is a false problem, as Novalis had already seen: to abandon oneself to the murmur of the unconscious requires a voluntary act; passivity involves an activity on which the former leans. I do not believe it is inappropriate to break up the word pre-meditation to show that it treats of an act prior to all meditation in which something that we could also call pre-reflection intervenes. Heidegger's criticism of the mechanical and unreflective "occupying oneself with tools"—in which the ultimate reference, man's radical pre-occupation, death, does not disappear but rather, hidden, continues to be the foundation of every occupation—is perfectly applicable to the surrealist doctrine of inspiration. The revelations of the unconscious imply a kind of consciousness of those revelations. Only by a free and voluntary act do those revelations come out in the open, just as the censorship of the ego involves a prior knowledge of what is going to be censored. When we repress certain desires or impulses, we do so by means of a will that is masked and disguised, and therefore we make it "unconscious," so that it will not compromise us. At the moment of the liberation of that "unconscious," the operation is repeated, but in the opposite direction: once again the will intervenes and chooses, now hidden under the mask of passivity. In both cases consciousness intervenes; in both, there is a decision, either to make unconscious that which offends us, or to bring it out in the open. This decision does not sprout from a separate faculty, will or reason, but rather it is the very totality of being that is expressed in it. Pre-meditation is the determinate trait of the act of creating and that which makes it possible. Without pre-meditation there is no inspiration or revelation of "otherness." But pre-meditation is anterior to will, to desire, or to any other inclination, conscious or unconscious, of the spirit. Because all willing and desiring, as Heidegger has shown, have their root and foundation in man's very being, which is now and has been since his birth a wanting to be, a permanent yearning for being, a continuous pre-being-himself. And thus, it is not in the unconscious or in consciousness, understood as "parts" or "compounds" of man, nor in impulse, in passivity, or in being alert, that we can find the source of inspiration, because they all are grounded upon man's being.

Breton never lost sight of the inadequacy of the psychological explanation, and, even at his moments of greatest adherence to Freud's ideas, he was careful to reiterate that inspiration was an inexplicable phenomenon for psychoanalysis. The doubt concerning the possibilities of real comprehension that psychology offers induced him to experiment with occultist hypotheses. Now, occultism can aid us only to the extent to which it ceases to be occultism, or, in other words, when it becomes revelation and shows us that which it hides. If inspiration is a mystery, occultist explanations make it doubly mysterious. Occultism claims, exactly as inspiration does, to be a revelation of "otherness"; therefore, it is incompetent to explain it except by analogy. If we are interested in knowing what inspiration is, it does not suffice to say that it is something like the revelation proclaimed by occultists, since we do not know in what that revelation consists, either. Moreover, the insistence with which Breton appeals to the possibility of an occult or supernatural explanation does not fail to be revealing. That insistence betrays his growing displeasure with the psychological explanation as well as the persistence of the phenomenon of "otherness." And thus, it is not so much the idea of inspiration that is valid in Breton, as his having made of inspiration an idea of the world. Although he may not succeed in giving us a description of the phenomenon, neither does he hide it or reduce it to a mere psychological mechanism. By this keeping "otherness" in abeyance, the surrealist doctrine does not end in a summary, and ultimately superficial, psychological affirmation but rather it opens the door to an interrogation. Surrealism not only acclimatized inspiration among us as an idea of the world, but, because of the same and admitted inadequacy of the psychological explanation adopted, it made visible the very core of the problem: "otherness." The answer is perhaps rooted in this and not in the absence of premeditation.

The difficulties experienced by spirits such as Novalis and Breton may perhaps lie in their conception of man as something given, that is, as the master of a nature: poetic creation is an operation during which the poet plucks or extracts certain words from within him. Or, if one utilizes the opposite hypothesis, from the substratum of the poet, at certain privileged moments, words pour out. Now, there is no such substratum, man is not a thing and even less a static, motionless thing, in whose depths lie stars and serpents, jewels and viscous animals. Arrow extended, always tearing the air, always ahead of himself, throwing himself beyond himself, shot, exhaled, man ceaselessly advances and falls, and at each step he is *another* and he himself. "Otherness" is in man himself. From this perspective of incessant death and resurrection, of unity that is resolved into "otherness" to be rearranged in a new unity, it may perhaps be possible to penetrate the enigma of the "other voice."

Here is the poet before the paper. It does not matter whether or not he has a plan, if he has meditated for a long time about what he is going to write, or if his consciousness is as empty and blank as the immaculate paper that alternately attracts and repels him. The act of writing involves, as the first movement, a separating oneself from the world, something like throwing oneself into the void. Now the poet is alone. All that was his everyday world and his usual preoccupations a moment ago, disappears. If the poet truly wishes to write and not to perform a vague literary ceremony, his act leads him to break away from the world and to interdict everything—not excluding himself. Then there are two possibilities: everything can turn to vapor and disintegrate, lose weight, float, and finally dissolve; or else, everything can close and turn aggressively into an object without meaning, matter that is unseizable and impenetrable to the light of significance. The world opens: it is an abyss, an immense yawn; the world—the table, the wall, the goblet, the remembered faces—closes and becomes a wall without fissures. In both cases, the poet is left alone, without a world to lean on. It is time to create the world anew and to name again with words that menacing external vacuity: table, tree, lips, stars, nothing. But the words have evaporated too, they too have slipped away. We are surrounded by the silence that precedes the word. Or the other side of silence: the senseless and untranslatable murmur, "the sound and the fury," the prattle, the noise that does not say anything, that only says: nothing. In being left without a world, the poet has been left without words. Perhaps, at that instant, he recoils and draws back: he wishes to remember language, to take from within it all that he learned, those beautiful words with which, a moment before, he made his way in the world and which were like keys that opened every door for him. But there is no longer a backward, there is no longer a within. The poet thrown forward, tense and attentive, is literally outside himself. And like him, the words are beyond, always beyond, put to flight as soon as he grazes them. Thrown out of himself, he will never be able to be one with the words, one with the world, one with himself.

He is always just beyond. The words are nowhere, they are not something given, which awaits us. They have to be created, they have to be invented, just as we create ourselves and create the world each day. How can words be invented? Nothing comes from nothing. Even if the poet could create from nothing, what sense would there be in talking about "inventing a language"? Language is, by its very nature, dialogue. Language is social and always implies, at least, two: the one who speaks and the one who hears. Thus, the word that the poet invents—the word that, for an instant that is every instant, had evaporated or been converted into an impenetrable object—is the word of every day. The poet does not take it from himself. Nor does it come to him from without. There is no without or within, as there is not a world before us: ever since we are, we are in the world and the world is one of the constituents of our being. And the same occurs with words: they are neither inside nor outside, but they are we ourselves, are part of our being. They are our own being. And because they are part of us, they are alien, they belong to others: they are one of the forms of our constitutive "otherness." When the poet feels cut off from the world and everything, even language itself, flees from him and scatters, he himself flees and is annihilated. And at the second moment, when he decides to face the silence or the noisy and deafening chaos, and he stammers and tries to invent a language, he himself is the one who invents himself and takes the mortal leap and is reborn and is another. In order to be he himself he must be another. And the same happens with his language: it is his because it belongs to the others. To make it truly his, he resorts to image, to adjective, to rhythm, that is, to everything that makes it distinct. Thus, his words are and are not his. The poet does not listen to a strange voice, his voice and his word are the strange ones: they are the words and the voices of the world, to which he gives new meaning. And not only his words and his voice are strange; he himself, his entire being, is something ceaselessly alien, something that is always being another. The poetic word is a revelation of our original condition because by it man actually names himself another, and thus he is, at the same time, this and that, he himself and the other.

The poem makes our condition transparent because at its core the

word becomes something that is the poet's exclusively, without ceasing
on that account to be the world's, that is, without ceasing to be word.
That is why the poetic word is personal and instantaneous—emblem
of the instant of creation—as well as historical. Because they are in-
stantaneous and personal emblems, all poems say the same thing. They
reveal an act that is repeated ceaselessly: that of the incessant destruc-
tion and creation of man, his language, and his world, that of the per-
manent "otherness" in which being man consists. But also, because it
is historical, because it is word in common, each poem says something
distinct and unique: Saint John does not say the same thing as Homer
or Racine; each one alludes to his world, each one re-creates his world.

Inspiration is a manifestation of man's constitutive "otherness." It is
not inside, within us, or behind, like something that suddenly sprouted
from the slime of the past, but rather it is, so to speak, ahead of us: it
is something (or rather, someone) that calls us to be ourselves. And
that someone is our very being. And in truth inspiration is not any-
where, it simply *is not*, nor is it a thing: it is an aspiration, a moving, a
forward thrust: toward that which we ourselves are. Thus, poetic
creation is the exercise of our freedom, of our decision to be. This
freedom, as has been said many times, is the act by which we go beyond
ourselves, in order to be more completely. Freedom and transcendence
are expressions, movements of temporality. Inspiration, the "other
voice," "otherness" are, in their essence, temporality gushing forth,
manifesting itself unceasingly. Inspiration, "otherness," freedom, and
temporality are transcendence. But they are transcendence, movement
of being—toward what? Toward ourselves. When Baudelaire main-
tains that the "highest and most philosophical of our faculties is the
imagination," he affirms a truth that can also be worded thus: by the
imagination—that is to say, by our capacity, inherent in our essential
temporality, to convert into images that same temporality's continuous
avidity to be incarnated—we can come out of ourselves, *go beyond
ourselves to the encounter of ourselves.* In its first movement, inspira-
tion is that by which we cease to be we; in its second movement, this
coming out of us is a being ourselves more fully. The truth of myths
and of poetic images—so manifestly mendacious—lies in this dialectic
of departure and return, of "otherness" and unity.

Man magnetizes the world. By him and for him, all the beings and objects that surround him are impregnated with meaning: they have a name. Everything points to man. But man—to what does he point? He does not know for certain. He wants to be another; his being always leads him to go beyond himself. And man constantly loses footing; at each step he plunges down and happens upon that other that he imagines himself to be and which slips from his grasp. Empedocles affirmed that he had been a man and a woman, a rock and, "in the Briny Deep, a mute fish." He is not the only one. Every day we hear phrases of this kind: when so-and-so is excited, he is "unrecognizable," he "becomes a different person." Our name also shelters a stranger, about whom we know nothing except that he is we ourselves. Man is temporality and change and "otherness" constitutes his own mode of being. Man realizes or fulfills himself when he becomes another. In becoming another he recovers himself, reconquers his original being, prior to the fall or the plunge into the world, prior to the split into self and "other."

The distinctive essence of man does not consist so much in being an entity of words as in this possibility that he has of being "another." And because he can be another he is an entity of words. They are one of the means he possesses to make himself another. But this poetic possibility is only realized if we take the mortal leap, that is, if we actually come out of ourselves and surrender and lose ourselves in the "other." There, in the very act of leaping, man, suspended in the abyss, between the this and the that, for a lightning instant is this and that, what he was and what he will be, life and death, in a being himself that is an absolute being, a present plenitude. Now man is all that he wished to be: rock, woman, bird, the other men and the other beings. He is image, marriage of opposites, poem saying itself to itself. He is, finally, the image of man being incarnated in man.

The poetic voice, the "other voice," is my voice. Man's being already contains that other that he wishes to be. "The beloved," Machado says, "is one with the lover, not at the end of the erotic process, *but at its beginning*." The beloved is already in our being, as thirst and "otherness." Being is eroticism. Inspiration is that strange voice that takes man out of himself to be everything that he is, everything that he desires: another body, another being. The voice of desire is the very voice of being, because being is nothing but desire for being. Beyond, outside of me, in the green and gold thicket, among the tremulous branches, sings the unknown. It calls to me. But the unknown is familiar *and therefore we do know, with a knowledge of memory, where the poetic voice comes from and where it goes.* I was here before. The rock of the homeland still bears the traces of my footsteps. The sea knows me. That star once blazed to the right of me. I know your eyes, the weight of your tresses, the temperature of your cheek, the paths that lead to your silence. Your thoughts are transparent. In them I see my image confused with yours a thousand times a thousand to the point of incandescence. Because of you I am an image, because of you I am another, because of you I am. All men are this man who is another and I myself. I is you. And also he and we and you and this and that. The pronouns of our languages are modulations, inflections of another secret, unutterable pronoun, which sustains them all, origin of language, end and limit of the poem. Languages are metaphors of that original pronoun that I and the others, my voice and the other voice, every man and each man, am. Inspiration is to throw oneself into being, yes, but also and above all it is to remember and to be again. *To return to Being.*

Poetry and History

9. The Consecration of the Instant

ON PRECEDING PAGES I tried to distinguish the poetic act from other related experiences. Now it becomes necessary to show how that irreducible act is inserted into the world. Although poetry is not religion, or magic, or thought, in order to be realized as a poem it always leans on something alien to it. Alien, but without which it could not become incarnate. The poem is poetry and something else as well. And this *as well* is not something false or added on, but a constituent of its being. A pure poem would be that in which the words abandoned their particular meanings and their references to this or that, to signify only the act of poetizing—an exigency that would cause their disappearance, because words are nothing but the meanings of this and that, that is, of relative and historical objects. A pure poem could not be made of words and would be, literally, unsayable. At the same time, a poem that did not struggle against the nature of words, obliging them to go beyond themselves and their relative meanings, a poem that did not try to make words say the unsayable, would remain a simple verbal manipulation. What characterizes the poem is its necessary dependence on the word as much as its struggle to transcend it. This circumstance permits an investigation of its nature as something unique and irreducible and, simultaneously, permits us to regard it as a social expression that is inseparable from other historical manifestations. The poem, a being of words, goes beyond words and history does not deplete its meaning; but the poem would have no meaning—or even an existence—without history, without the community that nourishes it and is nourished by it.

The poet's words, precisely because they are words, are his and others'. On the one hand, they are historical: they belong to a people and to a moment of the speech of that people: they are datable. On the other hand, they are prior to any date: they are an absolute beginning. Without the combination of circumstances we call Greece, neither the *Iliad* nor the *Odyssey* would exist; but without those poems, the historical reality that was Greece would not have existed either. The poem is a fabric of perfectly datable words and an act that precedes every date: the original act with which all social or individual history begins; the expression of a society and, simultaneously, the foundation of that society, the condition of its existence. Without a common word there is no poem; without a poetic word, there is no society, state, church, or community whatever. The poetic word is historical in two complementary, inseparable, and contradictory senses: it constitutes a social product and it is a previous condition for the existence of every society.

The language that nourishes the poem is, after all, nothing but history, name of this or that, reference and meaning that alludes to a closed historical world and whose sense is depleted with that of its central personage: a man or a group of men. At the same time, that whole combination of words, objects, circumstances, and men that constitute a history stems from a beginning, that is, from a word that grounds it and gives it meaning. That beginning is not historical nor is it something that belongs to the past, but it is always present and ready to be incarnated. What Homer relates to us is not a datable past and, strictly speaking, not even a past: it is a temporal category that floats, so to speak, above time, always avid to be present. It is something that happens again as soon as two lips utter the old hexameters, something that is always beginning and that does not cease to manifest itself. History is the place where the poetic word is incarnated.

The poem is mediation between an original experience and a cluster of subsequent acts and experiences, which only acquire coherence and meaning in relation to that first experience that the poem consecrates. And this is as applicable to the epic poem as to the lyric and dramatic one. In them all, chronological time—the common word, the social or individual circumstance—suffers a decisive transformation: it ceases to flow, it stops being succession, instant that comes before and after other identical instants, and is transformed into the beginning of something else. The poem traces a line that separates the privileged instant from the temporal current: in that here and in that now, something begins: a love, a heroic act, a vision of the godhead, a momentary wonder at that tree or the face of Diana, smooth as a wall of polished stone. That instant is anointed with a special light: it has been consecrated by poetry, in the best sense of the word consecration. Unlike what occurs with the axioms of mathematicians, the truths of physicists, or the ideas of philosophers, the poem does not abstract the experience: that time is alive, it is an instant packed with all of its irreducible particularity, and it is perpetually susceptible to repeating itself in another instant, to reengendering itself and illuminating new instants, new experiences with its light. The loves of Sappho, and Sappho herself, are unrepeatable and belong to history; but her poem is alive, it is a temporal fragment that, thanks to rhythm, can be reincarnated indefinitely. And I am wrong to call it a fragment, because it is a complete world in itself, unique, archetypal time, which is no longer past or future but present. And this virtue of being present now forever, by means of which the poem escapes from succession and from history, binds it more inexorably to history. If it is present, it exists only in this here and now of its presence among men. In order to be present, the poem needs to become present among men, to be incarnated in history. Like all human creations, the poem is a historical product, fruit of a time and a place; but it is also something that transcends the historical and is situated in a time prior to all history, at the beginning of the beginning. Before history, but not outside it. Before, because it is archetypal reality, impossible to date, absolute beginning, total and self-sufficient time. Within history because it only lives incarnated, by reengendering itself, repeating itself at the instant of the poetic communion. Without history—without men, who are the origin, the substance, and the end of history—the poem could not be born or incarnated; and without the poem there would be no history either, because there would be no origin or beginning.

It may be concluded that the poem is historical in two ways: first, as a social product; second, as a creation that transcends the historical but that, to actually be, needs to be incarnated again in history and repeated among men. And this second manner comes from its being a special temporal category: a time that is always present, a potential present that cannot be truly realized except by becoming present concretely in a determinate here and now. The poem is archetypal time; and because it is, it is time that is incarnated in the concrete experience of a nation, a group, or a sect. This possibility of being incarnated among men makes it a spring, a fountain: the poem lets us drink the water of a perpetual present that is, likewise, the most remote past and the most immediate future. The poem's second manner of being historical is, therefore, polemical and contradictory: that which makes it unique and separates it from other human works is its transmuting time without abstracting it; and that same operation leads it, in order to be completely fulfilled, to return to time.

Seen from the outside, the relations between poem and history do not present any fissure: the poem is a social product. Even when discord reigns between society and poetry—as happens in our time— and the former condemns the latter to exile, the poem does not escape from history: in its very solitude, it continues to be a historical testimony. A poetry such as ours is consistent with a split society. Moreover, throughout the centuries states and churches have confiscated the poetic voice for their ends. This rarely involves an act of violence: poets coincide with those ends and do not hesitate to consecrate with their word the enterprises, experiences, and institutions of their epoch. Undoubtedly Saint John of the Cross believed he was serving his faith—and indeed he did serve it—with his poems, but can we reduce the infinite charm of his poetry to the theological explanations that he gives us in his commentaries? Bashō would not have written what he wrote if he had not lived in the Japanese seventeenth century; but it is not necessary to believe in the enlightenment preached by Zen Buddhism to be engulfed by the motionless flower formed of the three lines of his haiku. The ambivalence of the poem does not spring from history, understood as a unitary and total reality that encompasses all works; it is a consequence of the poem's dual nature. The conflict is not in history but in the bowels of the poem and consists in the twofold movement of the poetic operation: transmutation of historical time into archetypal time and incarnation of that archetype in a determinate and historical now. This twofold movement constitutes poetry's proper and paradoxical mode of being. Its historical mode of being is polemical. Affirmation of the very thing that it denies: time and succession.

Poetry is not felt: it is said. Or rather: the proper way to feel poetry is to say it. Now, every utterance is always an utterance of something, a speaking of this and that. The poetic utterance does not differ in this from other ways of speaking. The poet speaks of the things that are his and his world's, even though he may speak to us of other worlds: nocturnal images are made of the fragments of diurnal ones, re-created according to another law. The poet does not escape from history, even if he denies it or attempts to ignore it. His most secret or personal experiences are transformed into social, historical words. At the same time, and with those same words, the poet says something else: he reveals man. That revelation is the ultimate meaning of every poem and is almost never said in an explicit manner, but it is the foundation of every poetic utterance. Transparent in the images and rhythms, more or less clearly, is a revelation that no longer relates to what the words say, but to something earlier and on which every word of the poem leans: man's ultimate condition, that movement that hurtles him onward without ceasing, always conquering new territories that turn to ashes the moment they are touched, in a continuous rebirth and redeath and rebirth. But this revelation that poets make to us is always embodied in the poem and, more precisely, in the concrete and determinate words of this or that poem. Otherwise there would be no possibility of poetic communion: for the words to speak to us of that "something else" that every poem speaks of, they must also speak to us of this and that.

The discord latent in every poem is a condition of its nature and is not given as cleavage. The poem is unity that can only be constituted of the complete fusion of opposites. The worlds that strive within it are not two strange worlds: the poem is struggling with itself. Therefore it is alive. And from this continuous quarrel—which is manifested as higher unity, as smooth and compact surface—springs also that which has been called the dangerousness of poetry. Although he receives communion at the social altar and shares with complete good faith the beliefs of his time, the poet is a being apart, he is heterodox by congenital fatality: he always says *something else*, even when he says the same things that the other men in his community say. The distrust of poetry by states and churches stems not only from the natural imperialism of these powers: the very nature of the poetic utterance arouses suspicion. It is not so much what the poet says, but what is implicit in his utterance, its ultimate and irreducible duality, that which gives his words a taste of liberation. The frequent accusation made to poets, that they are frivolous, distracted, absentminded, never completely in this world, proceeds from the character of their utterance. The poetic word is never completely of this world: it always takes us beyond, to other lands, to other skies, to other truths. Poetry seems to escape from history's law of gravity because its word is never completely historical. The image never means this or that. Instead, as we have seen, the opposite is true: the image says this and that at the same time. And even: this is that.

The poetic word's dual condition is no different from that of the nature of man, a temporal and relative being but one who is always thrown to the absolute. That conflict creates history. From this perspective, man is not mere succession, simple temporality. If the essence of history were nothing but the succession of one instant by another, one man by another, one civilization by another, change would be resolved to uniformity, and history would be nature. Indeed, whatever their specific differences may be, one pine tree is the same as another pine tree, one dog the same as another dog. But the opposite occurs with history: whatever their common characteristics may be, one man is irreducible to another man, one historical instant to another instant. And what makes the instant an instant, time time, is man, who fuses with them to make them unique and absolute. History is exploit, heroic act, conglomeration of meaningful instants because man makes of each instant something self-sufficient and thus separates the today from the yesterday. In each instant he wishes to realize himself as a totality, and each one of his hours is a monument to a momentary eternity. To escape from his temporal condition, his only recourse is to submerge himself more completely in time. The only way he has to conquer it is to fuse with it. He does not achieve eternal life, but he creates a unique and unrepeatable instant and thus gives origin to history. His condition leads him to be another; only by being another can he be himself completely. He is like the mythical Gryphon described in Canto XXXI of the Purgatory: "Without ceasing to be he himself he is transformed into his image."

The poetic experience is nothing but the revelation of the human condition, that is, of that transcending oneself unceasingly in which, precisely, one's essential freedom lies. If freedom is movement of being, man's continuous transcending himself, that movement will always have to be related to something. And so it is: it is an aiming at a value or a determinate experience. Poetry does not escape from this law, as the manifestation of temporality that it is. Indeed, that which is characteristic of the poetic operation is utterance, and all utterance is utterance of something. And what can that something be? In the first place, that something is historical and datable: what the poet actually speaks of, whether it be his loves with Galatea, the siege of Troy, the death of Hamlet, the taste of wine one evening, or the color of a cloud over the sea. The poet always consecrates a historical experience, which can be personal, social, or both at once. But as he speaks to us of all those events, feelings, experiences, and persons, the poet speaks to us of *something else*: of what he is doing, of what he is being in relation to us and in us. He speaks to us of the poem itself, of the act of creating and naming. And more: he induces us to repeat, to re-create his poem, to name what he names; and in doing so, he reveals to us that which we are. I do not mean that the poet makes

poetry of poetry—or that in his utterance about this or that he sud-
denly changes direction and begins to speak about his own utterance—
but that, in re-creating his words, we also relive his adventure and
exercise that freedom in which our condition manifests itself. Also we
fuse with the instant in order to transcend it better, also, in order to be
ourselves, *we are others*. The experience described in the preceding
chapters is repeated by the reader. This repetition is not identical, of
course. And precisely because it is not, it is valid. It is very possible
that the reader will not understand with complete exactitude that
which the poem says: it was written many years or centuries ago and
the living language has changed; or it was composed in a remote
region, where the people speak differently. None of this matters. If
the poetic communion is truly realized, I mean, if the poem still keeps
its powers of revelation intact and if the reader actually penetrates its
electric ambit, a re-creation is produced. Like every re-creation, the
poem of the reader is not the exact double of the poem written by the
poet. But if it is not identical with regard to the this and the that, it *is*
identical as for the very act of creation: the reader re-creates the instant
and creates himself.

The poem is a work that is always unfinished, always ready to be
completed and lived by a new reader. The novelty of the great poets of
antiquity springs from their capacity to be others without ceasing to be
themselves. Thus, what the poet speaks of (the this and the that: the
rose, death, the sundrenched afternoon, the assault on the ramparts,
the hoisting of the colors) is changed, for the reader, into that which
is implicit in every poetic utterance and is the nucleus of the poetic
word: the revelation of our condition and its reconciliation with itself.
This revelation is not a knowledge of something or about something,
because then poetry would be philosophy. It is an actual being again
that which the poet reveals that we are; therefore it is not produced
as a judgment: it is an act that is inexplicable except by means of itself
and that never assumes an abstract form. It is not an explanation of
our condition, but an experience in which our condition, itself, is
revealed or manifested. And therefore it is also indissolubly linked to a
concrete utterance about this or that. The poetic experience—original
or derived from reading—does not teach us or tell us anything about

freedom: it is freedom itself unfurling itself to achieve something and thus, for an instant, to realize man. The infinite diversity of poems recorded by history stems from the concrete character of the poetic experience, which is experience of this and that; but this diversity is also unity, because in all these and those the human condition becomes present. Our condition consists in not being identified with anything in which it is incarnated, but also in not existing except by being incarnated in that which is not itself.

The personal character of the lyric seems more adapted to these ideas than the epic or the drama. Epic and drama are forms in which man recognizes himself as a collectivity or community, while in the lyric he sees himself as an individual. Thus it is thought that in the epic and drama, the common word—the utterance about this or that— occupies all the space and leaves no room for the "other voice" to manifest itself. The epic poet does not speak of himself, or of his experience: he speaks of others, and his utterance does not tolerate any ambiguity whatever. The objectivity of that which he relates makes it impersonal. The words of the theater and the epic coincide completely with those of their community and rarely—except in the case of a polemical theater, such as that of Euripides or the modern theater—reveal truths different or contrary to those of their historical world. The epic form—and, to a lesser degree, the dramatic—do not offer the possibility of saying things that are different from the things they expressly say; the inner freedom that, as it unfolds, permits the revelation of man's paradoxical condition, is not given in them; therefore, there is not established that conflict between history and poetry that I tried to describe earlier and that seemed to constitute the essence of the poem. The correspondence between history and poetry, between common word and poetic word, is so complete that it leaves no opening through which a truth that is not historical can filter. This opinion, which in part contradicts everything that has hitherto been said, must be examined further.

Epic and drama are above all works with heroes, protagonists, or personages. It is not an exaggeration to say that precisely in the heroes —perhaps with greater plenitude than in the lyric poet's monologue—

is given that revelation of freedom that makes of poetry, simultane-
ously and indissolubly, something that is historical and that, being so,
denies and transcends history. What is more: that conflict or knot of
contradictions that is every poem is manifested with greater and more
complete objectivity in the epic and the tragedy. In them, contrary to
what happens in the lyric, the conflict ceases to be something latent,
never completely explicit, and is bared and revealed in all its crudity.
The tragedy and the comedy show in an objective way the conflict be-
tween men and destiny and, thus, the struggle between poetry and
history. The epic, in turn, is the expression of a people as collective
consciousness, but it is also the expression of something prior to the
history of that community: the heroes, the founders. Achilles is before,
not after, Greece. In short, the mystery of freedom is incarnated in the
characters of the drama and the epopee, and the "other voice" speaks
through them.

Every poem, whatever its nature may be: lyric, epic, or dramatic,
manifests a peculiar mode of being historical; but to truly lay hold
upon this singularity it is not enough to enunciate it abstractly as we
have done up to now. Instead, we must approach the poem in its his-
torical reality and see more concretely what is its function within a
given society. Thus, the theme of the ensuing chapters will be the
Greek tragedy and epic, the novel, and the lyric poetry of the modern
period. The choice of epochs and genres is no accident. In the heroes
of the Greek myth and, in another sense, in those of the Spanish and
Elizabethan theater, it is possible to perceive the relations between
the poetic and the social word, history and man. In them all the central
theme is human freedom. The novel, as has been said many times, is
the modern epic; likewise, it is an anomaly in the epic genre and thus
it deserves a special meditation. Finally, modern poetry constitutes,
like the novel, another exception: for the first time in history, poetry
fails to serve other powers and tries to remake the world in its image.
Undoubtedly Baudelaire's poems are not essentially different, in pro-
portion as they are poems, from those of Li Po, Dante, or Sappho. The
same can be said of the other modern poets, as creators of poems. But
the attitude of these poets—and that of the society that surrounds

them—is radically different from that of the ancients. In them all, with greater or lesser emphasis, the poet is allied with the theorist, the creator with the prophet, the artist with the revolutionary or with the priest of a new faith. They all regard themselves as beings apart from society and some consider themselves founders of a new history and a new man. Thus, for the purposes of this book, they are studied in this aspect rather than as mere creators of poems.

Before we dwell on the meaning of the hero, it seems necessary to ask where the heroic character has been produced with greatest purity. Until recently, everyone would have answered without hesitation: Greece. But each day more and more epic writings are being discovered, belonging to all peoples, from the epopee of Gilgamesh to the legend of Quetzalcóatl, which has been reconstructed in our country by Father Ángel María Garibay K. These discoveries compel us to justify our choice. Whatever the relations between epic, dramatic, and lyric poetry may be, it is obvious that epic and dramatic poetry are distinguished from the lyric by their objective character. The epic relates; the drama presents. And presents starkly. Moreover, both have as subject not the individual man but the collectivity or the hero who embodies it. Furthermore, drama and epic are distinguished from each other by this: in the epic, the people see themselves as origin and as future, that is, as a unitary destiny, which the heroic action has endowed with a particular meaning (to be worthy of heroes is to continue them, to prolong them, to assure a future to that past that always presents itself to our eyes as a model); in the theater, society is not seen as a whole but split from within, struggling with itself. In general, every epic represents an aristocratic and closed society; the theater —at least in its highest forms: the political comedy and the tragedy— requires, as atmosphere, democracy, that is, dialogue: in the theater, society dialogues with itself. And so, while the epic heroes are problematical only at isolated moments, those of the theater are problematical continuously, except at the instant of the denouement. We know what the epic hero will do, but the dramatic character offers himself as several possible courses of action, among which he has to choose. These differences reveal that there is a kind of filiation between epic and drama. The epic hero seems to be destined to reflect on himself in the theater, and thus Aristotle affirms that dramatic poets take their myths —that is, their plots or themes—from epic material. The epopee creates the heroes as beings cut from the same cloth; dramatic poetry takes those characters and drives them, as it were, in on themselves: it makes them transparent, so we may contemplate ourselves in their abysses and contradictions. Therefore the heroic character can only be studied completely if the epic hero is also a dramatic hero, that is, in that poetic tradition that makes of the primitive epic material the subject of examination and dialogue.

It is by no means certain that all great civilizations possess an epic, in the sense of the great Indo-European epopees. The *Book of Songs*, in China, and the *Manyōshū*, in Japan, are predominantly lyric collections. In other cases, a great dramatic poetry flouts its epic tradition: Corneille and Racine looked for heroes outside the French epic material. This circumstance does not make their characters less French, but it does reveal a break in the spiritual history of France. The "Grand Century" turns its back on medieval tradition, and the choice of Spanish and Greek themes reveals that that society had decided to exchange its heroic models and archetypes for others. Now, if we conceive the theater as the dialogue of society with itself, as an examination of its foundations, it does not fail to be symptomatic that in the French theater the Cid and Achilles supplant Roland, and Agamemnon, Charlemagne.

If the epic myth constitutes the substance of dramatic creation, there must be a necessary relation of filiation between epic and theater, as happens among the Greeks, Spanish, and English. In the epopee the hero appears as unity of destiny; in the theater, as consciousness and examination of that same destiny. But the problematical aspect of the tragic hero can only be unfolded where the dialogue is realized effectively and freely, that is to say, in the midst of a society where theology does not constitute the monopoly of an ecclesiastical bureaucracy and, further, where political activity consists above all in the free exchange of opinions. All this leads us to study the heroic character in Greece, because only among the Greeks is the epic the raw material of theology, and only among them did democracy permit the tragic characters to relive as theatrical conflicts the theological theses that animated the heroes of the epopee. So then, without denying other epopees or a theater like the Japanese Nō, it is obvious that Greece must be the center of our reflection on the figure of the hero. Only among the Greeks—and the exceptional nature of their culture is rooted in this— are all the conditions given that permit the full unfolding of the heroic character: the epic heroes are also tragic heroes; the tragic hero's reflection on himself is not limited by an ecclesiastical or philosophical coaction; and, finally, that reflection relates to the very foundations of man and the world, because in Greece the epic is, simultaneously, theogony and cosmogony and it constitutes the common sustenance of philosophical thought and popular religion. The tragic hero's reflection, and his conflict itself, are of a religious, political, and philosophical order. The sole theme of the Greek theater is *sacrilege*, or rather: freedom, its limits and its punishments. The Greek conception of the struggle between cosmic justice and human will, their final harmony and the conflicts that divide the heroes' souls, constitutes a revelation of being and, thus, of man himself. A man who is not outside the cosmos, like a strange guest of the earth, as occurs in the idea of man that modern philosophy gives us; nor a man immersed in the cosmos, as one of its blind components, a mere reflection of the dynamism of nature or the will of the gods. For the Greek, man forms part of the cosmos, but his relation with the whole is grounded upon his freedom. The tragic quality of the human being resides in this ambivalence. No other people has undertaken to reveal the human condition with the same daring and grandeur.

10. The Heroic World

WHAT DISTINGUISHES Greek heroes from all others is that they are not mere tools in the hands of a god, as occurs with Arjuna. Homer's theme is not so much the Trojan war or the return of Odysseus as the destiny of the heroes. That destiny is intermingled with the destiny of the gods and the very health of the cosmos, so that it is a religious theme. And here another distinguishing trait of Greek epic poetry becomes evident: that it is a religion. Homer is the Hellenic Bible. But it is hardly a dogmatic religion. Burckhardt points out that the originality of the Greek religion lies in the fact that it is a free creation of poets and not the speculation of a clergy. And being a free poetic creation, and not church dogma, it later permitted criticism and favored the birth of philosophical thought. But before analyzing the vision of the world offered us by the epopee and the heroes' place in that world, it is necessary to clarify the meaning of the cult of heroes among the Greeks.

Ancient Greece knew two religions: that of the gods and that of the dead. The former adored natural divinities and could be symbolized by the solar figure of Zeus; the latter was a cult of the men in whom the whole community recognized itself and whose best representation is Agamemnon.[1] Both cults underwent decisive transformations. The Aegean civilization was dispersed; the Mycenaean spread and was transplanted partially in Asia Minor, while it died out on the continent. In the Asiatic colonies the religion of the gods grew stronger, while the cult of the dead languished, linked as it was to the local or domestic tomb. It weakened, but did not die: the royal ancestors left their earthly dwelling, broke the magic ties that bound them to the earth, and entered the realm of the myth. The heroes, no longer the dead deposited in a tomb, were transformed into mythical figures in which the exiled people saw its past as something remote and familiar at the same time. Moreover, the myth separated from the religious hymn and the prayer and, taking the heroes as its own material, was transformed into the substance of the epopee.[2] The victory of the religion of the gods did not produce a canonical book like the Bible or the Vedas. The liberty that the epic poet could take with the heroes, thanks to the disappearance of the tombs, was also exercised in the depiction of the gods. After the sacred bond between the spirit of the tomb and man was broken, the god-hero, the "lord," was humanized. For the myth the hero was a semi-god, a son of gods, which is not completely inaccurate because we have already seen that he was a humanized god, a figure now free from the terrible power of blood and the earth. This humanization produced, by contagion, the humanization of the Olympian god. Thus, Homer is both an end and a beginning. The end of a long religious evolution that culminates with the triumph of the Olympian religion and the defeat of the cult of the dead. The beginning of a new aristocratic and chivalrous society, to which the Homeric poems give a religion, an ideal of life and an ethic. That religion is the Olympian religion; those ideas and that ethic are the cult of heroes, of the divine man in whom the two worlds— the natural and the supernatural—meet and struggle. From the time of his birth, the figure of the hero offers the image of a knot in which

---

[1] I am deliberately omitting the Minoan religion, with its great Goddess and its agrarian and subterranean cults.

[2] Raffaele Pettazzoni, *La religion dans la Grèce antique* (Paris, 1953).

opposing forces are bound together. His essence is the conflict between two worlds. All tragedy is already latent in the epic conception of the hero.

To understand clearly the essence of the hero's conflict, it is necessary to have an idea of the world in which he moves. According to Jaeger, "What characterizes the Greek spirit, and is unknown to earlier peoples, is the clear consciousness of an *immanent legality* of things."[3] This idea has two sides: the dynamic conception of a whole, animated by cosmic laws, impulses, and rhythms; and the notion of man as an active part of that whole. The idea of cosmic legality and the idea of man's responsibility in that legality, as one of its active components, does not fail to be contradictory. In it is found the root of the heroic and, later, the consciousness of the tragic. The epopee does not postulate this conception as a problem, because Homer "conceives *ate* and *moira* in a strictly religious way, as divine forces that man can scarcely resist. Nevertheless, man appears to be, especially in the ninth canto of the *Iliad*, if not the master of his destiny, at least an unconscious co-author of it."[4] The Greeks insert man into the general movement of nature, and this is the beginning of the conflict and of the exemplary value of the heroic. This conflict is not of a moral order, in the modern sense of the word: "The moral forces are as real as the physical ones . . . and the final limits of ethics for Homer are, as for the Greeks in general, the laws of being, not the conventions of pure duty."

The epopee and naturalistic philosophy are nourished by the same conception of being. The idea of a universal legality is expressed still more clearly in the famous fragment of Anaximander: "Things have to pay the penalty and suffer the expiation they owe one another on account of their injustice, according to the decrees of Time." This is not an anticipation of the scientific conception of nature, with its laws of cause and effect, but a vision of being as a cosmos not unlike Solon's

---

[3] Werner Jaeger, *Paideia*, fifth edition (Mexico City: Fondo de Cultura Económica, 1962). This affirmation of Jaeger's is disputable. The cosmic legality appears in Vedic poetry, among the Chinese, the ancient Mexicans, etc. What does not appear in those civilizations is the tragic conflict.

[4] Ibid.

political world, governed by justice.[5] Both political and cosmic justice are not properly laws that are over the nature of things, but things themselves in their mutual movement, engendering themselves and devouring each other, produce justice. Thus, justice is identified with the cosmic order, with the natural movement of being and with the political movement of the city and its free play of interests and passions, each punishing the excesses of the other. Once again: justice and order are categories of being. And their other name, it occurs to me, is harmony, movement or concerted dance as well as rhythmical clash of opposites.

The world of heroes and gods is no different from the world of men: it is a cosmos, a living whole in which the movement is called justice, order, destiny. Being born and dying are the two extreme notes of this concert or living harmony, and between them both appears the dangerous figure of man. Dangerous because in him the two worlds meet. Therefore he is an easy victim of *hubris*, which is the sin *par excellence* against political and cosmic health. The wrath of Achilles, the pride of Agamemnon, the envy of Ajax are manifestations of *hubris* and its destructive power. By reason of the total nature of this conception, individual health is in direct relation to cosmic health, and the hero's disease or madness infects the whole universe and endangers heaven and earth. Ostracism is a public health measure; the destruction of the hero who oversteps his limits and goes beyond the norms is a remedy to restore the cosmic health. Now, the sin of immoderation will not be fully understood if moderation is conceived as a limit imposed from without. Moderation is the real space that each one occupies in keeping with his nature. To go beyond one's self is both to transgress the limits of one's being and to violate the limits of other men and entities. Each time we break the harmony, we hurt the whole cosmos. On this harmonious model is built the political constitution of cities, social and individual life, and on it tragedy is grounded. The whole history of Greek culture can be seen as its development.

The maxim of Anaximander—things expiate their own excesses—already contains, in the germ, Heraclitus' whole polemical vision of

---

[5] Werner Jaeger, *The Theology of the First Greek Philosophers* (Mexico City: Fondo de Cultura Económica, 1952).

being: the universe is in tension, like the bowstring or the strings of the lyre. The world, "changing, rests." But Heraclitus not only conceives being as becoming—an idea that is somehow already implicit in the conception of the epic—but makes of man the meeting place of the cosmic war. Man is polemical because all earthly and divine forces converge and wage war in him. Consciousness and freedom—although Heraclitus does not use these words—are his attributes. To attain to the understanding of being is also to attain to the understanding of man. His mystery consists in being a wheel of the cosmic order, a chord of the great concerto and, likewise, in being freedom. Pain is disharmony; consciousness, harmony with the rhythm of being. The mystery of destiny consists in the fact that it is also freedom. Without freedom, destiny is not fulfilled.

Unlike the epopee, the tragedy is the offspring of continental Greece. The great individualistic creation of Asiatic Greece—the elegy —is transformed in the homeland into collective forms, as is observed in Spartan choral poetry. The tragedy receives a dual heritage: the elegiac lyric tradition and the aristocratic poetry of the epic. The origin of the tragedy, as we know, is popular and agrarian. Thanks to the reforms of the time of Pisistratus, the popular classes are elevated, and with this social elevation comes the entrance of the popular cults— the religion of Dionysus and Demeter—into the closed and aristocratic *polis*. But just as the emigration to Asia Minor brought about the transformation of the cult of the dead into a religion of heroes, with the popular triumph comes "a parallel religious evolution in the meaning of the traditional Olympian forms: the lower classes adopt them as a sign and a consecration."[6] The Dionysian pantomime is transformed into the cult of the *polis*. The substance of the tragedy is not the agrarian myth but the heroic tradition of the epopee. The peasant chorus changes tone and content and is transformed into a vehicle of the highest art and the freest and most passionate meditation on man's fate. The heroic myth, which founds Greece in the epopee, is transformed into a dialogue: the tragedy and the comedy are a dialogue of Greece with itself and with the foundations of its being.

[6] R. Pettazzoni, *La religion dans la Grèce antique.*

Aeschylus conceives destiny as a superhuman and superdivine force, but a force in which man's will participates. Pain, misfortune, and catastrophe are, in the literal sense of the word, punishments inflicted on man because he has exceeded moderation, that is, he has transgressed that maximum limit of expansion of each being and has tried to go beyond himself: to be a god or a demon. Beyond moderation, the space on which each one can unfold himself, sprout discord, disorder, and chaos. Aeschylus steadfastly accepts the avenging violence of destiny; but his piety is virile, and he rebels against man's fate. To see in Aeschylus' theater the sad and somber victory of destiny is to forget what Jaeger calls "the problematical tension of the soldier of Salamis." That tension is relieved when pain is transformed into consciousness of destiny. Then man accedes to the vision of cosmic legality, and his misfortune appears as a part of the universal harmony. Having paid his penalty, man is reconciled with the whole. But Aeschylus does not give us a solution, or a moral or philosophical formula. We are in the presence of a mystery that his words do not succeed in unveiling completely, because if it is just for man to pay, the cries of Prometheus in the last scene of the tragedy contradict this belief: "Ether, you who make the common light revolve for all, see how unjustly I suffer." This cry does not admit of any consolation: it is a dart thrust into the heart of that just cosmos. No one can pull it out because it symbolizes the tragic condition of man.

Also for Sophocles the tragic action not only implies the sovereignty of Destiny but also man's active participation in the fulfillment of cosmic justice. Resignation is ignoble unless it is transformed into consciousness of pain. And it is by means of this pain that one arrives at the tragic vision, which says "yes to the Sphinx whose mystery no mortal is able to solve."[7] The tragedy does not preach unconscious resignation, but rather the voluntary acceptance of Destiny. In it and in the face of it the human temper is refined and only in that "yes" is human freedom reconciled with external fatality. Thanks to the hero's tragic acceptance, the chorus can say to Oedipus: "The gods who injured you will raise you up again." In these words of Sophocles' there

[7] W. Jaeger, *Paideia*.

is an answer to the cry of Prometheus: as soon as Destiny becomes con-
sciousness, it is transformed and punishment ceases. Neither Aeschylus
nor Sophocles denies that Destiny is the expression of the immanent
legality of things, but both try to insert man into that universal law
without sacrificing his consciousness. Sophocles accentuates the re-
demptive character, so to speak, of consciousness, which he conceives
as the higher intuition of the forces that govern the cosmos, and the
light of that understanding illuminates the blind footsteps of Oedipus
in Colonus. Again and again the Greek genius affirms that man is
something more than a "tool" in the hands of a god. How is it possible
to reconcile this affirmation with that of Destiny? This problem was
never solved completely, and in it resides precisely that which is called
the tragic conflict. It has to do with two incompatible terms that, never-
theless, complement one another and as a result of which man is man
and the world is the world. The tragic aspect lies in the mutual and
equally absolute affirmation of opposites. If man were not guilty, Des-
tiny would not destroy him; but that guilt does not diminish, rather it
magnifies Prometheus, Antigone, and Oedipus. Through them and in
them Being is realized and chaos does not return. The consciousness of
Destiny is the only thing that can free us from its atrocious weight and
give us a glimpse of the universal harmony. Freedom and Destiny are
contrary and complementary terms. Their mystery belongs to the very
nature of things. The Greek pessimism is different from the Christian.

Euripides is the first to dare openly to question the sanctity and
justice of the cosmic legality. When he does so, he abandons the realm
of Being and moves into the sphere of moral criticism. Guilt ceases to
be an objective curse and is turned into a subjective and psychological
concept. Destiny is mad, capricious, and unjust, Euripides' heroes tell
us. Aeschylus had expressed similar complaints, but his work is not
a philosophical defense of the rights of man or a criticism of the gods,
but rather the expression of the human condition as a manifestation of
the cosmic legality. As soon as the justice of Destiny is denied, pain
also loses justification and chaos returns. Faced with the invasion of
chance, man can do nothing but take refuge in himself or create for
himself an ideal city. Stoicism, personal mysticism, and political utopia
are ways out of a world that has lost its objective legality. Euripides'

greatness as a lyric poet, his understanding of passions, and his psychological penetration do not compensate for what has been called his "sin against the myth," or rather his having made a psychological cause of what was formerly cosmic justice. In breaking the tragic tension, he opened the door to relativism and psychology, and undermined the foundations of the idea of being. But can we forget that Euripides also affirms man's innocence? That innocence, contrary to what occurs with Aeschylus, is not posited in relation to the legality and sanctity of Destiny but vis-à-vis the irrationality and madness of that same Destiny. Euripides' answer to the question that Aeschylus and Sophocles had asked is thus two-sided: it denies the sanctity of Destiny and upholds man's innocence. Its negation breaks the tragic conflict, because it is not the same to be a victim of blind chance or passion as to be a victim of a cosmic justice; its affirmation, on the other hand, is indeed eminently tragic: man is innocent because his guilt is not really his. Euripides takes up the ancient notion of objective guilt, contrasts it with the ideas of subjective responsibility, and affirms man's ultimate innocence. This affirmation is tragic, because in it there is also a conflict that nothing, except the higher consciousness of our condition, resolves. We pay and we expiate, because being innocent we are guilty.

Transparent in the three great tragic poets is a conflict that admits of no solution, except by suppressing one of the two contrary terms: Destiny or human consciousness. In that conflict the "other voice," revelatory of the fundamental human condition, is manifested with a plenitude and a profundity that, in my opinion, make the tragedy man's highest poetic creation. Man is Destiny, fatality, nature, history, chance, appetite, or whatever one wishes to call that condition that takes him beyond himself and beyond his limits; but, also, man is consciousness of himself. In this contradiction lies the mystery of his being, his polemical nature and that which distinguishes him from other beings. But the greatness of the tragedy does not consist in having attained to this conception but in having really lived it and embodied the unresolvable contradiction of the two terms. The tragic heroes—even at the moments of greatest madness and aberration—do not lose consciousness and do not fail to wonder about the ultimate reasons for their condition: are we really free? Are we guilty? Are those gods, who injure us so unmercifully, just or unjust? Do they really exist? Are there other laws—as Sophocles says—above the whims of the godhead? The Greek tragedy is a question about the very foundations of Being: is Destiny holy, is man guilty, what is the meaning of the word justice? These were not rhetorical questions, because they concerned the basic principles of Greek society and cast doubt on the whole system of values on which the *polis* was built. Neither Calderón nor Shakespeare ever asked himself such questions, which perhaps have no answer. The holiest actions and the most atrocious sacrileges are pitilessly examined by the tragic poets in order to show us the obverse and the reverse of each act. When he frees Thebes from the Sphinx, Oedipus is lost; when he kills his mother, Orestes reestablishes the cosmic order. The tragedy is a vast meditation on sacrilege and an examination of its ambiguous value: it saves and condemns, condemns and saves. All the heroes are lost because they violate a sacred limit: that of their own being; and order prevails again if a new violation—divine or human, of the offended divinity or the avenging hero—restores the equilibrium. Nothing equals the audacity with which the tragic poets examine the conventions most generally accepted as holy by their people. Only in freedom can an art be born whose only theme is sacrilege, as in the tragedy, or political health, as in the Aristophanesque comedy. The absence of an ecclesiastical dogma and of a clergy that is the guardian of traditional truths, on the one hand, and the climate of the Athenian democracy, on the other, explain the sovereign liberty that poets took with the heroic myth. But liberty does not suffice without valor of spirit and boldness of vision. The Greek theater offers a pessimistic view of man, but it is also a criticism of the gods. Its pessimism encompasses the whole cosmos. The freedom of the tragedy does not reject fatality but is proved in it. The Greeks never had illusions and, as Nietzsche has said, the tragedy was possible only because of their psychic health. He who has known victory as the Greeks knew it after Salamis and Marathon, he who *has discovered geometry and knows that he is mortal*, he, and he alone, has the tragic temper.

The Greeks are the first to have seen that Destiny requires the action of freedom in order to be realized. Destiny leans on the freedom of men; or rather: freedom is the human dimension of Destiny. Without men, Destiny is not realized and the cosmic harmony is broken. For the Greeks man is not "a useless passion," because freedom is one of the faces of Destiny. Without human action there would be no fatality or harmony or cosmic health, and the world would collapse. The tragedy is an image of the cosmos and of man. In it each element lives in relation to its opposite. And there is a moment when opposites fuse, not to produce an illusory synthesis, but in a tragic act, a knot that nothing but catastrophe can untie. Every tragic act, every conflict, can be reduced to this: freedom is a condition of necessity. Herein lies the originality of the tragedy, and the revelation that it gives us could be reduced to this. For the Greek, life is not a dream, or a nightmare, or a shadow, but an exploit, an act in which freedom and destiny form an indissoluble knot. That knot is man. Bound together in him are the human and the divine laws, and the unwritten laws that govern both. Man is the pointer of the scales, the cornerstone of the cosmic order, and his freedom prevents the return of the original chaos. (Let us remember the verse of Hölderlin, the only one of the moderns who, until Nietzsche, has known how to retrieve the Greek heritage: man is the guardian of creation and his mission consists in preventing the return of chaos.) Resting on human freedom is Destiny, the visible form of the universal rhythm, the manifestation of a Justice that is not reward and punishment, good and evil, but cosmic harmony. And man, the mortal, the child who grows old and falls ill, subject to the caprices of passion and the inconstancy of opinions, is the only free being, precisely because he is the subject chosen by Destiny. That choice demands his acceptance. And therefore his crimes cause the universe to tremble, and his actions reestablish the course of life. Because of him the world moves.

Our theater is also nourished by an epic tradition, and its vitality and originality stem from this fact. This is a dual tradition: on the one hand, the treasure of medieval romances and legends; on the other, what we would call the Christian epic: the lives of the saints and the martyrs. But this heroic material could not be freely re-created and put to the test by the dramatic poets. Monarchy by divine right and Catholic dogma are not comparable to the cult of the *polis* and the Olympian religion. Although Menéndez y Pelayo points out that during those centuries Spain was a "nation of theologians" and a "friarly democracy," the limits that state and church set for creative thought were quite narrow. When Lope takes up a topic from a previous century, like that of *Fuente-Ovejuna*, he resolves the conflict in accordance with the ideas of his time and exalts the monarch as supreme arbiter in the dispute of peasants and feudal lords. The work does not attack the established order, but tends rather to strengthen it. It is the same with *Peribáñez y el comendador de Ocaña*, *El mejor alcalde: el rey*, *El alcalde de Zalamea*, and other dramas. At any rate it is worth noting that through them all shines the famous "none beneath the king," a phrase in which the political conception of medieval Spain can be summarized. And even the cult of the monarch continues the tradition of the Cid: "Oh, God, how good a vassal, if his master were the same!" The best example of this attitude is *La estrella de Sevilla*, a beautiful fresco in which don Busto Tavera prolongs the figure of the *hidalgo* or nobleman as epic poetry had imagined him. Every man is bound by a dual loyalty: to his lord and to his honor. When this pair of loyalties becomes incompatible, the drama irrupts. Thus, our theater is rich in violent conflicts and its heroes move fiercely within the inexorable limits of honor and loyalty to the monarch. The clash of characters, the transports of passion, and the havoc wreaked on souls by the tyranny of the inflexible norms of honor produce extreme situations in which man seems to touch his ultimate possibilities. Nevertheless, in all those works we miss the boldness of the questions about destiny and the mystery of the human condition that the Greek heroes ask themselves. Unlike the Greeks and the English, Spanish dramatic poets possess a repertory of ready-made answers, applicable to every human situation. There are certain questions—those, precisely, that refer to man and his position in the cosmos—that our poets did not ask themselves or to which they already had the answers provided by Catholic theology.

The same must be said of the comedy: it is a play with a complicated plot or a criticism of customs, never a political comedy as in Aristophanes or a social satire as in Ben Jonson. The real Spanish comedy is a kind of poetic ballet, in which the speed of the action, the intricacy of the situations, and the wit of the dialogue make the spectacle a dazzling fireworks display. But there is a part of the Spanish theater—undoubtedly the most original and, at the same time, the most universal—that has man's freedom and the grace of God as its central theme. In such works as *La vida es sueño, El mágico prodigioso*, or *El condenado por desconfiado*, the Spanish theater fuses a national dramatic conception with the defense and elucidation of the Catholic doctrine of free will. And here it must be said that our theater is the only one in the Western world that really deserves to be called philosophical, at least until Goethe. In relation to Calderón, the thought of Racine or Shakespeare is mere prattle. But what surprises us is not the richness of Calderón's philosophical thought or Mira de Mescua's—because then they would only be esteemed as philosophers—but that they were able to transmute all those concepts into poetic images and dramatic action. No less astonishing was the passion with which the spectators followed those long baroque tirades on freedom, grace, and sin. As in Athens, so too in the Spanish *corrales* was established that sympathy between poets and audience without which the existence of great theater is not possible. That audience was not well versed in "the exact understanding of the natural laws and the sciences based on calculus"—Menéndez y Pelayo says—but on the other hand "it nourished its mind and fed its fancy on dogmatic theology and philosophy, which were not the patrimony of persons accustomed to the lecture hall but the everyday food of the masses. . . ." For the modern spectator, the language of Calderón or Tirso de Molina is unintelligible. And not only because our Spanish is so poor: the scarcity of words is the result of intellectual penury.

The central theme of our dramatic poetry is the soul's destiny; its greatness and what makes it comparable to the Greek tragedy is rooted in this. But for Aeschylus or Euripides this is a problem that had no answer except the one the poet was able to give, while our dramatists make use of a dogma that does not admit of any emendation. They apply formulas, they instruct, argue, prove their point, and win their theses brilliantly. Their art would deserve to be called "theater of

propaganda," if it were not for the fact that its authors never con-
fused intellectual conviction with the vile proselytism of our epoch.
Not one of them abased his conceptions to the point of transforming
them into magic formulas, or simplified them "to put them within
reach of the masses." Lope, who was not ashamed to write for the mul-
titude, would have blushed to hear the poets who now speak for the
people. Commercial propaganda was not yet the favorite rhetorical
model of politicians and writers "in the service of humanity." Our
poets wrote for their peers, that is, for beings endowed with reason
and in control of a will. Their very Catholicism prevented them from
regarding their fellows as tools or things. On the other hand, the prin-
ciple that governs propaganda—and which its beneficiaries have taken
from the commercial methods of the bourgeoisie—rejects reason and
freedom: man is a complex of reactions that must be stimulated or
neutralized according to the circumstances.

For our great authors, freedom is a gift of God. Thus they postulate
a terrible mystery, one that is analogous to the conflict of Greek trage-
dy. They too move between two incompatible poles: if a Providence
exists, how can man be free? And moreover, what can be the meaning
of human freedom, if it does not relate to God? Freedom is what dif-
ferentiates men from brutes, so that the essence of man is the free will;
well, if the free act leads man to realize his essence, how can that act
be contrary to God, in Whom essence and existence, act and potential,
are resolved into unity? The answer is paradoxical, as it was with the
Greeks. When Segismundo obeys his inner voice, he becomes a prison-
er of the stars, that is, of his untamed nature. To affirm his nature thus
implies not to be more, but to be less and, literally, to lose being, to
lose himself. But as soon as he denies himself and restrains his being,
he is saved. True freedom is exercised by subjecting ourselves to God.
This negation is also an affirmation and resembles the "yes" with
which Oedipus and Antigone answer Destiny. Nevertheless, there is
one capital difference: the freedom of the Spanish heroes consists in
saying "no" to human nature; the affirmation of Destiny, on the other
hand, is also an affirmation of man's tragic being. Although the mystery
of freedom as a gift of God is as impenetrable as the mystery of the
Destiny that is only realized in the hero's freedom, their consequences

are different. In the Greek's "yes," man exceeds himself, draws the bowstring of his will to its extreme limit and thus participates in the cosmic concert. Our theater proclaims man's nothingness; the Greek theater, his heroic condition. Segismundo's freedom is not cosmic justice realizing itself as an act of consciousness but Providence reflecting itself. Man is not a cluster of opposing forces but a stage occupied by two actors: God and the Devil. The triumphant freedom of the stars, as Calderón's beautiful verses express it, but also a freedom that consists in denying the one who exercises it. The hero, in the Greek sense, disappears. There is no tragedy but rather the *auto sacramental* or liturgical drama.

The doctrine of free will and that of predestination are a theological labyrinth at the end of which nothing or being awaits us. This was felt, wholeheartedly, by our authors and their audience. There is no other theater—aside from the Greek and the Japanese Nō—that emits metaphysical flashes of such brilliance. The brevity of its splendor does not prevent us from glimpsing the so-called abysses of being. Sacrilege is the central theme of the Spanish theological theater, as it is in the Greek. But, not without reason, criticism has shown that our authors do not excel in the creation of characters. All theater of ideas offers the same weakness; and perhaps the genius of the Spanish poets consists, precisely, in the fact that they have been able to create with such abstract themes human characters and not mere puppets. Characters, types, beings of blood and fire whose furious trajectory across the stage is always like the wind and the lightning, but not heroes in the sense of Oedipus and Prometheus, Orestes and Antigone. God has disinhabited man. Life is a dream and men are the ghosts of that dream.

Lisarda, the chief protagonist of *El esclavo del demonio*, is one of those feminine temperaments that abound in the Elizabethan theater, which Sade would rediscover and carry to atrocious extremes, but which are exceptional in our dramatic tradition. Possessed by her frightful and beautiful genius like a catastrophe in which fire is the principal actor, she plans to kill her father and sister. When she is before her victims, grace—that enigmatic grace that others seek in vain—descends and stays her homicidal hand. If this episode is compared with the attitude of the incestuous brother and sister in *'Tis Pity She's a Whore*, it is possible to determine all that separates the Spanish theater from the English. Mira de Mescua uses Lisarda to prove his thesis, and the heroine's passions have a theological resonance. John Ford's protagonists are a reality that irrupts, and the slaughter with which his play ends is rather like the final eruption of a volcano. Unlike Mira de Mescua, the English poet conceives passion as something sacred. Nothing more revealing of this consecration of nature as a divine force than Giovanni's words concerning the counsel of his confessor and spiritual father:

> *Shall a peevish sound,*
> *A customary form, from man to man,*
> *Of brother and of sister, be a bar*
> *'Twixt my perpetual happiness and me?*
> *Say that we had one father; say one womb—*
> *Curse to my joys!—gave both us life and birth;*
> *Are We not therefore each to other bound*
> *So much the more by nature? by the links*
> *Of Blood, of reason? nay, if you will have't,*
> *Even of religion, to be ever one,*
> *One soul, one flesh, one love, one heart, one all?*

The place occupied by God and free will in the Spanish theater, by freedom and Destiny in the Greek, is held by human nature in the English. But the sacred character of nature does not come from God or from the cosmic legality, but from its being a force that has rebelled against those old powers. Tamerlane, Macbeth, Faust, and even Hamlet belong to a blasphemous race, which has no law other than its passions and desires. And that law is terrible because it is the law of a nature that has forsaken God and has consecrated and anointed itself. The Elizabethans have just discovered man. The tide of his passions drives God from the stage. Like the Destiny of the ancients and the God of the Spanish, nature is an ambiguous divinity:

> *O, nature, what hadst thou to do in hell,*
> *When thou didst bower the spirit of a fiend*
> *In mortal paradise of such sweet flesh?*

The young Juliet's complaint can be repeated by the Duchess of Malfi and the old Lear, but not by Antigone or Agamemnon. The ambiguity of man and his nature is of a different order from that of the ancient divinities. Segismundo and Oedipus are not deceived by any man or woman, but by the gods. Thus their complaint has a super-human resonance. The heroes of Shakespeare and Webster are alone, in the most radical sense of the word, because their shouts are lost in the void: God and Destiny have deserted their heavens. With the dis-appearance of the gods the cosmos loses coherence and chance irrupts. The Greek necessity and the divine grace of the Spanish are impene-trable mysteries, but they command a secret logic. As soon as the human happening loses its former sacred references, it turns into a suc-cession of meaningless acts, which also lose connection with one an-other. Man becomes a plaything of chance. It is true that Romeo and Juliet are victims of the hate of their families and that the play could be explained as a consequence of caste rivalries. But it is also true that they could have been saved had it not been for the intervention of a series of circumstances that no power, except chance, has brought to-gether. In Shakespeare's world, chance replaces necessity. At the same time, innocence and guilt turn into words with no value. The dialectical equilibrium is broken, the tragic tension is relaxed. Despite their dev-astating passions and their cries that cause the earth to tremble, the characters in the Elizabethan theater are not heroes. There is some-thing childish in them all. Childish and barbarous. Violent or gentle, candid or treacherous, brave or cowardly, they are a heap of bones, blood, and nerves doomed to calm for an instant the appetite of a deified nature. Sated, the tiger withdraws from the stage and leaves the theater covered with bloody traces: men. And what is the meaning of all that residue? Life is a tale told by an idiot.

Torn between two laws, Antigone chooses piety: she sins against the law of the city to restore the equilibrium of the divine balance. Orestes does not shrink from matricide in order to implement justice and set the world, paralyzed by Clytaemnestra's crime, in motion again. Universal harmony is realized in man's freedom. Freedom is the foundation of being. If man renounces freedom, chaos irrupts and being is lost. In Shakespeare's world we witness the return of chaos.

The limits between things and beings disappear, crime can be virtue, and innocence, guilt. The loss of legality causes the world to vacillate. Reality is a dream, a nightmare. And again we move among ghosts.

The Spanish theater is nourished by the Spanish epic tradition and by theology. The English theater also leans on a national chronicle, and about a third of Shakespeare's work is composed of historical dramas. Moreover, as Pound states, for Shakespeare and his contemporaries the unity of Europe was still a reality and therefore, freely, like those who draw upon a common property, they are inspired by Italian, Danish, or Spanish themes and works.[8] The Elizabethan poet's vision of the world reveals even more profoundly the filiation between European Renaissance thought and the English theater. The substance of the thought of Marlowe, Shakespeare, Ford, Webster, or Jonson is a free interpretation of Montaigne and Machiavelli. The individualism of a Macbeth or a Faust is the reflection of the conditions of those times, but among those conditions is found, precisely, the thought of the period. Eliot has said that it is hardly necessary to emphasize how easily, in an epoch such as that, the Senecan attitude of pride, the cynicism of Machiavelli, and the skepticism of Montaigne were fused in the Elizabethan individualism. What the theology of Homer and philosophy were for the Greek tragedians, what neo-scholasticism was for the Spanish, the thought of Montaigne was for the Elizabethans. Europe gives the English poets a philosophy, conceived not so much as an aggregation of doctrines as a manner of understanding the world and man. That philosophy was not dogmatic but fluid, and it admitted of variations, emendations and unpublished solutions, a circumstance not unlike the Greeks' attitude toward the myth.

The French theater does not transform a national epic material, nor does it reflect on a theology or a philosophy to put it to the test in dramatic action. It does not examine the foundations on which French society rests, it neither goes back to its epic origins nor is a defense or a criticism of the principles that nourish France. It is true that the at-

[8] European literature is a whole, and the different national literatures that compose it are fully comprehensible only in terms of that whole. Concerning the conception of Western poetry as a "unity of sense," see the work by Ernst Robert Curtius, *European Literature and the Latin Middle Ages* (Mexico City: Fondo de Cultura Económica, 1955).

titude of Corneille and Molière toward Spanish and Italian works and
themes was no different from that of the Elizabethans, but in the end
the Graeco-Latin model replaces the freest and most immediate Euro-
pean tradition. The image of European unity is supplanted by the ab-
stract figure of an ideal Greece. So then it is a case of an external clas-
sicism: the French theater does not reproduce the evolution of the
Greek tragedy—the re-creation of an epic hero and the free meditation
on a national theology—but selects it as an aesthetic model. The laws
that govern Racine's tragedies are primordially aesthetic laws: the
theater is an ideal space where the characters move according to a de-
terminate rhythm. The humanity he gives us is very singular: nothing
more human than his characters or, likewise, nothing less human.
Racine's man has undergone a kind of surgical operation, which if
it has made him purer and more abstract—so that we can all recog-
nize ourselves in him—has also cut away that mysterious dimension
that makes him escape from his own humanity and puts him in rela-
tion with the higher and lower worlds.

Racine's theater—and in this he approaches the Elizabethan—is a
theater of characters and situations. The situation—or rather the com-
plicated tangle of circumstances and relations within which the pro-
tagonists move—is a substitute for God and necessity. The character,
the individual reaction to a given situation, occupies the place of free-
dom. In this sense Shakespeare and Racine are absolutely modern. But
Shakespeare's universe is that of the passions in rebellion. And that
same rebellion gives it a Luciferian, that is, a sacred quality. In Ra-
cine's theater the passions are terrible, but they never have a super-
human tone. His characters move in a pure and vacuous atmosphere,
from which not only every idea of cosmos and divinity has disap-
peared, but also every concrete particularity. The references to this
world or to the other have been suppressed. Men are victims of their
passions, but we are told nothing about the ultimate origin of those
passions. Racine's heroes live suspended in an abstract space which
does not touch the animal world or the supernatural one. Their psy-
chology is absolutely human, and that is precisely the source of their
inhumanity: man is always, in addition to man, something else: an-
gel, demon, beast, god, fatality, history—something impure, alien,

"other." Racine's situations are ideal, in the sense that a chess game is ideal, gratuitous, aesthetic. The product of the interweaving of circumstances and characters, fatality possesses an aesthetic tonality; it is a game from which divine ambiguity and the caprice of chance have previously been excluded. Chaos has been expelled again, only not to exalt destiny, but in favor of a geometry of the passions. Racine offers us a transparent image of man, but that very transparency dissolves the obscure, ambiguous area, the real mouth of shadows through which we catch a glimpse of the beyond that is every man.

The romantics tried to resume the Spanish and English tradition. Their endeavor was doomed to failure; Hegel said that the romantic theater could not be written by the Germans, because Shakespeare and the Spanish had already written it. Goethe's great Faustian myth is a kind of vast monologue of the Western spirit reflecting itself interminably in its own creations: all is mirror. The German poet struggled all his life against that subjectivism, and his homage to "mothers"—an echo of the ancient mysteries—is an attempt to recover the divinity of the natural whole. The dramatic poets who succeed him carry subjectivism to the extreme. Kleist's characters live in a world where reality has become atrocious, because the dream and subjectivity cannot penetrate it: they are prisoners whose only way out is death; Grabbe corrodes the hitherto sacred foundations of society and creates heroes who conspire against the health of the world. Neither Shakespeare, nor Racine, nor Calderón interdicted the world; the romantics condemned it, and their theater is a bill of indictment. The poet's relation with history changes radically.

It is true that not all modern theater condemns the world in the name of subjectivity. This also applies to the novel. But when they do not condemn it, they deny and dissolve it in a trick of mirrors. Just as lyric poetry becomes poetry of poetry in Hölderlin, the theater unfolds and is transformed into a vertiginous representation of itself. Although that play of reflections culminated in Strindberg, Synge, and Pirandello, it began in the Renaissance: Cervantes wrote a novel of the novel, Shakespeare, a criticism of the play in the play, Velázquez painted himself painting. The artist meditates on his work and sees in it only his own face that, astonished, contemplates him. Modern heroes are as ambiguous as the reality that sustains them. This movement culminates in Pirandello, the dramatic poet who has perhaps carried the revelation of man's *irreality* to its furthest limits. For the ancients the world rested on solid pillars; no one doubted appearances because no one doubted reality. In the modern age humor appears, dissociating appearances and making the unreal real, the real unreal. The "realistic" art *par excellence*, the novel, proscribes the reality of so-called reality. The poetry of the past consecrates the heroes, be they named Prometheus or Segismundo, Andromache or Romeo. The modern novel examines them and denies them, even when it pities them.

11. Ambiguity of the Novel

IT HAS BEEN SAID many times that the distinctive essence of the modern age—this age that is expiring now, before our eyes—consists in grounding the world on man. And the stone, the foundation on which the structure of the universe rests, is consciousness. Of course, not every modern philosophy shares this idea. But even in a philosophy that could seem most remote from these tendencies, consciousness appears as the ultimate and the highest conquest of history. Although Marx does not base the world on consciousness, he makes of history a long march at the end of which the alienated man will at last be master of himself, that is, of his own consciousness. Then consciousness will cease to be determined by the laws of production, and the leap from "necessity to freedom" will have been taken. As soon as man is the master and not the victim of historical relations, social existence will be determined by consciousness and not the other way around, as it is now.

Moreover, it is very strange that the most objective and rigorous sciences have developed freely within these intellectual convictions. The strangeness disappears if one observes that, unlike the ancient

Greek conception of science, that of the modern period is not so much an ingenuous version of nature—or rather a vision of the natural world as we see it—as a creation of the objective conditions that will permit the verification of certain phenomena. For the Greeks nature was above all a visible reality: what the eyes see; for us, a cluster of reactions and stimuli, an invisible network of relations. Modern science selects and isolates portions of reality and conducts its experiments only when it has created certain conditions favorable for observation. In a certain way, science invents the reality on which it operates. The final mission that Marx assigns to the human species at the end of the labyrinth of history—the autonomy of consciousness and its almost demiurgic possibility of creating and modifying existence— has been achieved by modern man in determinate areas of reality. For modern scientific thought also, objective reality is an image of consciousness and the most perfect of its products.

Whether one posits consciousness as the foundation of the universe, or affirms that we cannot operate on external reality unless we first reduce it to a datum in consciousness or, finally, conceives history as a progressive liberation of consciousness from that which determines and alienates it, the position of modern man vis-à-vis the cosmos and vis-à-vis himself is radically different from that which he assumed in the past. The revolution of Copernicus showed that man was not the center of the universe or the king of creation. Man became an orphan and was dethroned, but he had the ability to remake his earthly dwelling. As we know, the first consequence of this attitude was the disappearance of the notions that were the justification for life and the foundation of history. I refer to that complex system of beliefs that, to simplify, is known as the sacred, the divine, or the transcendent. This change did not only occur in the sphere of ideas—if it is possible to speak of discarnate or pure ideas—but rather in the less precise, but much more active area of intellectual convictions. It was a historical change and, what is more, a revolutionary change, because it consisted in the substitution of one world of values for another. Now, every revolution aspires to establish a new order on positive and unshakable principles, which tend to occupy the place of the deposed divinities. Every revolution is, at the same time, a profanation and a consecration.

The revolutionary movement is a profanation because it tears down the old images; but this degradation is always accompanied by a consecration of what had been regarded as profane up to that time: revolution consecrates sacrilege. Great reformers have been considered sacrilegious because they actually profaned the sacred mysteries, denuded them and exposed them as frauds or incomplete truths. And simultaneously they consecrated truths that had hitherto been unknown or regarded as profane. Buddha denounces as illusory the metaphysic of the Upanishads: the ego does not exist and the atman is a deceitful play of reflections; Christ breaks with Judaism and offers salvation to all men; Lao-Tse ridicules the Confucian virtues and turns them into crimes, as he sanctifies what his adversaries considered sin. Every revolution is the consecration of a sacrilege, which becomes a new sacred principle.

The modern revolution reveals a characteristic that makes it unique in history: its inability to consecrate the principles on which it is based. In fact, since the Renaissance—and especially after the French Revolution, which consummates the triumph of modernity—myths and secular religions have arisen that collapse as soon as they are touched by the living air of history. It seems unnecessary to recall the failures of the religion of humanity or of science. And as the sacrilege was not followed by the consecration of new principles, a vacuity in consciousness was produced. That vacuity is called the secular spirit. The secular spirit or neutrality. Now, "where gods die, ghosts are born." Our ghosts are abstract and implacable. The fatherland ceases to be a community, a land, something concrete and palpable, and becomes an idea to which all human values are sacrificed: the nation. The old lord—tyrannical or merciful, but who can always be assassinated—is succeeded by the state, immortal like an idea, efficient like a machine, like them impersonal, against which neither entreaties nor daggers are effective because nothing causes it to feel pity or kills it. At the same time the cult of technology wins souls and replaces the old beliefs in magic. But magic is grounded on a two-edged principle: the universe is a whole in motion, governed by rhythm; and man is in a living relation with that whole. Everything changes because everything communicates. The metamorphosis is the expression of this vast and vital community of which man is one of the terms. We can change, be stones or stars, if we know the right word that opens the doors of analogy. The man of magic is in constant communication with the universe, forms part of a whole in which he recognizes himself and on which he can act. Modern man uses technology as his ancestor used magic formulas, although it opens no doors for him. On the contrary, it puts an end to any possibility of contact with nature and with his fellows: nature has become a complex system of causal relations in which qualities disappear and are transformed into pure quantities; and his fellows have ceased to be persons and are utensils, tools. Man's relation with nature and with his neighbor is not essentially different from that which he maintains with his automobile, his telephone, or his typewriter. In short, the grossest credulity—as is seen in political myths—is the other side of the positive spirit. No one has faith, but everyone has illusions. But the illusions evaporate and then nothing is left but the void: nihilism and vulgarity. Like Balzac's series, the history of the secular or bourgeois spirit could be entitled *Lost Illusions*.

The bourgeois revolution proclaimed the rights of man, but at the same time it trampled on them in the name of private ownership and free trade; it declared that freedom was sacrosanct, but subjected it to the combinations of money; and it affirmed the sovereignty of nations and the equality of men, while it conquered the planet, reduced old empires to slavery, and established the horrors of colonialism in Asia, Africa, and America. The final fate of bourgeois ideals is not surprising. Empires and churches recruit their functionaries and officials from among the old revolutionaries and their sons. Thus, the real problem lies not in the fatal debasement of principles, or in their confiscation, for its own use, by a class or a group, but in the very nature of those principles. How can man be the foundation of the world if he is the being who is, by his very nature, change, perpetual becoming who never overtakes himself and who ceases to transform himself only to die? How is it possible to escape or transcend the contradiction that is contained in the critical spirit and, therefore, in all modern revolutionary movements? Only, perhaps, by a revolution grounded on the original principle of every revolution: change. Only a movement that turned inward, to produce the "revolution of revolution," could prevent the fatal fall into Caesarean terror or bourgeois mystification. Such a revolution would make impossible the transformation of the critical spirit into ecclesiastical orthodoxy, of the revolutionary instant into a holy date, of the leader into Caesar, and of the dead hero into a divinized mummy. But that revolution would unceasingly destroy itself and, carried to its extreme, would negate the very principle that moved it. Nihilism would be its final result. Thus, what distinguishes the revolution of the modern age from the old revolutions is not so much or exclusively the corruption of the original ideals, or the degradation of its liberating principles into new tools of oppression, as the impossibility of consecrating man as the foundation of society. And this impossibility of consecration is due to the very nature of the instrument used to overthrow the old powers: the critical spirit, rational doubt.

Rational criticism has always been a tool of liberation, personal or social. Buddha presents himself as a critic of tradition and urges his listeners not to accept his words without first examining them. But Buddhism—at least in its original form—does not aim to explain the foundations of the world, but to offer us a means of escape. This explains Gautama's reticence in the face of certain questions: "The religious life does not depend on the dogma of the eternity of the cosmos or its perishable nature. . . . Whatever our opinion of these matters may be, the truth is that we are born, we die, we grow old and suffer misery, grief, and despair." The doctrine leads to the extinction of pain and evil. Its criticism has a precise function: to illuminate man, to cleanse him from the illusion of the ego and of desire. Modern thought, on the contrary, sees its foundation in the critical reason. It sets the constructions of reason in opposition to the creations of religion; its paradises are not outside time, in the other life or in that instant of enlightenment that denies the temporal stream, but in time itself, in the historical event: they are social utopias. While the myth is situated outside of history, the utopia is a promise that tends to be realized here, among us, and in a determinate time: the future. But utopias, as offspring of the rational spirit, are subject to rational criticism. A society that defines itself as rational—or that tends to be rational—has to be critical and unstable, because reason is, above all, criticism and inquiry. Thus the distance between principles and reality —present in every society—is changed among us into a real and insuperable contradiction. The liberal state is founded on freedom of inquiry and on the exercise of the critical spirit; to deny those principles would be to deny its historical legitimacy and its very existence. They alone justify it. At the same time, it is true that the state and the ruling class do not hesitate to resort to force whenever that spirit of inquiry causes the social order to vacillate. And therefore words change their meaning and become ambiguous: repression is practiced in the name of freedom of inquiry. In ancient societies the exercise of power did not entail any hypocrisy, because its foundations were never disputed; on the other hand, the foundation of modern authority is precisely the possibility of disputing it. This is the origin of the duplicity and the feeling of illegitimacy that tinge the bourgeois consciousness. The bourgeois man's right to lead society is not clear; it is the result of prestidigitation, of a quick change of hands. The criticism that enabled him to dethrone the monarchy and the nobility now permits him to occupy their place. He is a usurper. Like a secret wound that will not heal, modern society carries within it a principle that denies it, which it cannot renounce without renouncing itself and destroying itself. Criticism is its food and its poison.

At the beginning of this third part of our study it was noted that the most immediate function of poetry, that which could be called its historical function, consists in the consecration or transmutation of an instant, personal or collective, into an archetype. In this sense, the poetic word builds nations. Without an epic no society is possible, because there is no society without heroes in whom it can recognize itself. Jacob Burckhardt was one of the first to observe that the epic of modern society is the novel. But he stopped with this affirmation and did not explore the contradiction involved in giving the name of epic to an ambiguous genre, which runs the gamut from the confession and autobiography to the philosophical essay.

The singular character of the novel stems, first of all, from its language. Is it prose? If one thinks of the epopee, it obviously is. As soon as one compares it with the classic genres of prose—essay, discourse, tractate, epistle, or history—one perceives that it does not obey the same laws. In the chapter devoted to verse and prose it was stated that the prose writer struggles against the seduction of rhythm. His work is a constant battle against the rhythmic nature of language. The philosopher arranges ideas according to a rational order; the historian narrates events with the same linear rigor. The novelist does not demonstrate or relate: he re-creates a world. Although his task is to relate a happening—and in this sense he resembles the historian—he is not interested in telling what happened, but in reliving an instant or a series of instants, re-creating a world. Therefore he resorts to the rhythmic powers of language and the transmuting virtues of the image. His entire work is an image. Thus, on the one hand, he imagines, poetizes; on the other, he describes places, events, and souls. He touches on poetry and history, image and geography, myth and psychology. Rhythm and examination of conscience, criticism and image, the novel is ambiguous. Its essential impurity springs from its constant oscillation between prose and poetry, concept and myth. Ambiguity and impurity result from its being the epic genre of a society grounded on analysis and reason, that is, on prose.

The epic hero is an archetype, a model. As archetypes, Achilles or Siegfried are invulnerable; as men, they are subject to the fate of every mortal; there is always a secret chink in the hero's body or soul through which death or defeat can penetrate. Achilles' heel is the stamp of his mortality, the mark of his human nature. And when he falls, wounded by fatality, he recovers his divine nature: the heroic action is the reconquest of divinity. Two worlds, the supernatural and the human, combat in the hero, but that struggle does not involve any ambiguity. It is a case of two principles fighting for a soul and one will conquer the other in the end. There is nothing like that in the novel. Reason and madness in Don Quixote, vanity and love in Rastignac, avarice and generosity in Benigna form a single cloth. One never knows where jealousy ends and love begins for Swann. Therefore none of these personages can really be an archetype in the sense that Achilles, the Cid, or Roland is. The epic of heroes who reason and doubt, the epic of doubtful heroes—we know not whether they are crazy or sane, saints or demons. Many are skeptics, others frankly rebellious and antisocial and all are in open or secret contention with their world. The epic of a society in conflict with itself.

Neither Achilles nor the Cid doubts the ideas, beliefs, and institutions of his world. The heroes of the epopee are securely rooted in their universe and therefore their relations with their society are the natural relation of the plant with its own earth. Arjuna does not pass judgment on the cosmic order or the social hierarchies, Roland is completely loyal to his lord. The epic hero is never a rebel, and the heroic act generally tends to reestablish the ancestral order, violated by a mythical lack. This is the meaning of Odysseus' return or, in the tragedy, of Orestes' vengeance. Justice is a synonym of natural order. On the other hand, the novelistic hero's doubt concerning himself is also projected on the reality that sustains him. Do Don Quixote and Sancho see windmills or giants? Neither of the two possibilities is the true one, Cervantes seems to be telling us: they are giants and they are windmills. The realism of the novel is a criticism of reality and even a suspicion that reality may be as unreal as Don Quixote's dreams and fantasies. Was Albertine a lesbian, did Gilberte tell the truth, did Mathilde love Julien Sorel, did Smerdyakov kill the old Karamazov? Where is reality and what kind of strange realism is that of all these novelists? The world that surrounds these heroes is as ambiguous as they themselves.

The transition from the epic ideal to the novelistic one can be observed very clearly in Ariosto and Cervantes. Orlando is not only an extemporaneous attempt at an epic poem: it is also a mockery of the chivalric ideal. The perfection of the stanzas, the brilliance of the images, and the intricacy of the invention help to emphasize the grotesque tone. Ariosto's idealism is unrealism. The true epic is realistic: although Achilles speaks with gods and Odysseus descends into hell, no one doubts their reality. That reality is composed of the mixture of the mythical and the human, so that the passage from the quotidian to the marvelous is imperceptible: nothing more natural than for Diomedes to wound Aphrodite in battle. In Ariosto everything is unreal. And as he treats of sublime feelings and events, their very irreality makes them grotesque. The grotesque sublime is close to humor, but it is still not humor. Neither Homer nor Virgil knew humor; Ariosto seems to have a presentiment of it, but it is only born with Cervantes. Because of humor, Cervantes is the Homer of modern society. For Hegel irony consists in inserting subjectivity into the order of objectivity; one could add that it is a critical subjectivity. Thus, Cervantes' most outrageous characters possess a certain consciousness of their situation; and that consciousness is critical. In its presence, reality vacillates, although it does not give in completely: the windmills are giants for a moment, only to become windmills with greater force and aplomb. Humor makes ambiguous what it touches: it is an implicit judgment of reality and its values, a kind of provisional suspension, which causes them to oscillate between being and nonbeing. Ariosto's world is insolently unreal, and the same is true of his characters. In Cervantes' work there is a continuous communication between reality and fantasy, madness and common sense. The Castilian reality, by its very presence, makes Don Quixote a farcical, unreal character; but suddenly Sancho doubts and is not sure if Aldonza is Dulcinea or the peasant girl he knows, if Clavileño is a charger or a piece of wood. And now it is the Castilian reality that vacillates and seems nonexistent. The inharmony between Don Quixote and his world is not resolved, as in the traditional epic, by the triumph of one of the principles but by their fusion. That fusion is humor, irony. Irony and humor are the great invention of the modern spirit. They are the equivalent of the tragic conflict and therefore our great novels resist the proximity of the Greek drama. The fusion of irony is a provisional synthesis, which prevents any effective denouement. The novelistic conflict cannot give birth to a tragic art.

Epic of a society that is grounded upon criticism, the novel is an implicit judgment of that same society. First, as we have seen, it is a question about the reality of reality. This question—which has no possible answer, because its very formulation excludes any reply—is an acid that corrodes the whole social order. Although the feudal world is not seen in a favorable light in Cervantes' novel, his own epoch does not deserve absolution either. In *The Red and the Black*, there is an evident nostalgia for the heroic world and in the name of that nostalgia Julien Sorel condemns the reality that surrounds him; but is not the figure of Mathilde also a condemnation of the past? The opposition between the novelistic world and that of the old poetry is stated more clearly in Balzac. His work is a reply to the *Divine Comedy*. Like the latter, *The Human Comedy* has its hell, its paradise, its purgatory, and even its limbo. But Dante's poem is a song and thus it ends: as a praise of creation. One could hardly say the same of Balzac's work. Description, analysis, history of a rising class, account of its crimes, its passions and its secret renunciations, *The Human Comedy* partakes of the encyclopedia and the epopee, of mythical creation and pathology, of the chronicle and the historical essay, with inspiration and scientific investigation, utopia and criticism grafted on. It is a mythical history, a myth that has chosen the forms of history for its incarnation and one that ends in a judgment. A Last Judgment, in which society condemns itself and its principles. A century later, on the last pages of another novel, when the narrator attends a reception at the home of the Prince de Guermantes, Proust repeats the gesture and again condemns the society he had meant to revive and describe. The novel is an epic that turns against itself and denies itself in a threefold way: as poetic language, eaten away by prose; as the creation of heroes and worlds, made ambiguous by humor and analysis; and as song, because that which its word tends to consecrate and exalt is transformed into an object of analysis and finally into an unappealable condemnation.

It is natural that France should have had a predilection for the novel. French is the most analytical of the modern languages and in that country the modern spirit is incarnated with greater precision and clarity than in others. In the rest of Europe it seems that history has proceeded by leaps, breaks, and interruptions; in France, at least from the seventeenth century to the first quarter of the twentieth, everything seems to have occurred in an orderly fashion: the Academy prepares the way for the Encyclopedia; the latter, the Revolution; the Revolution, the Empire, and so on successively. Spain, Italy, Germany, and even England do not possess such a fluid and coherent history. Moreover, this impression is no doubt illusory and is dependent on the peculiar historical perspective of our time. But if it is illusory to see the history of France as the model of the evolution of modern Western society, it is not an illusion to regard the French novel as a true archetype. Of course, we cannot forget Cervantes and Pérez Galdós, Dick-

ens and Melville, Tolstoi and Dostoevski. But no country or language
has such an uninterrupted succession of great novelists, from Laclos to
Proust. French society sees itself in those creations and, alternately,
divinizes and examines itself. It extols itself, but also judges and con-
demns itself.

The crisis of modern society—which is a crisis of the principles of
our world—has been manifested in the novel as a return to the poem.
The movement begun by Cervantes is repeated now, but in the oppo-
site direction, in Joyce, Proust, and Kafka. Cervantes separates the
novel from the burlesque epic poem; his world is hazy, like the world
of dawn, and thus the hallucinatory character of the reality he offers
us. His prose sometimes borders on verse, not only because he resorts
to hendecasyllables and octosyllables with a certain frequency, but be-
cause of the deliberate use of poetic language. His obsession for poetry
is revealed above all in the limpid language of *Los trabajos de Persiles
y Sigismunda*, which he regarded as his best work and which abounds
in selections of real poetry. Insofar as the spirit of analysis scores
greater conquests, the novel abandons the language of poetry and ap-
proximates that of prose. But criticism is destined to refute itself.
Prose denies itself as prose. The author of *Madame Bovary* is also the
author of *Salammbô* and of *Saint Julian the Hospitaler*. The triumphs
of reason are also its defeats, as is seen in Tolstoi, Dostoevski, Swift,
or Henry James. Since the beginning of the century the novel has
tended to be a poem again. It is not necessary to emphasize the poema-
tic character of Proust's work, with its slow rhythm and its images
stirred by a memory whose operation does not fail to have analogies
with poetic inspiration. Neither is it necessary to dwell on the experi-
ment of Joyce, who causes the word to recover its autonomy so that it
may break the thread of discursive thought. Kafka's world is an infer-
nal Comedy, where Predestination plays the same role as Grace in Cal-
derón's theater. I do not know if D. H. Lawrence and Faulkner are
great novelists, but I am sure that they belong among the great poets.
This return to the poem is still more visible in German writers like
Ernst Jünger. In other works the invasion of the rhythmic tide is not
as decisive as the reconquest of the heroic temperature. At the height

of the action, Malraux's heroes doubt—but they would prefer not to doubt. There is a sentence in *La Condition Humaine* that shocked Trotski: "Marxism is not a philosophy but a destiny." In it I see the germ of a future theater because it condenses the contradictions of the modern spirit and of the history we are living.

The same tendencies can be observed in the contemporary theater. After the decline of romanticism, the theater fell into the gravitational orbit of prose, and Ibsen represents the apogee of this direction. But with Strindberg poetry returns—and in a terrible, fulminating way. The last great dramatist of the critical strain was Shaw, and it is indeed significant that his successors are named Synge, Yeats, and Eliot. In them, as in García Lorca, the poetic rhythm conquers the prose and the theater is poetry again. In short, the two principal playwrights of this period, Paul Claudel and Bertold Brecht, are poets, first and foremost. It is revealing that these two names are linked, almost involuntarily, when one thinks of the modern theater. In life, everything set them in opposition: aesthetics, philosophy, beliefs, and personal destiny. And yet, in his own way each denies the modern world; both seek and find in the tradition of the Far East a system of signs that will permit them to transform the neutral stage of our theater into a meaningful space; both, in short, in their best works, have achieved that fusion of the idea and the act, the person and the word, in which the *exemplary* character of great theater consists. Because the theater is the proof of the act by the word and of the latter by the former; I mean: it is the objectivization of language in actions and, also, the opposite: the word illumines the act, makes it lucid, causes history to reflect. In sum, the struggle between prose and poetry, consecration and analysis, song and criticism, latent since the birth of modern society, is resolved by the triumph of poetry. And this is true even in Brecht: the famous "distancement" does not tend to dissolve our judgment about the reality of what takes place on stage but invites us to support or oppose the action. But the victory of poetry is the sign of the extinction of the modern age. The theater and the novel of our time extol not a birth but a funeral: the funeral of their world and of the forms it engendered.

Poetry is the revelation of the human condition and the consecration

of a concrete historical experience. The modern novel and theater lean
on their epoch, even when they deny it. In denying it, they consecrate
it. The destiny of the lyric has been different. With the old deities dead
and objective reality denied by consciousness, the poem has nothing
to sing about, except its own being. The poet sings to song. But song
is communication. The monologue can only be followed by silence, or
an adventure desperate and extreme among all others: now poetry will
not be incarnated in the word but in life. The poetic word will not
consecrate history, but will be history, life.

12. The Discarnate Word

THE NOVEL and the drama are forms that permit of a compromise between the critical and the poetic spirit. Moreover, the novel demands it; its essence consists precisely in being a compromise. On the other hand, lyric poetry sings of passions and experiences that cannot be reduced to analysis and that constitute a waste and an extravagance. To exalt love is a provocation, a challenge to the modern world, because it is something that escapes analysis and that constitutes an unclassifiable exception; that is the reason for the strange prestige of adultery in modern times: if for the ancients it was a crime or an unimportant thing, in the nineteenth century it becomes an affront to society, a rebellion, and an act consecrated by the ambiguous light of the accursed. (Now we are witnessing the opposite phenomenon: the fact that eroticism is in style suppresses its powers of destruction and creation. Transition from a sin to an anonymous diversion. . . .) Dream, divagation, play of rhythms, fantasy, are also experiences that alter the economy of the spirit without a possible compensation and unhinge the mind. For the bourgeois man, poetry is an amusement—but whom does it amuse, except a few eccentrics?—or a dangerous activity; and the poet, an inoffensive—although costly—clown, or a madman and potentially a criminal. Inspiration is a fraud or a disease, and poetic images can be classified as the products of mental illness—a curious confusion that still persists.

The *poètes maudits* are not a creation of romanticism: they are the fruit of a society that expels that which it cannot assimilate. Poetry neither enlightens nor entertains the bourgeois man. Therefore he exiles the poet and transforms him into a parasite or a vagabond. And therefore, also, for the first time in history, poets do not live from their work. Their efforts are not worth anything and this *are not worth anything* is translated precisely into *do not earn anything*. The poet must seek another occupation—from diplomacy to chicanery—or die of hunger. This situation coincides with the birth of modern society: the first "mad" poet was Tasso; the first "criminal" poet, Villon. The Spanish Golden Age was populated by beggarpoets and the Elizabethan period by ruffianlyrists. Góngora was a beggar all his life, he cheated at cards and ended besieged by his creditors; Lope trafficked with procurers; in Cervantes' old age there is an unfortunate incident in which women of his family appear in an equivocal light; Mira de Mescua, a canon in Granada and playwright in Madrid, accepted payment for work he did not do; Quevedo, with variable fortune, engaged in politics;[1] Alarcón took refuge in high bureaucracy. . . . Marlowe was assassinated in an obscure intrigue after having been accused of atheism and libertinage; Jonson was a poet laureate and received, in addition to a sum of money, a cask of wine each year: both inadequate; Donne was a turncoat and thus rose to become Dean of Saint Paul's. . . . In the nineteenth century the social position of poets deteriorates. With the disappearance of wealthy patrons their incomes diminish, although there are some exceptions, such as Hugo. Poetry does not have a price; it is not a commodity that can be converted into money like a painting. The "deluxe editions" of the new poetry have been not so much a manifestation of its sectarian spirit as a means of selling at a higher price, by reason of the small number of copies, books that the

---

[1] Concerning Quevedo, a realistic politician, see the essay by Raimundo Lida, "Quevedo's Letters," published in number 1 of *Cuadernos Americanos* (Mexico, 1953).

general public will not buy in any case. The *Communist Manifesto* af-
firms that "the bourgeoisie has turned the doctor, the lawyer, the
priest, the poet, and the man of science into paid servants." This is
true, with one exception: the coffers of the bourgeoisie were closed to
the poets. Neither menials nor buffoons: pariahs, ghosts, vagrants.

To complete this description it must be added that the antagonism
between the modern spirit and poetry begins as an agreement. With
the same decision of philosophical thought, poetry tries to ground the
poetic word on man himself. The poet does not see in his images the
revelation of a strange power. Unlike sacred writings, poetic writing
is the revelation of himself that man makes to himself. From this it
follows that modern poetry is also theory of poetry. Moved by the need
to ground his activity on principles that philosophy denies him and
theology concedes him only in part, the poet doubles as a critic. Cole-
ridge is one of the first to meditate on poetic creation, to ask what the
poem really means or says. For the English poet imagination is man's
highest gift and in its primordial form "the original faculty of all hu-
man perception." This conception is inspired by Kant's. According to
Heidegger's interpretation of the *Critique of Pure Reason*, the "tran-
scendental imagination" is the root of sensibility and understanding
and that which makes judgment possible. . . . Imagination unfolds or
projects objects, and without it there would be neither perception nor
judgment; or rather: as a manifestation of the temporality that it is, it
unfolds itself and presents objects to the sensibility and the under-
standing. Without this operation—in which what we call "imagining"
properly consists—perception would be impossible.[2] Reason and ima-
gination ("transcendental" or "primordial") are not contrary facul-
ties: the latter is the foundation of the former and that which permits
man to perceive and to judge. Moreover, Coleridge, in a second ac-
ceptance of the word, conceives imagination not only as an organ of
cognition but as the faculty to express it in symbols and myths. In
this latter sense the knowledge given us by the imagination is not real-
ly a cognition: it is the supreme knowledge, "it's a form of Being, or
indeed it is the only Knowledge that truly is, and all other Science is

[2] Martin Heidegger, *Kant and the Problem of Metaphysics* (Mexico City: Fondo
de Cultura Económica, 1954).

real only as it is symbolical of this."[3] Imagination and reason, original-
ly one and the same thing, end by fusing in an evidence that is inex-
pressible except by means of a symbolic representation: the myth. In
short, the imagination is, primordially, an organ of cognition, since it
is the necessary condition of all perception; and, moreover, it is a facul-
ty that expresses, by means of myths and symbols, the highest knowl-
edge.

Poetry and philosophy culminate in the myth. The poetic experience
and the philosophical one are confused with religion. Religion is not
a revelation, but a state of mind, a kind of ultimate agreement of
man's being with the being of the universe. God is a pure substance,
about which the reason can express nothing, except that it is inexpres-
sible: "the divine truths of religion should have been revealed to us in
the form of poetry; and at all times poets, not the slaves of any particu-
lar sectarian opinion, should have joined to support all those delicate
sentiments of the heart. . . ."[4] Religion is poetry, and its truths, beyond
any sectarian opinion, are poetic truths: symbols or myths. Coleridge
strips religion of its constitutive quality: being a revelation of a divine
power; and reduces it to the intuition of an absolute truth, which man
expresses through mythical and poetic forms. Moreover, religion *is the
poetry of Mankind*. Thus, he grounds poetic-religious truth on man
and changes it into a historical form. Because the phrase "religion is
the poetry of mankind" actually means: the way that poetry has of
being incarnated in men, and becoming rite and history, is religion. In
this idea, common to all great poets of modern times, is found the root
of the opposition between poetry and modernity. Poetry is proclaimed
as a rival principle of the critical spirit and as the only principle that
can replace the former sacred principles. Poetry is conceived as the
original principle on which the truths of religion rest as secondary and
historical manifestations, if not as tyrannical superimpositions and
concealing masks. Thus the poet can only view with favor the criti-
cism that the rational spirit makes of religion. But as soon as that same
critical spirit proclaims itself the successor of religion, he condemns it.

Undoubtedly the foregoing reflections simplify the problem over-

[3] *On Method.* Essay XI
[4] *Biographia Literaria.*

much. It is obvious enough that reality is richer than our intellectual schemes. Nevertheless, reduced to the essential, this is the position of German romanticism since Hölderlin and, from that moment on, of all European poets, be they called Hugo or Baudelaire, Shelley or Wordsworth. Moreover, it is worth repeating that all these poets coincide at some moment with the revolution of the critical spirit. It could not be otherwise, because it has already been seen that the poetic adventure coincides laterally with the revolutionary one. The poet's mission consists in being the voice of that movement that says "no" to God and His hierarchs and "yes" to men. The Scriptures of the new world will be the poet's words revealing a man free of gods and lords, now without intermediaries vis-à-vis death and life. Revolutionary society is inseparable from society grounded on the poetic word. It is therefore not strange that the French Revolution aroused an unbounded expectation in every spirit and won the sympathy of German and English poets. Of course, hope was followed by hostility; but later— after the double scandal of revolutionary terror and Napoleonic Caesarism has been mitigated or justified—the heirs of the first romantics again identify poetry and revolution. For Shelley the modern poet will occupy his former place, usurped by the priest, and will again be the voice of a society without monarchs. Heine demands the warrior's sword for his tomb. All see in the great rebellion of the critical spirit the prologue to an even more decisive event: the advent of a society grounded on the poetic word. Novalis observes that "religion is merely practical poetry," that is, poetry incarnated and lived. More daring than Coleridge, the German poet affirms: "Poetry is the original religion of mankind." To reestablish the original word, the poet's mission, is to reestablish the original religion, prior to the dogmas of churches and states.

   William Blake's attitude illustrates unsurpassably the direction of poetry and the place it occupies at the beginning of our epoch. Blake does not soften his attacks and sarcasms against the prophets of the century of enlightenment and especially against the Voltairian spirit. But, with equal fury, he does not cease to ridicule official Christianity. The poet's word is the original word, prior to Bibles and Gospels: "The Poetic Genius is the true Man. . . . The Religions of all Nations

are derived from each Nation's different reception of the Poetic Gen-
ius. . . . The Jewish & Christian Testaments are An original derivation
from the Poetic Genius."[5] The man and the Christ of Blake are the
reverse of those proposed to us by the official religions. The original
man is innocent, and each one has an Adam within him. Christ Him-
self is Adam. The Ten Commandments are the invention of the Devil:

> *Was Jesus Chaste? or did he*
> *Give any Lessons of Chastity?*
> *The morning blush'd fiery red:*
> *Mary was found in Adulterous bed.*
>
> . . . .
>
> *Good & Evil are no more!*
> *Sinai's trumpets, cease to roar!*

The poet's mission is to reestablish the original word, turned askew
by priests and philosophers. "Prisons are built with stones of Law;
Brothels, with bricks of Religion." Blake sings of the American and
the French Revolutions, which destroy prisons and take God out of
the churches. But the society prophesied by the poet's word cannot be
confused with political utopia. Reason creates darker jails than theolo-
gy. Man's enemy is named Urizen (Reason), the "god of systems,"
the prisoner of himself. Truth does not proceed from reason, but from
poetic perception, that is, from imagination. The natural organ of
knowledge is not the senses or ratiocination; both are limited and in-
deed contrary to our ultimate essence, which is infinite desire: Less
than all cannot satisfy man. Man is imagination and desire:

> *Abstinence sows sand all over*
> *The ruddy limbs & flaming hair,*
> *But Desire Gratified*
> *Plants fruits of life & beauty there.*

By means of imagination man sates his infinite desire and turns him-
self into infinite being. Man is an image, but an image in which he
himself is incarnated. Amorous ecstasy is that incarnation of man in
his image: one with the object of his desire, he is one with himself.
Therefore, man's true history is the history of his images: mythology.

[5] *All Religions are One* (1778).

In his prophetic books Blake tells us the story of man in mythical images. A continuing story that is happening right now, at this instant and one that issues in the founding of a new Jerusalem. Blake's great poems are merely the history of the imagination, that is, of the avatars of the primordial Adam. Mythical history: sacred scripture: writing of origins. Revelation of the original past, which unveils archetypal time, prior to the times. A writing of origins and a prophecy: that which was, will be, and is being from all eternity. And what do these sacred poetic writings prophesy to us? The coming of a man who has recovered his original nature and has thus conquered sin's law of gravity. Relieved of guilt, Blake's man flies, he has a thousand eyes, fire in his hair, he kisses what he touches, kindles what he thinks. Now he is image, now act. Desire and realization are the same. Christ and Adam are reconciled, Urizen is redeemed. Christ is not the eternal thief of energies but energy itself, tense and thrown toward the act. Imagination made desire, desire made act: "Energy, Eternal Delight." The poet cleanses the sacred books of error and writes innocence where one used to read sin, freedom where authority was written, instant where eternity was graved. Man is free, desire and imagination are his wings, heaven is within his grasp and its name is fruit, flower, cloud, woman, act. Eternity is enamored of the works of time. The kingdom prophesied by Blake is that of poetry. Once again the poet is a Diviner, and his divination proclaims the establishment of a city whose foundation stone is the poetic word. The poetic society, the new Jerusalem, is delineated for the first time, separated from the dogmas of religion and the utopia of philosophers. Poetry enters into action.

German romanticism proclaims similar ambitions. In the review *Athenäum*, which served as the organ of the first romantics, Friedrich Schlegel defines its program thus: "Romantic poetry is not just a progressive universal philosophy. Its purpose is not only to unite all the different forms of poetry and to reestablish communication between poetry, philosophy, and rhetoric. It must also mix and fuse poetry and prose, inspiration and criticism, natural poetry and artificial poetry, it must enliven and socialize poetry, make life and society poetic, poetize the spirit, fill and saturate artistic forms with a unique and diverse substance, and animate the whole with irony." In Novalis the tendencies of the Jena group find the clearest voice and the purest and boldest thought, combined with the authenticity of the great poet. The religion of night and death of the *Hymns*, the moving *Fragments*—each like a piece of sidereal stone carved with the signs of universal analogy and the correspondences that link man with the cosmos—the search for the lost Middle Ages, the resurrection of the myth of the poet as a three-fold figure in which the knight-errant, the lover, and the seer are united, form a many-faceted star. One of these facets is a plan for historical reform: the creation of a new Europe, formed of the alliance of Catholicism and the Germanic spirit. In the famous essay *Christianity or Europe*—written in 1799, the year of the fall of the Directory—Novalis proposes a return to medieval Catholicism. Not a return to Rome, but something new, although inspired by the Roman universality. Novalis' universality is not an empty form; the Germanic spirit will be its substance, because the Middle Ages are alive and well in the depths of the German popular soul. And what are the Middle Ages but the prophecy, the dream of the romantic spirit? The romantic spirit: poetry. History and poetry are fused. A great Peace Council will reconcile freedom with the papacy, philosophical reason with imagination. Once again, and by unexpected paths, poetry enters history.

The dream of Novalis is a disquieting harbinger of other, more ferocious ideologies. But, if one is to be just, certain speeches of Saint-Just, another pure young man, which are also a prophecy of the future deeds of the geometric spirit, must cause us to feel the same disquietude. Moreover, Novalis' attitude reflects a dual crisis, personal and historical, which cannot be analyzed here. Suffice it to say that the French Revolution put the best German spirits on the horns of a dilemma, as it did with the Spanish. After the initial seduction and not without a split, the Jena group disavowed many of its conceptions of the first moment. Some threw themselves into the arms of the Holy Alliance, others chose a less militant Catholicism, and the rest penetrated the great romantic night of death. These oscillations were the counterpart of revolutionary crises and convulsions, from the Terror to Thermidor and its final culmination in the adventure of Bonaparte. It is impossible to understand the romantic reaction if the historical circumstances are forgotten. To defend Germany from the Napoleonic invasions was to fight against foreign oppression, but also to strengthen internal absolutism. A dilemma without a solution for most of the romantics. As Marx has said: "The struggle against Napoleon was a regeneration accompanied by a reaction." We, the contemporaries of the Revolution of 1917 and the Moscow Trials, can understand better than anyone the alternatives of the romantic drama.

Novalis' conception appears as an attempt to insert poetry into the center of history. Society will become a poetic community and, more precisely, a living poem. The relation between men will cease to be in the form of master and slave, employer and servant, to be converted into poetic communion. Novalis foresees communities dedicated to the collective production of poetry. This communion is, above all, a penetrating of death, the great mother, because only death—which is night, sickness, and Christianity, but also the erotic embrace, the banquet at which the "stone becomes flesh"—will give us access to health, to life and to the sun. Novalis' communion is a reconciliation of the two halves of the sphere. In the night of death, which is also the night of love, Christ and Dionysus are one. There is a magnetic point at which great poetic currents meet: in such a poem as *Bread and Wine*, the vision of Hölderlin, the solar poet, momentarily grazes that of *Hymn V* of Novalis, poet of the night. In the *Hymns* burns a secret sun, sun of poetry, black grape of resurrection, star covered with black armor. And there is no accident in the irruption of that image of the sun like a knight whose arms and plumed crest are draped in mourning, because Novalis' communion is a mystic and heroic supper at which the commensals are knights who are also poets. And the bread distributed at that banquet is the solar bread of poetry. "We shall drink that wine of light, we shall be stars," the *Hymn* says. Communion in poetry, the supper of German romanticism is a rhyme or reply to Blake's Jerusalem. In both visions we descend to the origin of the times, in search of the original man, the Adam who is Christ. In both, woman—who is the "highest corporeal food"—is mediation, gate of access to the other shore, yonder where the two halves come together and man is one with his images.

Since its birth modern poetry has presented itself as an autonomous

and conflictive endeavor. Incapable of coming to terms with the criti-
cal spirit, neither does it manage to find a place in the churches. It is
revealing that for Novalis the triumph of Christianity does not involve
the negation but rather the absorption of pre-Christian religions. In
the romantic night, "all is delight, all is eternal poem and the sun that
illuminates us is the august face of God." The night is sun. And what
is most surprising is that this solar victory of Christ's is accomplished
not before but after the scientific era, that is, in the romantic age: in
the present. The historical Christ who preached in Galilee is clearly not
the same as the sun-night deity invoked by the *Hymns.* The same is
true of the Virgin, who is also Persephone and Sophia, the poet's be-
loved, the death that is life. Novalis' new Catholicism is, literally, new
and different from historical Catholicism; and it is also more ancient,
because it calls up the divinities adored by the pagans. From this per-
spective the essay *Christianity or Europe* is illuminated with another
meaning; once again poetry shows a double face: it is the most revo-
lutionary of revolutions and, simultaneously, the most conservative of
revelations, because it consists only in reestablishing the original word.
The attitude of the other great precursors—Hölderlin, Blake, Nerval
—is even clearer: their Christ is Dionysus, Lucifer, Orpheus.

The root of the break between modern poetry and religion is differ-
ent from that which pits the poetic spirit against the rational one, but
its consequences are similar: like the bourgeoisie, the churches also
expel the poets. The opposition between poetic and sacred writings is
of such a nature that every alliance made by modern poetry with an
established religion always ends in scandal. Nothing less orthodox
than the Christianity of a Blake or a Novalis; nothing more suspect
than that of a Baudelaire; nothing more alienated from the official re-
ligion than the visions of a Shelley, a Rimbaud, or a Mallarmé, not to
mention the one who made of rupture and negation the most mordant
dirge of the century: Isidore Ducasse.[6]

It is not necessary to follow the episodes of the sinuous and subter-
ranean course of the poetic movement of the last century, always oscil-
lating between the two poles of Revolution and Religion. Each ad-

---

[6] Concerning the case of Whitman, see Appendix III.

herence ends in a break; each conversion, in scandal. Monnerot has compared the history of modern poetry to that of the Gnostic sects and the adepts of the occult tradition. This is true in two senses. The influence of Gnosticism and hermetic philosophy is undeniable in such poets as Nerval, Hugo, Mallarmé, not to mention the poets of this century: Yeats, George, Rilke, Breton. Moreover, each poet creates around him little circles of initiates, so that without exaggeration one can speak of a secret society of poetry. The influence of these groups has been immense, and it has transformed the sensibility of our time. From this standpoint it is not inexact to affirm that modern poetry has been incarnated in history, not openly, but as a nocturnal mystery and a clandestine rite. An atmosphere of conspiracy and of an underground ceremony surrounds the cult of poetry.

Condemned to live in the substratum of history, the modern poet is defined by loneliness. Although no decree obliges him to leave his land, he is an exile. In a certain sense, Dante never left Florence, because the old society always kept a place for the poet. The ties with his city were not broken: they were transformed, but the relation continued to be a living and dynamic one. To be an enemy of the state, to lose certain civil rights, to be subject to the vengeance or justice of the native city, is something quite different from lacking a personal identity. In the latter case the person disappears, turns into a ghost. The modern poet has no place in society because, indeed, he is "no one." This is not a metaphor: poetry does not exist for the bourgeoisie or for the masses of our time. The practice of poetry can be a distraction or a disease, never a profession: the poet does not work or produce. Therefore poems have no value: they are not products susceptible to commercial exchange. The effort expended on their creation cannot be reduced to work value. Commercial circulation is the most active and total form of exchange our society knows and the only one that produces value. As poetry is not a thing that can enter into the exchange of mercantile goods, it is not really a value. And if it is not a value, it has no real existence in our world. The volatilization operates in two directions: the thing the poet speaks of is not real—and it is not real, primordially, because it cannot be reduced to a commodity—and also poetic creation is not an occupation, a task, or a definite activity, since it cannot be remunerated. That is why the poet has no social status. The controversy over "realism" would be seen in a different light if those who attacked modern poetry for its scorn of the "social reality" realized that they were merely duplicating the attitude of the bourgeoisie. Modern poetry does not speak of "real things" because it was decided beforehand to abolish one whole part of reality: precisely the part that, since the origin of the times, has been the wellspring of poetry. "What is admirable about the fantastic"—Breton says—"is that it is not fantastic but real." No one recognizes himself in modern poetry because we have been mutilated and have forgotten what we were like before this surgical operation. In a world of cripples, the one who says that there are beings with two sound legs is a visionary, a man who evades reality. When the world was reduced to the data of consciousness and all works of art were reduced to merchandise-work value, the poet and his creations were automatically expelled from the sphere of reality.

To the extent that the poet disappears as a social existence and the open circulation of his works becomes rarer, his contact increases with that which, for lack of a better expression, we shall call man's lost half. All the endeavors of modern art are intended to reestablish dialogue with that half. The upsurge of popular poetry, the recourse to dream and delirium, the use of analogy as key to the universe, the attempts to recover the original language, the return to myths, the descent into night, the love for the art of the primitives—all this is a search for the lost man. A ghost in a city of stone and money, dispossessed of his concrete and historical existence, the poet stands on the sidelines and perceives that we have all been uprooted from something and cast into the void: into history, into time. The situation of exile, from one's self and one's fellows, leads the poet to intuit that condemnation will cease only if he touches the furthest point of the solitary condition. Because there where it seems that there is no longer anything or anyone, on the last frontier, appears the *other*, we *all* appear. Man alone, cast out into this night—we know not if it is the night of life or the night of death —defenseless, with nothing left to hold on to, descending interminably, is the original man, the real man, the lost half. The original man is every man.

The most desperate and total attempt to break the siege and make of poetry a common property occurred in the place where objective conditions had become critical: in Europe, after the First World War. Of all the adventures of that period, the most lucid and ambitious was surrealism. To examine it will be to give an account of the pretensions of contemporary poetry, in its most extreme and radical form.

The surrealist program—to transform life into poetry and thus to bring about a decisive revolution in spirits, customs, and social life— is no different from the plan of Friedrich Schlegel and his friends: to make life and society poetic. To accomplish it, both appeal to subjectivity: the disintegration of objective reality, first step for its poetization, will be brought about by the insertion of the subject into the object. Romantic "irony" and surrealist "humor" join hands.

In both movements love and woman occupy a central place: complete erotic freedom is united with the belief in a single love. Woman opens the doors of night and of truth; the amorous union is one of man's highest experiences, and in it he touches the two sides of being: death and life, night and day. Romantic heroines, beautiful and terrible like that marvelous Karoline von Günderode, are reincarnated in women like Leonora Carrington. The political vicissitudes are also similar: between the Bonapartist reaction and the Holy Alliance, Schlegel bows to Metternich and others take refuge in Catholicism; in an opposite direction, but denying their past no less, poets like Aragon and Éluard, facing the bourgeois world and the Stalinist reaction, embrace the latter. Others scatter (until the concentration camp or the insane asylum swallows them up: Desnos and Artaud), continue their adventure, action and creation alone, like René Char, or persist, like Breton and Péret, in their search for a way to reconcile poetry and revolution.

The differences are no less noteworthy. Among the surrealists the metaphysical glance is less keen and broad; even in Breton and Artaud —the only ones with a truly philosophical vocation—the vision is partial and split. The romantics are enveloped by the atmosphere of German philosophy; surrealism, by Apollinaire's poetry; contemporary art, Freud and Marx. On the other hand, the surrealists' historical consciousness is clearer and deeper and their relation with the world more direct and fearless. The romantics end by denying history and taking refuge in the dream; the surrealists do not give up—even if this means, as is the case with Aragon, subjecting the word to the needs of the action. The differences and similarities are fused in a common circumstance: both movements are a protest against the spiritual sterility of the geometric spirit, they coincide with revolutions that are transformed into Caesarean or bureaucratic dictatorships and, in short, they constitute attempts to transcend reason and religion and thus to found a new sacred. In the face of similar historical crises they are simultaneously twilight and dawn. The first betrays the common insufficiency of feudalism and of the Jacobinic spirit; the second, the ultimate nihilism of capitalism and the dangers of bureaucratic Bolshevism. They do not achieve a synthesis, but at the height of the historical tempest they raise the banner of poetry and love.

Like the romantics, the surrealists attack the notions of subject and object. There is no need to expound further on their attitude, which was already described in another chapter. On the other hand, it is useful to emphasize that the affirmation of inspiration as a manifestation of the unconscious, and the attempts to create poems collectively involve a socialization of poetic creation. Inspiration is a common property; one has only to close his eyes for the flow of images to begin; we are all poets and *yes*, we must gather figs from thistles. Blake had said: "All men are alike in the Poetic Genius." Surrealism tries to show this by resorting to the dream, the dictation of the unconscious and the collectivization of the word. The hermetic poetry of Mallarmé and Valéry—and the conception of the poet as one who has been chosen, a being apart—suffer a terrible onslaught: we can all be poets. "We return the talent that is lent to us. Speak to me of the talent of that meter of platinum, of that mirror, that door. . . . We have no talent," Breton says in the *First Manifesto*. The destruction of the subject implies the destruction of the object. Surrealism interdicts works. Every work is an approximation, an attempt to achieve something. But when poetry is within reach of everyone, poems and paintings are superfluous. We can all make them. And what is more: we can all be poems. To live in poetry is to be poems, to be images. The socialization of inspiration leads to the disappearance of poetic works, dissolved into life. Surrealism does not propose the creation of poems as much as the transformation of men into living poems.

Among the resources destined to bring about the abolition of the antinomy poet and poetry, poem and reader, you and I, the most radical is automatic writing. With the husk of the self destroyed, the partitions of consciousness broken, man, possessed by the other voice that rises from the depth like an emerging water, returns to that from which he was separated when consciousness was born. Automatic writing is the first step toward the restoration of the golden age, in which thought and word, fruit and lips, desire and act are synonyms. The "higher logic" that Novalis asked for is automatic writing: I is you, this is that. The unity of opposites is a state in which knowledge ceases, because he who knows has been fused with what is known: man is a purveyor of evidences.

The practice of automatic writing runs into a number of difficulties. In the first place, it is an activity that is accomplished in a direction contrary to all the accepted notions in our world; above all, it attacks one of the basic tenets of the prevailing morality: the value of effort. Moreover, the passivity required by poetic automatism involves a violent decision: the will not to intervene. The tension thus produced is unbearable and only a few succeed in arriving, if indeed they do arrive, at that state of passive activity. Automatic writing is not within everyone's reach. And I shall even say that the actual practice of it is impossible, since it presupposes the identity of the individual man's being and the word, which is always social. The ambiguity of language lies precisely in that opposition. Language is symbolic because it tries to relate two heterogeneous realities: man and the things he names. The relation is doubly imperfect because language is a system of symbols that reduces, on the one hand, the heterogeneity of each concrete thing to equivalences and, on the other, constrains the individual man to use general symbols. Poetry, precisely, proposes to find an equivalence (that is the metaphor) in which neither things in their concrete particularity nor the individual man will disappear. Automatic writing is a method for achieving a state of perfect coincidence between things, man, and language; if that state were achieved, it would consist in an abolition of the distance between language and things

and between language and man. But that distance is the distance en-
gendered by language; if the distance disappears, language evaporates.
Or in other words: the state to which automatic writing aspires is not
the word but silence.

Now, after the Second World War and the tense years that have
followed it, it is possible to see more clearly the essence of surrealism's
revolutionary failure. None of the revolutionary movements of the
past had adopted the closed form of the Communist party; no previous
poetic school had presented itself as such a compact and militant
group. Surrealism not only proclaimed itself the poetic voice of the
Revolution, but identified the Revolution with poetry. The new com-
munist society would be a surrealist society, in which poetry would
circulate through social life like a perpetually creative force. But in
the historical reality that new society had already engendered its
myths, its images, and a new sacred. Before the cult of leaders was
born, the guardians of the holy books and a caste of theologians and
inquisitors had already sprung up. Finally, the new society began to
resemble the old ones too much and many of its acts were reminiscent
not so much of the terror of the Committee of Public Safety as of the
exploits of the pharaohs. The transformation of Lenin's workers'
state into a vast and efficient bureaucracy precipitated the break, but
was not its cause. With Trotski in power the difficulties would not
have been completely different. One has only to read *Literature and
Revolution* to understand that artistic freedom also had certain limits
for Trotski; if the artist exceeds them, the revolutionary state is duty-
bound to take him by the shoulders and shake him.[7] Compromise was
impossible, for the same reasons that had prevented the poets of a
century before from forming any permanent union with the church,
the liberal state, or the bourgeoisie.

After this break, surrealism is again what the ancient poetic circles
were: a semisecret society. It is true that Breton has not ceased to
affirm the ultimate identity of the revolutionary movement and the

---

[7] Years later, when he was in exile, Trotski changed his beliefs and affirmed that
the only possible system for the artist would be anarchy, absolute freedom, inde-
pendently of the circumstances that the revolutionary state might endure. But these
are the affirmations of a man of the opposition.

poetic one, but its action in the field of reality has been sporadic and has not influenced political life. At the same time, it would be unjust to forget that, beyond this historical failure, the sensibility of our epoch and its images—particularly the incandescent triangle formed of liberty, love, and poetry—are in large measure a creation of surrealism and of its influence on the majority of contemporary poets. For the rest, surrealism is not a survival of the period that followed World War I, or an archaeological object. In reality, it is the only tendency that has managed to reach the half-century mark alive, after enduring a war and a spiritual crisis without parallel. What distinguishes romanticism and surrealism from other modern literary movements is their power of transformation and their capacity to penetrate beneath the historical surface and then reappear again. Surrealism cannot be buried because it is not an idea but a direction of the human spirit. The undeniable decadence of the surrealist poetic style, transformed into a formula, is that of a determinate art form and does not essentially affect its ultimate powers. Surrealism can create new styles, fertilize old ones, or, also, dispense with any form and be converted into a method of inner search. Now, aside from what the future may hold for this group and its ideas, it is obvious that aloneness continues to be the dominant note of present-day poetry. Automatic writing, the golden age, the night that is an eternal banquet, the world of Shelley and Novalis, of Blake and Hölderlin, is not within the reach of men. Poetry has not been incarnated in history, the poetic experience is an exceptional state and the only way still open to the poet is the old way of the creation of poems, paintings, and novels. But this turning back to the poem is not a simple return or a restoration. Cervantes does not renounce Don Quixote: he assumes his madness, he does not sell it for a few crumbs of common sense. The future poem, to be truly a poem, will have to start with the great romantic experience. The questions that the greatest poets have been asking themselves for a century and a half—have they an answer?

Epilogue

13. Signs in Rotation

The history of modern poetry is the history of an immoderation. After tracing a brief and enigmatic sign, all its great protagonists have crashed against the rock. Lautréamont's black star rules the destiny of our most eminent poets. But this century and a half has been as rich in disasters as in works: the failure of the poetic adventure is the opaque side of the sphere; the other is formed of the modern poems' light. Thus, to examine poetry's possibilities of being incarnated is not to ask questions about the poem but about history: is it idle fancy to think of a society that will reconcile the poem and the act, that will be living word and lived word, creation of the community and creative community? This book did not propose to answer that question: its theme was a reflection on the poem. Nevertheless, the compelling naturalness with which it appears at the beginning and end of the meditation—is this not an indication of its central character? That question is the question. Since the dawn of modern times, the poet has never ceased to ask it—and therefore he has written. And History, also unceasingly, has rejected it—has answered with *something else*. I shall not try to answer it. I should not be able to. But still I cannot remain silent either. I shall hazard something that is more than an opinion and less than a certainty: a belief. It is a belief nourished by uncertainty and grounded upon nothing but its negation. In reality I seek that point of insertion of poetry that is also a point of intersection, fixed and vibrant center where contradictions are constantly annulled and reborn. Wellspring-heart.

The question embraces two antagonistic and complementary terms: there is no poetry without society, but poetry has a contradictory way of being social: it simultaneously affirms and denies speech, which is social word; there is no society without poetry, but society can never be realized as poetry, it is never poetic. Sometimes the two terms aspire to break apart. They cannot. A society without poetry would lack a language: everyone would say the same thing or no one would speak, transhuman society in which all would be one or each person would be a self-sufficient unit. A poetry without a society would be a poem without an author, without a reader and, in fact, without words. Condemned to a perpetual association that is resolved to instant discord, the two terms seek a mutual conversion: to poetize social life, to socialize the poetic word. Transformation of society into creative community, into living poem; and of the poem into social life, image incarnate.

A creative community would be that universal society in which the relations between men, far from being an imposition of external necessity, would be like a living fabric, made of each one's fatality in being bound up with the freedom of all. That society would be free because, as its own master, society alone would be able to determine itself; and it would be unified because human activity would not consist, as it does today, in some men's domination over others (or in the revolt against that domination), but would seek the recognition of each person by his equals or, rather, his fellows. The cardinal idea of the modern revolutionary movement is the creation of a universal society that, in abolishing oppression, will simultaneously unfold the original identity or similarity of every man and each man's radical difference or singularity. Poetic thought has not been alien to the vicissitudes and conflicts of this literally superhuman endeavor. Since German romanticism, the history of Western poetry has been that of its breaks and its reconciliations with the revolutionary movement. At one time or another, all our great poets have believed that in a revolutionary, communist, or libertarian society the poem would cease to be that nucleus of contradictions that simultaneously affirms and denies history. In the new society, poetry would at last be *practical*.

The conversion of society into a community and the poem into practical poetry are not within view. It is just the opposite: each day they seem more remote. The predictions of revolutionary thought have not come true or have been realized in a way that is an affront to the supposed laws of history. It has become a commonplace to insist on the palpable discord between theory and reality. I can only repeat, with no joy whatever, for the sake of the argument, some facts known by all: the absence of revolutions in the countries that Marx called civilized and that today are called industrial or developed; the existence of revolutionary regimes that have abolished private ownership of the means of production without also abolishing the exploitation of man or the differences of class, rank, or function; the almost complete replacement of the classic antagonism between the proletariat and the bourgeoisie, capital and labor, by a dual and ferocious contradiction: the opposition between rich and poor countries and the quarrels between states and groups of states that join together or separate, form alliances or fight one another, stirred by the needs of the moment, by geography and the national interest, independently of their social systems and the philosophies they claim to profess. A description of the surface of contemporary society would have to include other no less disturbing traits: the aggressive rebirth of racial, religious, and linguistic particularisms along with the docile adoption of forms of thought and conduct elevated to a universal canon by commercial and political propaganda; the raising of the standard of living and the degrading of the *standard of life*; the sovereignty of the object and the dehumanization of those who produce and use it; the predominance of collectivism and the evaporation of the notion of one's fellow man. The means have become ends: economic policy instead of political economy; sex education and not an understanding of eroticism; the perfection of the communications system and the nullification of those who communicate with one another; the triumph of the sign over the

image in the arts and, now, of the thing over the sign. . . . A cir-
cular process: plurality is resolved to uniformity without suppressing
the discord between nations or the split in consciousnesses; the per-
sonal life, exalted by advertising, melts into a life of anonymity; the
novelty of each day ends by being repetition and agitation issues in im-
mobility. We go from no place to nowhere. *Like the movement in a
circle*, said Raimundo Lulio, *so is the punishment in hell.*

Perhaps Rimbaud was the first poet who saw, in the sense of percep-
tion and clairvoyance, the present reality as the infernal or circular
form of movement. His work is a condemnation of modern society,
but his final word, *Une Saison en Enfer*, is also a condemnation of
poetry.[1] For Rimbaud, the new poet would create a *universal language,
from the soul for the soul*, that would announce the action instead of
rhythming it. The poet would not merely express the *march toward
Progress*, but would be *vraiment un multiplicateur de progrès*. The
novelty of poetry, Rimbaud says, *is not in the ideas or the forms*, but
in its capacity to define the *quantité d'inconnu s'éveillant en son temps
dans l'âme universelle*. The poet does not limit himself to discovering
the present: he awakens the future, brings the present to the encounter
of that which is coming: *cet avenir sera matérialiste*. The poetic word
is no less "materialistic" than the future it announces: it is movement
that engenders movement, action that transmutes the material world.
Animated by the same energy that moves history, it is prophecy and
the actual consummation, in real life, of that prophecy. The word is
incarnated, it is practical poetry. *Une Saison en Enfer* condemns all
this. The alchemy of the word is a delirium: *vieillerie poétique,
hallucination, sophisme de la folie*. The poet renounces the word. He
does not return to his former belief, Christianity, or to his own people;
but before abandoning everything, he proclaims a singular *Noël sur la*

---

[1] In my opinion, the theme of the chronology of Rimbaud's writings has been
stated unilaterally. The dates on which the poems were written are one thing, and
their place in the work is another. No psychological problem is involved here: there
is no doubt that when Rimbaud wrote *Une Saison en Enfer*, he believed it was his
last word, a farewell; but even if it had not been, that text is actually an examination
and a final judgment of the poetic experience, as conceived by the so-called *Lettre du
Voyant* and *Les Illuminations*. If one regards Rimbaud's poems as one work, if they
are a whole and not a collection of separate texts, then *Une Saison en Enfer* follows
Les Illuminations, even though some of the latter were written later.

terre: le travail nouveau, la sagesse nouvelle, la fuite des tyrans et des démons, la fin de la superstition. It is the farewell to the old world and the hope of changing it by poetry: *Je dois enterrer mon imagination.* The chronicle of hell closes with an enigmatic declaration: *Il faut être absolument moderne.* Whatever may be the interpretation given to this phrase, and there are many, it is evident that here *modernity* stands in opposition to *alchemy of the word.* Rimbaud no longer exalts the word, but the action: *point de cantiques.* After *Une Saison en Enfer* one cannot write a poem without overcoming a feeling of shame: is it not a ridiculous act or, what is worse, a kind of deceit? Two paths are still open, the paths tried by Rimbaud: action (industry or revolution) or the writing of that final poem that will also be the end of poetry, its negation and its culmination.

Revolutionary action and the practice of poetry have never seemed so incompatible as in the last thirty years. Nevertheless, something unites them. Born at almost the same time, modern poetic thought and the revolutionary movement meet, after a century and a half of quarrels and ephemeral alliances, before the same landscape: a space fully packed with objects, but devoid of future. The condemnation of poetry's intent to be incarnated in history also touches the principal protagonist of the modern era: the revolutionary movement. They are the two sides of the same phenomenon. This condemnation, moreover, is an exaltation: it condemns us to ourselves, not to revolution or to poetry. It is very easy now to criticize revolutionary thought, especially its Marxist branch. Its insufficiencies and limitations are obvious. Has anyone observed that they are also our own insufficiencies and limitations? Its errors are those of the boldest and most generous segment of the modern spirit, in its dual direction: as criticism of the social reality and as universal plan for a just society. Not even the crimes of the Stalinist period or the progressive degeneration of the official Marxism, transformed into bureaucratic Manichaeism, are alien to us: they are an integral part of the same history. A history that encompasses us all and that we have all made together. Although the society envisaged by Marx is far from being a reality of history, Marxism has permeated history so deeply that we all, in one way or another, sometimes without knowing it, are Marxists. Our moral categories and judgments, our idea of the future, our opinions of the present or of justice, peace or war, everything, not excluding our negations of Marxism, is impregnated with Marxism. Marxist thought is now part of our intellectual blood and our moral sensibility.

The contemporary situation has a certain similarity with that of the medieval philosophers who had no tool with which to define the Judeo-Christian God, a creative and personal God, except Aristotle's metaphysical notions about entity and being. (If God, the idea of God, is dead, it died of a philosophical death: Greek philosophy.) Criticism of Marxism is indispensable, but it is inseparable from that of modern man and must be made with the critical ideas of Marxism itself. To learn what is alive and what is dead in the revolutionary tradition, contemporary society must examine itself. Marx had already said that the only way for Christianity "to make the earlier mythologies understood objectively was by criticizing itself," and that "bourgeois economy did not understand the feudal, ancient, and oriental societies until bourgeois society began to criticize itself."[2] Within the Marxist system, moreover, are the germs of the creative destruction: dialectic and, above all, the *force of abstraction*, as Marx called social analysis, today applied to a real and historically determinate subject: twentieth-century society. The notion of the proletariat as a universal agent of history, that of the state as a simple expression of the class in power, that of culture as a "reflection" of the social reality, all this, and many other things besides, will disappear. Not the vision of a communist society. The idea of a universal community in which, by the abolition of classes and of the state, the domination of some by others will cease and the morality of power and punishment will be replaced by that of freedom and personal responsibility—a society in which, with the disappearance of private property, each man will be the proprietor of himself and that "individual property" will be literally common, shared by all thanks to collective production; the idea of a society in which the distinction between work and art is obliterated—that idea is unrenounceable. It is not only the heritage of Western moral and political thought since the epoch of Greek philosophy, but it is part

[2] *General Introduction to a Critique of Political Economy.*

of our historical nature. To renounce it is to renounce being what modern man has wished to be, to renounce being. Not just a morality or a political philosophy is involved here. Marxism is Western thought's last attempt to reconcile reason and history. The vision of a universal communist society is linked to another: history is the place where reason is incarnated; or more accurately: the movement of history, as it unfolds, is revealed as universal reason. The reality of history often belies this idea; again and again we seek a meaning for the bloody agitation. We are condemned to seek the reason for the unreason. Indeed, if a new revolutionary thought is to emerge, it will have to absorb two traditions scorned by Marx and his heirs: the libertarian and the poetic traditions, the latter being understood as the experience of *otherness*; and it is no less certain that this thought, as Marxism was, will be critical and creative; knowledge that embraces society in its concrete reality and in its general movement—and changes it. Active reason.

Doubtless the new poetry will not repeat the experiences of the last fifty years. They are unrepeatable. And still submerged are the poetic worlds waiting to be discovered by an adolescent whose face we shall surely never see. But from the outside it may perhaps not be too reckless to describe some of the circumstances that the new poets face. One is the loss of the world image; another, the appearance of a universal vocabulary composed of active signs: technology; still another, the crisis of meanings.

In antiquity the universe had one form and one center; its movement was governed by a cyclical rhythm and that rhythmical figure was for centuries the archetype of the city, the laws, and the works. The political order and the order of the poem, public festivals and private rites—and even discord and the transgressions of the universal rule—were manifestations of the cosmic rhythm. Later, the figure of the world widened: space became infinite or transfinite; the Platonic year turned into a linear, unending succession; and stars ceased to be the image of cosmic harmony. The center of the world was displaced and God, ideas, and essences disappeared. We were alone. The figure of the universe changed and man's idea of himself changed; nevertheless, the worlds did not cease to be the world nor man men. Everything was a whole. Now space expands and breaks apart; time becomes discontinuous; and the world, the whole, explodes into splinters. Dispersion of man, wandering in a space that is also dispersed, wandering in his own dispersion. In a universe that breaks up and separates from itself, a whole that has ceased to be thinkable except as absence or a collection of heterogeneous fragments, the self also breaks apart. Not that it has lost reality or that we regard it as an illusion. On the contrary, its very dispersion multiplies and strengthens it. It has lost cohesion and has ceased to have a center, but each particle is conceived as a unique self, more closed and clinging to itself than the former self. Dispersion is not plurality, but repetition: always the same self that blindly combats another blind self. Propagation, pullulation of the identical.

The growth of the self threatens language in its twofold function: as dialogue and as monologue. The former is grounded on plurality; the latter, on identity. The contradiction of dialogue consists in the fact that each one speaks with himself as he speaks with others; the contradiction of monologue is that it is never I, but another, who listens to what I say to myself. Poetry has always been an attempt to resolve this discord by a conversion of the terms: the I of the dialogue into the you of the monologue. Poetry does not say: I am you; it says: you are my self. The poetic image is *otherness*. The modern phenomenon of incommunication depends less on the plurality of subjects than on the disappearance of the you as a constitutive element of each consciousness. We do not speak with others because we cannot speak with ourselves. Yet the cancerous multiplication of the self is not the cause, but rather the result of the loss of the world image. Feeling himself alone in the world, ancient man discovered his own self and, thus, that of the others. Today we are not alone in the world: there is no world. Each place is the same place and nowhere is everywhere. The conversion of the I into you—image that comprises every poetic image —cannot be realized if the world does not first reappear. The poetic imagination is not an invention but a discovery of the presence. To discover the image of the world in that which emerges as fragment and dispersion, to perceive in the one the other, will be to restore to language its metaphorical virtue: to give it presence for the others. Poetry: search for the others, discovery of *otherness*.

If the world, as image, disappears, a new reality covers the whole earth. Technology is a reality so powerfully real—visible, palpable, audible, ubiquitous—that the real reality has ceased to be natural or supernatural: industry is our landscape, our heaven and our hell. A Mayan temple, a medieval cathedral, or a baroque palace were something more than monuments: sensible points of space and time, privileged observatories from which man could contemplate the world and the transworld as a totality. Their orientation corresponded to a symbolic vision of the universe; the form and arrangement of their parts opened a plural perspective, a veritable crossing of visual paths: upward and downward, toward the four points of the compass. Total view of the totality. Those works were not only a vision of the world, but they were made in its image: they were a representation of the shape of the universe, its copy or its symbol. Technology comes between us and the world, it closes every prospect from view: beyond its geometries of iron, glass, or aluminum there is exactly nothing, except the unknown, the region of the formless that is not yet transformed by man.

Technology is neither an image nor a vision of the world: it is not an image because its aim is not to represent or reproduce reality; it is not a vision because it does not conceive the world as shape but as something more or less malleable to the human will. For technology, the world presents itself as resistance, not as archetype: it has reality, not shape. That reality cannot be reduced to any image and is, literally, unimaginable. The ultimate purpose of ancient knowledge was the contemplation of reality, either sensible presence or ideal form; technological knowledge aspires to substitute a universe of machinery for the real reality. The artifacts and utensils of the past existed in space, which is radically altered by modern machinery. Space is not only populated by machines that tend toward automatism or are already automatons, but it is a field of forces, a knot of energies and relations—something very different from that more or less stable expanse or area of the former cosmologies and philosophies. The time of technology is, on the one hand, a break in the cosmic rhythms of the old civilizations; on the other, the acceleration and, in the end, the cancellation of modern clock time. From both standpoints it is a discontinuous and vertiginous time that eludes representation, if not measurement. In short, technology is grounded upon a negation of the world as image. And one would have to add: because of that negation, technology exists. It is not technology that denies the image of the world; it is the disappearance of the image that makes technology possible.

The works of the past were replicas* of the cosmic archetype in the dual sense of the word: copies of the universal model and human response to the world, rhymes or stanzas of the poem that the cosmos says to itself. Symbols of the world and dialogue with the world: the former, because they were a reproduction of the image of the universe; the latter, because they were the point of intersection between man and external reality. Those works used to be a language: a vision of the world and a bridge between man and the whole that surrounded and sustained him. The constructions of technology—factories, airports, power plants, and other grandiose establishments—are absolutely real but they are not presences; they do not represent: they are signs of action and not images of the world. Between them and the natural landscape that contains them there is no dialogue or correspondence. They are not works but tools; their duration depends on their performance and their form has no significance other than their efficiency. A mosque or a Roman triumphal arch are works impregnated with significance: they endure because they were built upon lasting meanings, not only because of the greater or lesser resistance of their materials. Even the caves of the Paleolithic period seem to us like a text that is perhaps indecipherable but not devoid of meaning. The trappings and mechanisms of technology become meaningless as soon as they cease to function: they say nothing, except that they have ceased to be of service. Thus, technology is not properly a language, a system of permanent meanings grounded on a vision of the world. It is a repertoire of signs that possess temporal and variable meanings: a universal vocabulary of activity, applied to the transformation of reality,

* TRANSLATOR'S NOTE: The Spanish word is *réplicas*, which means both replicas and replies.

which is organized in this or that way vis-à-vis this or that resistance. The poet of the past was nourished from the language and mythology that his society and his time offered him. That language and those myths were inseparable from the world image of each civilization. The universality of technology is unlike that of the old religions and philosophies: it does not offer us a world image but a blank space, the same for all men. Its signs are not a language: they are the marks that designate the boundaries, always shifting, between man and the unexplored reality. Technology liberates the imagination from all mythology and pits it against the unknown. It pits it against itself and, in the absence of a world image, causes it to be configured. That configuration is the poem. Erected on the formless like the signs of technology and, like them, in search of a ceaselessly elusive meaning, the poem is an empty space but one charged with imminence. It is not yet presence: it is a swarm of signs that seek their meaning and whose only meaning is that they are a search.

The consciousness of history seemed to be modern man's great attainment. That consciousness has been transformed into a question about the meaning of history, a question without an answer. Technology is not an answer. If it were, it would be a negative one: the invention of weapons for total annihilation interdicts every hypothesis or theory about the meaning of history and the supposed reason inherent in the movements and struggles of nations and classes. But let us suppose that those weapons had not been invented or that the powers possessing them decided to destroy them: technical thought, lone survivor of the philosophies of the past, would not be able to tell us anything about the future either. Technology can foresee these or those changes and, up to a certain point, construct future realities. In this sense technology can produce the future. None of these marvels will answer the only question that man asks himself as historical being and, I must add, as man: the why and wherefore of changes. This question already contains, in the germ, an idea of man and an image of the world. It is a question about the meaning of individual and collective human existence; to ask it is to affirm that the answer, or lack of it, belongs to different spheres of technology. And thus, although technology invents something new every day, it can tell us nothing about the future. In some manner, its action consists in being an incessant destruction of the future. Indeed, in proportion as the future it builds is less and less imaginable and appears devoid of meaning, it ceases to be future: it is the unknown that intrudes on us. We have ceased to recognize ourselves in the future.

The loss of the image of the future, Ortega y Gasset said, implies a mutilation of the past. So it is: everything that once seemed loaded with meaning now appears before our eyes as a series of efforts and creations that are a non-sense. The loss of meaning affects the two halves of the sphere, death and life: death has the sense that our living gives it; and the ultimate meaning of our living is being life in relation to death. Technology can tell us nothing about all this. Its philosophical virtue consists, so to speak, in its absence of philosophy. Perhaps this is not a misfortune: thanks to technology man finds himself, after thousands of years of philosophies and religions, on his own. The consciousness of history has been revealed as tragic consciousness; the now is no longer projected into a future: it is an instantaneous always. I say tragic consciousness not because I think of a return to Greek tragedy, but to designate the *temper* of a new poetry. History and tragedy are incompatible terms: for history, nothing is definitive except change; for tragedy all change is definitive. Therefore the genres, today mortally wounded, that are characteristic of the historical sensibility are the novel, the drama, the elegy, the comedy. The modern poet lived in a time that was distinguished from other times because it was the epoch of the historical consciousness; that consciousness now perceives that history has no meaning or, if it has one, that meaning is inaccessible to it. Our time is that of the end of history as imaginable or foreseeable future. Reduced to a present that grows more and more narrow, we ask ourselves: where are we going? What we should really ask ourselves is: what times are we living in? I don't believe anyone can answer that question with certainty. The acceleration of the historical happening, especially after World War I, and the universality of technology, which has made of the earth a homogeneous space, are revealed at last as a kind of frenzied immobility in one place that is every place. Poetry: search for a now and a here.

The foregoing description is incomplete and inadequate. But perhaps not so incomplete and inadequate that it will prevent our discerning the possible direction of the coming poetry. First: the dispersion of the world image into disconnected fragments is resolved to uniformity and, thus, to loss of *otherness*. Technology, for its part, has not given us a new world image and has made it impossible to return to the old mythologies. As long as this time that is our time lasts, there is no past or future, no golden age prior to history or social utopia to come. The poet's time: living for each day; and living it, simultaneously, in two contradictory ways: as if it were endless and as if it would end right now. Thus, the imagination can only endeavor to recuperate and exalt—to discover and project—the concrete life of today. Discovery designates the poetic experience; projection relates to the poem properly so called and will be dealt with later.

As to the discovery, I shall begin by saying that the concrete life is the real life, as against the uniform living that contemporary society tries to impose on us. Breton has said: *la véritable existence est ailleurs.* That elsewhere is here, always here and in this moment. Real life opposes neither the quotidian nor the heroic life; it is the perception of the spark of *otherness* in each one of our acts, not excluding the most trivial. These states are often massed together under a name I consider inexact: the *spiritual experience*. Nothing permits us to affirm that this concerns something predominantly spiritual; moreover, nothing causes us to think that the spirit is really different from the corporeal life and from what, also inaccurately, we call matter. Those experiences are and are not exceptional. No external or internal method—meditation, drugs, eroticism, ascetic practices, or any other physical or mental means— can of itself bring on the apparition of *otherness*. It is an unforeseen gift, a sign that life makes to life, and one's receiving it does not involve any merit or difference whatever, either moral or spiritual. Of course, there are propitious situations and more receptive temperaments, but even in such cases there is no fixed rule. An experience made of the fabric of our daily acts, *otherness* is above all the simultaneous perception that we are others without ceasing to be what we are and that, without ceasing to be where we are, our true being is in another place. We are another place. In another place means: here, right now while I am doing this or that. And also: I am alone and I am with you, in a who-knows-where that is always here. With you and here: who are you, who am I, where are we when we are here?

Irreducible, elusive, indefinable, unforeseeable, and constantly present in our lives, *otherness* is confused with religion, poetry, love, and other similar experiences. It makes its appearance with man himself, and therefore it can be said that if man became man by means of work, he had consciousness of himself because of the perception of his radical *otherness*: being and not being the same as the other animals. From the Lower Paleolithic period to our days that revelation has nourished magic, religion, poetry, art, and also the daily imagining and living of men and women. Civilizations of the past integrated the images and perceptions of *otherness* into their vision of the world; contemporary society condemns these images and perceptions in the name of reason, science, morality, and health. The prohibitions of our time alter and deform them, give them greater virulence, do not suppress them. I would call *otherness* a basic experience, if it were not for the fact that it consists precisely in the opposite: it suspends man in a kind of motionless flight, as if the foundations of the world and those of his own being had disappeared.

Although this is an experience more vast than the religious experience and is prior to it, as I said in another part of this book, rationalist thought condemns it as vigorously as it condemns religion. It may not be useless to repeat that modern religious criticism reduces the divine to the Judeo-Christian notion of one personal and creative God. It thus forgets that there are other conceptions of the godhead, from primitive animism to the atheism of certain oriental sects and religions. Western atheism is polemical and antireligious; the atheism of the East, unacquainted with the notion of a creative god, is a contemplation of the totality in which the extremes between god and creature vanish. Moreover, despite its antitheism, our atheism is no less "religious" than our theism; a great French poet, known for the violence of his antireligious convictions, once said to me: *Atheism is an act of faith.* In that phrase, not devoid of grandeur, there is a kind of echo of Tertullian and even of Saint Augustine. In short, the very idea of religion is a Western notion abusively applied to the beliefs of other civilizations. The

Sanātana-dharma—which embraces a number of "religions," some atheistic like the Sankhya system—or Taoism could scarcely be called religions, in the sense that this word is given in the West: they postulate neither an orthodoxy nor an otherworldly life. . . . The experience of the divine is more ancient, immediate, and original than any religious conception. It is not limited to the idea of one personal God or even of many: every deity comes from the divine and returns to it.

Finally, I shall recall something that has been said many times: in extirpating the notion of divinity, rationalism diminishes man. It frees us from God but encloses us in an even more rigorous system. The humbled imagination avenges itself, and atrocious fetishes sprout from God's corpse: in Russia and other countries, the divinization of the leader, the cult of the letter of writings, the deification of the party; among us, the idolatry of the self. To be *one's self* is to condemn oneself to mutilation because man is perpetual longing to be another. The idolatry of the self leads to the idolatry of property; the real God of Western Christian society is named domination over others. It conceives the world and men as *my* properties, *my* things. The arid world of today, the circular hell, is the mirror of man severed from his poetizing faculty. There is no longer any contact with those vast territories of reality that reject measure and quantity, with everything that is pure quality, irreducible to genus and species: the very substance of life.

The revolt of the romantic poets and their modern heirs was not so much a protest against the exile from God as a search for the lost half, a descent into the region that puts us in communication with the *other*. Therefore they did not find a place in any orthodoxy, and their conversion to this or that faith was never total. Behind Christ or Orpheus, Lucifer or Mary they were seeking that reality of realities we call the divine or the *other*. The situation of the contemporary poets is radically different. Heidegger has expressed it admirably: *We were too late for the gods and too early for being*; and he adds: *whose poem, already begun, is being*. Man is that which is incomplete, although he may be complete in his very incompletion; and therefore he makes poems, images in which he realizes and completes himself without ever completing himself completely. He himself is a poem: he is being always in a perpetual possibility of being completely and thus fulfilling himself in his non-completion. But our historical situation is characterized by the *too late* and the *too early*. Too late: in the tremulous light, the gods, already disappeared, their radiant bodies submerged below the horizon that devours all the mythologies of the past; too early: being, the central experience coming out of our selves to the encounter of its true presence. We are lost among things, our thoughts are circular and we perceive but dimly something, as yet unnamed, that is emerging.

The experience of *otherness* embraces the two extreme notes of a rhythm of separation and union, present in every manifestation of being, from the physical to the biological. In man that rhythm is expressed as a fall, a sensation of being alone in a strange world, and as reunion, harmony with the whole. All of us without exception have known, for an instant, the experience of separation and union. The day on which we truly fell in love and knew that that instant was forever; when we sank into the infinity of our selves and time opened its entrails and we saw ourselves as a face that disappears and a word that is annulled; the afternoon on which we saw that tree in the middle of the field and divined, although we have forgotten now, what the leaves, the vibration of the sky, the reverberation of the white wall struck by the last light, were saying; one morning, lying on the grass, listening to the secret life of the plants; or at night, watching the water surge between the rocks. Alone or accompanied we have seen Being and Being has seen us. Is it the *other life*? It is real life, the life of every day. As to that other life promised us by religions, we cannot say for certain. It seems like too much vanity, too much fascination with our own self to believe in its survival; and to reduce all existence to the human and earthly model reveals a certain lack of imagination concerning the possibilities of being. There must be other forms of being, and perhaps dying is only a transition. I doubt that this transition may be a synonym for personal salvation or perdition. In any case, I aspire to being, to the being that changes, not to the salvation of the self. I am not concerned about the *other life* elsewhere but here. The experience of *otherness* is, here and now, the *other life*. Poetry does not seek to console man for death but to make him see that life and death are inseparable: they are the totality. To recuperate the concrete life means to unite the pair life-death, to reconquer the one in the other, the you in the I, and thus to discover the shape of the world in the dispersion of its fragments.

In the dispersion of its fragments. . . . The poem—is it not that vibrant space on which a few signs are projected like an ideogram that might be a purveyor of meanings? Space, projection, ideogram: these three words allude to an operation that consists in unfolding a place, a here, that will receive and support a writing: fragments that regroup and seek to form a figure, a nucleus of meanings. When I imagine the poem as a configuration of signs on an animated space I do not think of the page in the book: I think of the Azores Islands seen as an archipelago of flames one night in 1938, of the black tents of the nomads in the valleys of Afghanistan, of the mushrooms of the parachutes suspended over a sleeping city, of a diminutive crater of red ants on an urban patio, of the moon that is multiplied and extinguished and disappears and reappears over India's dripping breast after the monsoon. Constellations: ideograms. I think of a music never heard, music for the eyes, a music never seen. I think of *Un Coup de dés.*

Modern poetry, as prosody and writing, begins with free verse and the prose poem. *Un Coup de dés* closes that period and opens another, which we are only just beginning to explore. Its significance is twofold. On the one hand, it is the condemnation of "idealistic" poetry, as *Une Saison en Enfer* had been of "materialistic" poetry; if Rimbaud's poem declares that the attempt of the word to be materialized in history is madness and sophistry, Mallarmé's proclaims that the intent to make of the poem the ideal double of the universe is absurd and vacuous. On the other hand, *Un Coup de dés* does not imply a renunciation of poetry; on the contrary, Mallarmé offers his poem as the model of a new genre. A pretension at first glance extraordinary, if one thinks that it is the poem of the nullity of the act of writing, but which is entirely justified when one considers that it inaugurates a new poetic manner. In this text, poetic writing achieves its maximum condensation and its utmost dispersion. At the same time it is the apogee of the page, as literary space, and the beginning of another

space. The poem ceases to be a linear succession and thus escapes
from the typographical tyranny that imposes on us a longitudinal
vision of the world, as if images and things presented themselves one
after another and not, as actually happens, at simultaneous moments
and in different areas of the same space or in different spaces. Al-
though *Un Coup de dés* is read from left to right and from the top
downward, the phrases tend to be configured in more or less indepen-
dent centers, like solar systems within a universe; each cluster of
phrases, without losing its relation to the whole, creates its own do-
main on this or that part of the page; and those different spaces are
sometimes fused in a single area on which two or three words shine.
The typographical arrangement, a veritable portent of the space
created by modern technology, is a form that corresponds to a differ-
ent poetic inspiration. In that inspiration lies the real originality of
the poem. Mallarmé explained it several times in *Divagations* and
other writings: the novelty of *Un Coup de dés* consists in the fact that
it is a *critical poem.*

A critical poem: if I am not mistaken, the union of these two con-
tradictory words means: that poem that contains its own negation and
that makes of that negation the point of departure for the song, equal-
ly distant from affirmation and negation. Poetry, conceived by Mallar-
mé as language's only possibility of identification with the absolute, of
being the absolute, denies itself each time it is realized in a poem (no
act, including a pure and hypothetical act: without an author, time or
place, will abolish chance)—unless the poem is simultaneously a
criticism of that attempt. The negation of the negation annuls the ab-
surdity and dissolves chance. The poem, the act of throwing the dice
or uttering the number that will suppress chance (because its digits
will coincide with the totality), is and is not absurd: *devant son exis-
tence*, one of the rough drafts of *Igitur* reads, *la négation et l'affirma-
tion viennent échouer. Il contient l'Absurde—l'implique, mais a l'état
latent et l'empêche d'exister: ce qui permet à l'Infini d'être.*[3] Mallar-
mé's poem is not the work that caused him such prolonged attention

[3] I am following in part the interpretation of Mr. Garner Davies (*Vers une expli-
cation rationelle du "Coup de dés"* [Paris, 1953]), who was one of the first to per-
ceive the sense of affirmation of the poem.

and that he never wrote, that hymn that would express, or rather, consummate, the *intimate correlation between poetry and the universe*; but in a certain sense, *Un Coup de dés* contains it.

Mallarmé opposes two possibilities that seem mutually exclusive (the act and its omission, chance and the absolute) and, without suppressing them, resolves them to a conditional affirmation—an affirmation that is ceaselessly denied and thus is affirmed because it is nourished by its own negation. The impossibility of writing an absolute poem under conditions that are also absolute, the theme of *Igitur* and of the first part of *Un Coup de dés*, is changed, thanks to criticism, to negation, into the possibility, here and now, of writing a poem open to infinity. That poem is the only possible, fleeting and yet adequate, view of the absolute. The poem does not deny chance but neutralizes or dissolves it: *il réduit le hasard à l'Infini*. The negation of poetry is also a joyous exaltation of the poetic act, a veritable shot at infinity: *Toute pensée émet un coup de dés*. Those dice thrown by the poet, an ideogram of chance, are a constellation that rolls over space and that in each of its momentary combinations says, without ever saying it completely, the absolute number: *compte total en formation*. Its stellar course does not end until it touches *quelque point dernier qui le sacre*. Mallarmé does not say what that point is. It is not farfetched to assume that it is an absolute and relative, ultimate and transitory point: that of each reader or, more exactly, each reading: *compte total en formation*.

In an essay that is one of the densest and most luminous that has been written about this capital text for the poetry of the future, Maurice Blanchot points out that *Un Coup de dés* contains its own reading.[4] Indeed, the notion of *critical poem* is bound up with that of a reading, and Mallarmé referred more than once to an ideal writing in which the phrases and words would reflect each other and, in some manner, contemplate or read one another. The reading to which Blanchot alludes is not that of just any reader, or even that of that privileged reader who is the author. Although Mallarmé, unlike most authors, does not impose his interpretation on us, neither does he leave it up to the whim of the reader. The reading, or readings, depends on

[4] *Le Livre à Venir* (Paris, 1959).

the correlation and intersection of the different parts at each moment of the mental or sonorous recitation. The blanks, the parentheses, the appositions, the syntactical construction as well as the typographical arrangement, and, above all, the verbal time on which the poem leans, that *If*. . . , a conditional conjunction that keeps discourse in suspense, are the manners of creating between the phrases the necessary distance for the words to reflect each other. In its very movement, in its dual rhythm of contraction and expansion, of negation that is annulled and transformed into an affirmation that doubts itself, the poem engenders its successive interpretations. It is not subjectivity but rather, as Ortega y Gasset would say, the intersection of the different points of view that gives us the possibility of an interpretation. None of them is definitive, not even the last (*Toute pensée émet un coup de dés*), a phrase that absorbs chance as it shoots its *perhaps* toward infinity; and all of them, from their particular perspective, are definitive: total account in perpetual formation. There is no final interpretation for *Un Coup de dés* because its last word is not a final word. Destruction was my Beatrice, Mallarmé says in a letter to a friend; at the end of the journey the poet does not contemplate the Idea, symbol or archetype of the universe, but a space in which a constellation appears: his poem. It is not an image or an essence; it is an account being calculated, a handful of signs that are drawn, effaced, and drawn again. Thus, this poem that denies the possibility of saying something absolute, consecration of the word's impotence, is at the same time the archetype of the future poem and the plenary affirmation of the sovereignty of the word. It says nothing and it is language in its totality. Author and reader of itself, negation of the act of writing, and writing that is continually reborn from its own nullification.

It is an empty space, that horizon below the errant constellation formed of the last verses of *Un Coup de dés*. And even the constellation itself has no certain existence: it is not a shape but the possibility of becoming one. Mallarmé does not show us anything except a null place and a time without substance: an infinite transparency. If one compares this vision of the world with that of the great poets of the past—it is not necessary to think of Dante or Shakespeare: it is enough to remember Hölderlin or Baudelaire—one can perceive the change.

The world, as image, has evaporated. The whole poetic endeavor is re-
duced to the clenching of one's fist to keep those dice, the ambiguous
sign of the word *perhaps*, from escaping. Or to the opening of one's
fist, to show that they too have disappeared. Both gestures have the
same meaning. Throughout his whole life, Mallarmé spoke of a book
that would be the double of the cosmos. It still amazes me that he used
so many pages to tell us what that book would be like, and so few to
show us his vision of the world. The universe, he confides to his
friends and correspondents, seems to him like a system of relations
and correspondences, an idea that is not different from that of Baude-
laire and the romantics; and yet he never explained how he really saw
it or what it was that he saw. The truth is that he did not see it: the
world had ceased to have shape. The contrast with Blake and his uni-
verses crammed with symbols, monsters, and fabulous beings will
seem even more remarkable if one remembers that both poets speak in
the name of imagination and that both regard it as a sovereign power.
The difference depends not only on the diversity of temperaments and
sensibilities but on the hundred years that separate *The Marriage of
Heaven and Hell* (1790) from *Un Coup de dés* (1897). The change
of the poetic imagination depends on the change of the world image.

Blake sees the invisible because for him everything conceals a shape.
The universe in its essence is a longing for manifestation, desire that
is projected: the imagination has no mission other than to give sym-
bolic and sensible form to energy. Mallarmé nullifies the visible by a
procedure that he calls *transposition*, which consists in making every
real object imaginary: the imagination reduces reality to idea. The
world is no longer energy or desire. Indeed, nothing would exist with-
out poetry, which gives it the possibility of being incarnated in the
verbal analogy. For Blake the primordial reality is the world, which
contains all the symbols and archetypes; for Mallarmé, the word. The
whole universe becomes the imminence of a hymn; if the world is
idea, its own mode of existing cannot be anything other than that of
the absolute language: a poem that will be the Book of books. In a
second moment of his adventure, Mallarmé understands that neither
the idea nor the word is absolutely real: the only true word is *perhaps*
and the only reality in the world is called infinite probability. Lan-

guage becomes transparent like the world itself and *transposition*, which annuls the real in favor of language, now also annuls the word. The marriage of the word and the universe is consummated in an unusual way, which is neither word nor silence but a sign that seeks its meaning.

Although the horizon of *Un Coup de dés* is not that of technology —its vocabulary is still the vocabulary of symbolism, grounded on the *anima mundi* and on the universal correspondence—the space it opens is the same as that faced by technology: world without image, reality without world and infinitely real. Marx is frequently accused, not always with reason, of aesthetic blindness; but this does not prevent one of his observations from being an extraordinarily accurate forecast of the contemporary poet's situation: the modern world is "a society that develops by excluding any mythological relation with nature, relation that is expressed by means of myths, and then presupposes in the artist an imagination independent of mythology. . . ." The imagination free of any world image—a mythology is nothing else—turns back on itself and sets up its abode out in the cold, as it were: a now and a here without anyone. Unlike the poets of the past, Mallarmé does not offer us a vision of the world; nor does he say one word to us about what it means or does not mean to be a man. The *legacy* to which *Un Coup de dés* expressly refers—without an express legatee: *à quelqu'un ambigu* —is a form; and more than that, it is the form of possibility itself: a poem closed to the world but open to the space without a name. A now in perpetual rotation, a nocturnal noon—and a deserted here. To populate it: the future poet's temptation. Our legacy is not Mallarmé's word but the space opened by his word.

The disappearance of the world image enlarged the poet's image: the real reality was not without but within, in his head or in his heart. The death of the myths engendered his own myth: his figure grew so much that his works themselves had an accessory and derivative value, proofs of his genius more than of the existence of the universe. Mallarmé's method, creative destruction or *transposition*, but above all surrealism, destroyed forever the idea of the poet as an exceptional being. Surrealism did not deny inspiration, an exceptional state: it affirmed that it was common property. Poetry requires no special talent but rather a kind of spiritual daring, an unbinding that is also an unwinding. Breton has frequently affirmed his faith in the creative power of language, which is superior to that of any personal skill, no matter how eminent. Moreover, the general movement of contemporary literature, from Joyce and Cummings to the experiments of Queneau and the combinations of electronics, tends to reestablish the sovereignty of the language over the author. The figure of the poet suffers the same fate as the world image: it is a notion that slowly evaporates. His image, not his reality. The utilization of machines, the use of drugs to achieve certain exceptional states (Michaux calls them *misérable miracle* and *paix dans les brisements*), the intervention of mathematical chance and other combinatorial methods, are not, in the end, any different from what *automatic writing* set out to do: to displace the center of creation and give language back its own. Once again: men are served by words; the poet is their servant. Ours is the century of the return, by unsuspected paths, of a power denied or at least disdained since the Renaissance: the old inspiration. Language creates the poet, and only in proportion as words are born, die, and are reborn within him is he in turn a creator. The vastest and most powerful poetic work in modern literature is perhaps that of Joyce; its theme is immense and exiguous: the story of the fall, wake, and resurrection of Tim Finnegan, who is nobody else but the English language. Adam (every man), English (every language), and the book itself and its author are a single voice that flows in a circular discourse: the word, end and beginning of all history. The poem devours the poet.

Many of these procedures express the critical tendency adopted in our time by all creative activity. Their interest is twofold: one, of a scientific nature, is that of investigating the essence of the creative process, how and in what way the phrases, rhythms, and images of the poem are formed; the other, poetic, has to do with enlarging the sphere of creation, until recently regarded by our society as an individual domain. In this latter sense, which is the properly creative one, those procedures reveal the old nostalgia for a poetry created by all and for all. But it is necessary to distinguish between the attempt to make of the poem a creation in common and the aspiration to eliminate the creator, either personal or collective. The latter betrays a contemporary obsession: a fear and a resignation. A renunciation. Man is language because he is always men, the one who speaks and the one who listens. To suppress the subject who speaks would be to complete once and for all the process of man's spiritual subjugation. Human relations, today vitiated by differences of rank between the speakers, changed markedly when the book replaced the living voice, imposed on the listener a solitary reading, and took away his right to reply or ask questions. If the book reduced the listener to the passivity of the reader, these new techniques tend to annul man as the emitter of the word. With the disappearance of the one who speaks and the one who answers, language is annulled. A circular nihilism that ends by destroying itself: the sovereignty of noise. And as to the idea of a poetry created by all, the reservation formulated by Benjamin Péret some fifteen years ago still seems valid to me: *the practice of collective poetry is conceivable only in a world free from any oppression, in which poetic thought again becomes as natural for man as water and sleep.* I shall add that in such a world the practice of poetry would perhaps be superfluous: poetry itself would be, at last, *practical.* In short, the notion of a creator, personal or collective—which is not exactly the same as the contemporary author—is inseparable from the poetic work. In reality, every poem is collective. Intervening in its creation, as much or more than the active or passive will of the poet, is the language of his time, not as word already consummated but in formation: as a wanting to say of language itself. Later, whether the poet may wish it or not, the proof of his poem's existence is the reader or the listener, the real repository of the work, who re-creates it and gives it its final meaning as he reads.

Poetry, music, and the dance were originally a whole. The division of the arts did not prevent verse from continuing to be for many centuries, with or without musical accompaniment, song. In Provence, poets composed the music for their poems. It was the last time that Western poetry could be music without ceasing to be word. Since then, whenever one has tried to unite these two arts, the poetry is lost as word, dissolved in the sound. The invention of printing did not cause the separation but accentuated it so that poetry, instead of being something that is said and listened to, was changed into something that is written and read. Clearly, the reading of the poem is a private activity: we hear mentally what we see. It makes no difference: poetry enters us through our eyes, not through our ears. What is more: we read for ourselves, in silence. Transition from the public act to the private one: the experience becomes solitary. Moreover, printing made the art of calligraphy and that of illustrating and illuminating manuscripts superfluous. Although typography has resources that are not inferior to those of the pen or the pencil, rarely has there been a real fusion between what the poem says and its typographical arrangement on the page. It is true that illustrated editions are abundant; the illustrations almost always overshadow the text, or vice versa. The idea of representing with letters what those same letters mean has frequently tempted poets; the result has been to denaturalize both the design and the writing. I do not know if lines can speak (sometimes, as I look at certain drawings, I believe they can); on the other hand, I am sure that type cannot draw. Perhaps my opinion would be different if Apollinaire, to cite the last one who tried to draw with letters, had invented real poetic ideograms instead of *calligrammes*. But the ideogram is not a drawing or a painting: it is a sign and it belongs to a system of signs. Likewise, to call the strokes of some contemporary painters calligraphy is an abusive metaphor of criticism and a confusion. If there is a prefiguration of writing in those paintings it is because all our arts suffer a nostalgia for meaning—although the real language of painting and its meaning may be different. None of these efforts has endangered the realm of the black and white.

By the elimination of music, calligraphy, and illumination, poetry was reduced until it became almost exclusively an art of the intellect. Written word and internal rhythm: mental art. Thus, to the silence and seclusion required for the reading of the poem must be added concentration. The reader strives to understand the meaning of the text, and his attention is more intense than that of the listener or that of the medieval reader, for whom the reading of the manuscript was also contemplation of a symbolic landscape. At the same time, the modern reader's participation is passive. The changes in this sphere also correspond to the changes in the world image, from its appearance in prehistory to its eclipse in our own time. Spoken word, word written by hand, printed word: each requires a different space in order to manifest itself and implies a different society and a different mythology. The ideogram and painted calligraphy are real, sensible representations of the world image; type corresponds to the triumph of the principle of causality and to a linear conception of history. It is an abstraction and reflects the gradual decline of the world as image. Man does not see the world: he thinks it. Today the situation has changed again: we hear the world again, although we still cannot see it. Thanks to new methods of reproducing the sound of the word, the voice and the ear recover their former position. Some say that the era of printing is at an end. I do not believe this. But the letter will cease to occupy a central place in men's lives. The space that supported it is no longer that flat and homogeneous surface of classic physics on which all things, from stars to words, were placed or deposited. Space has lost, as it were, its passivity: it is not that which contains things but rather, in perpetual movement, it alters their course and intervenes actively in their transformations. It is the agent of mutations, it is energy. In the past, it was the natural support of verbal rhythm and of music; its visual representation was the page, or any other flat surface, over which the dual structure of melody and harmony would slide, horizontally and vertically. Today space moves, sits up, and becomes rhythmic. Thus, the reappearance of the spoken word does not imply a return to the past: the space is different, more vast and, above all, in dispersion. To space in movement, word in rotation; to plural space, a new phrase that will be like a verbal delta, like a world that explodes in mid sky. Word on its own, through inner and outer spaces: nebula contained in a pulsation, blinking of a sun.

The change affects the page and the structure. Journalism, advertising, the cinema, and other means of visual reproduction have transformed writing, which had been almost totally stereotyped by typography. As Mallarmé had foreseen, and above all because of Apollinaire, who understood admirably—even in his aberrations—the direction of the epoch, modern poetry has adopted many of these procedures. The page, which is nothing but the representation of the real space on which the word unfolds, is changed into an animated area, in perpetual communication with the rhythm of the poem. More than containing the writing, one would say that it tends itself to be writing. In turn, the typography aspires to a kind of musical order, not in the sense of written music but of visual correspondence with the movement of the poem and the unions and separations of the image. At the same time, the page evokes the canvas of the painting or the leaf of the sketchbook; and the writing presents itself as a figure that alludes to the rhythm of the poem and that in some manner calls up the object designated by the text. In utilizing these resources, poetry recovers something that it had lost, and it puts them again at the service of the word. But poetry is not music or painting. The music of poetry is the music of language; its images are the visions that the word stirs in us, not the line or the color. Between the page and the writing is established a relation, new in the West and traditional in Far Eastern and Arabic poetry, which consists in their mutual interpretation. Space becomes writing: the blank spaces (which represent silence, and perhaps for that very reason) say something that signs do not say. The writing projects a totality but leans on a lack: it is not music nor is it silence, and it is nourished by both. Ambivalence of poetry: it partakes of all the arts and lives only if it is liberated from any company.

All writing summons a reader. The writing of the future poem evokes the image of a ceremony: game, recitation, *passion* (never spectacle). The poem will be re-created collectively. In certain times and places, poetry can be lived by all: the art of the festival awaits its resurrection. The ancient festival was grounded upon the concentration or incarnation of mythical time in a closed space, suddenly turned into the center of the universe by the descent of the divinity. A modern festival would obey an opposite principle: the dispersion of the word in different spaces, and its coming and going from one to another, its perpetual metamorphosis, its bifurcations and multiplications, its final union in a single space and a single phrase. Rhythm formed of a dual movement of separation and union. Plurality and simultaneity; convocation and gravitation of the word in a magnetic here. And so, read in silence by one who is alone or heard and perhaps said by a group, the poem conjures up the notion of a play. The word, the rhythmic unit: the image, is the only character in that play; the stage is a page, a square, or a vacant lot; the action, the continuous union and separation of the poem, a solitary and plural hero in perpetual dialogue with himself: a pronoun that is dispersed in every pronoun and is reabsorbed in a single, immense one that will never be the I of modern literature. That pronoun is language in its contradictory unity: the I am not you and the you are my I.

Poetry is born in silence and mumbling, in not being able to say, but it aspires irresistibly to recuperate language as a total reality. The poet makes word of everything he touches, not excluding silence and the blanks in the text. The recent attempts to substitute mere sounds—letters and other noises—for the word are even more unfortunate and less ingenious than calligrams: the poetry is lost without a gain in the music. The poetry of music and the music of poetry are different things. The poem welcomes the cry, the shred of vocable, the gangrened word, murmur, noise, and absurdity: not in-significance. The destruction of meaning was meaningful at the time of the Dadaist rebellion, and it could even be meaningful now if it involved a risk and if it were not just one more concession to the anonymity of commercial advertising. At a time when the sense of words has disappeared, these activities are not unlike those of an army that machine-guns corpses. Today poetry cannot be destruction of meaning but rather search for it. We know nothing of that meaning because the significance is not in what is said now but beyond, on a horizon that is scarcely perceptible. A faceless reality that is there, before us, not like a wall: like an empty space. Who knows what that which is coming will really be like and what image is being formed in a world that, for the first time, has consciousness of being an unstable equilibrium floating in the middle of infinity, an accident among the innumerable possibilities of energy? Writing in a changing space, word in the air or on the page, ceremony: the poem is a cluster of signs that seek a meaning, an ideogram that revolves on itself and around a sun as yet unborn. Significance has ceased to illuminate the world; that is why today we have reality and not image. We revolve around an absence, and all our meanings are nullified in the presence of that absence. In its rotation the poem emits lights that successively gleam and darken. The meaning of that blinking is not the ultimate significance but it is the instantaneous union of the I and the you. Poem: search for the you.

The poets of the last century and the first half of this one conse-crated the word with the word. They exalted it even as they denied it. Those poems in which the word turns in on itself are unrepeatable. What or who can name the word today? Recuperation of *otherness*, projection of language in a space depopulated of any mythology, the poem assumes the form of an interrogation. It is not man who ques-tions: language interrogates us. That question encompasses us all. For more than 150 years, the poet felt cut off, at odds with society. Each reconciliation, with churches or parties, ended in a new break or in the poet's nullification. We love Claudel or Mayakovski not because of but in spite of their orthodoxies, for what their word has of irreducible aloneness. The new poet's aloneness is different: he is not alone be-fore his contemporaries but before the future. And he shares this feel-ing of uncertainty with every man. His exile is every man's exile. The ties that bound us to the past and the future have been cut with one slash. We live a present that is fixed and interminable and yet is con-stantly moving. A floating present. It does not matter that the rem-nants of every civilization are stored up in our museums; or that each day human sciences teach us something new about man's past. Those remote pasts are not ours: if we wish to recognize ourselves in them it is because we have ceased to recognize ourselves in the past that be-longed to us. Likewise, the future that is in preparation does not resemble the one that our civilization planned and wanted. We cannot even affirm that it has any similarity whatever: we not only have no inkling of its shape but we do not know that its essence consists in not having one. Unique situation: for the first time the future lacks form. Before the birth of the historical consciousness, the form of the future was not earthly or temporal: it was mythical and it occurred in a time outside time. Modern man caused the future to descend, rooted it in the earth and dated it: changed it into history. Now, in losing its mean-ing, history has lost its control over the future and also over the present. With the disfigurement of the future, history ceases to justify our present. The question that the poem asks itself—who is he who says this that I say and to whom is it said?—embraces the poet and the reader.

The poet's separation has ended: his word springs from a situation common to all. It is not the word of a community but of a dispersion; and it does not found or establish anything, except its interrogation. Yesterday, perhaps, his mission was *to give a purer sense to the words of the tribe*; today it is a question about that sense. That question is not a doubt but a quest. And more: it is an act of faith. Not a form but some signs that are projected on an animated space and that possess multiple possible meanings. The final meaning of those signs is not yet known to the poet: it is in time, the time we all make together and that unmakes us all. Meanwhile, the poet listens. In the past he was the man of vision. Today he strains his ear and perceives that the very silence is voice, murmur that seeks the word for its incarnation. The poet listens to what time says, even if it says: nothing. On the page a few words are scattered or joined together. That configuration is a prefiguration: imminence of presence.

An image by Heraclitus was the starting point of this book. As it draws to a close, the image appears before me: the lyre, which consecrates man and thus gives him a place in the cosmos; the bow, which shoots him beyond himself. All poetic creation is historical; every poem is a longing to deny succession and to establish an enduring realm. If man is transcendence, a going beyond himself, the poem is the purest sign of that continuous transcending himself, of that permanent imagining himself. Man is an image because he transcends himself. Perhaps the historical consciousness and the need to transcend history are nothing but the names we now give to this ancient and perpetual split of being, always separated from oneself, always in search of oneself. Man wants to be one with his creations, to unite with himself and with his fellows: to be the world without ceasing to be himself. Our poetry is consciousness of the separation and attempt to unite that which was separated. In the poem, being and desire for being come to terms for an instant, like the fruit and the lips. Poetry, momentary reconciliation: yesterday, today, tomorrow; here and there; you, I, he, we. All is present: will be presence.

Appendices

I. POETRY, SOCIETY, STATE

There is no more pernicious and barbarous prejudice than that of attributing to the state powers in the sphere of artistic creation. Political power is sterile, because its essence is the domination of men, whatever the ideology that may mask it. Although there has never been absolute freedom of expression—freedom is always defined in relation to certain obstacles and within certain limits: we are free in relation to this or that—it would not be difficult to show that where power invades every human activity, art languishes or is transformed into a servile and mechanical activity. An artistic style is a living thing, a continuous invention within a certain direction. Never imposed from without, born of the profound tendencies of society, that direction is to a certain extent unpredictable, as is the growth of the tree's branches. On the other hand, the official style is the negation of creative spontaneity: great empires tend to have a leveling effect on man's changing face and to transform it into a mask that is repeated indefinitely. Power immobilizes, stabilizes life's variety in a single gesture—grandiose, terrible, or theatrical and, in the end, simply monotonous. "I am the state" is a formula that signifies the alienation of human faces, supplanted by the stony features of an abstract self that is changed, until the end of time, into the model of a whole society. The style that, like a melody, advances and weaves new combinations, utilizing some of the same elements, is degraded into mere repetition.

There is nothing more urgent than the need to dispel the confusion that has been established between the so-called "communal" or "collective" art and the official art. One is art that is inspired by the beliefs and ideals of a society; the other, art subjected to the rules of a tyrannical power. Diverse ideas and spiritual tendencies—the cult of the *polis*, Christianity, Buddhism, Islam, and so on—have been incarnated in powerful states and empires. But it would be a mistake to regard Gothic or Romanesque art as creations of the papacy, or the sculpture of Mathura as the expression of the empire founded by Kanishka. Political power can channel, utilize, and—in certain cases—stimulate an artistic current. It can never create it. What is more: in the long run it generally has a sterilizing effect. Art is always nourished from the social language. That language is, likewise and above all, a vision of the world. Like the arts, states live by that language and sink their roots in that vision of the world. The papacy did not create Christianity, but the other way around; the liberal state is the offshoot of the bourgeoisie, not the latter of the former. The examples can be multiplied. And when a conqueror imposes his vision of the world on a people—for example: Islam in Spain—the foreign state and its whole culture remain as alien superimpositions until the people have truly made that religious or political conception their own. Only then, that is to say: when the new vision of the world becomes a shared belief and a common language, will there be an art or a poetry in which society recognizes itself. Thus, the state can impose one vision of the world, prevent others from emerging, and exterminate those that obscure it, but it lacks the fecundity to create such a vision. And the same thing happens with art: the state does not create it, it can hardly encourage it without corrupting it and, more frequently, as soon as it tries to utilize it, it deforms it, suffocates it, or converts it into a mask.

Egyptian and Aztec art, the art of the Spanish baroque and the Grand Century of France—to cite the best-known examples—seem to belie these ideas. They all coincide with the noonday of absolute power. Thus, it is not strange that many see in their light a reflection of the state's splendor. A brief examination of some of these cases will help to correct the error.

Like every art of the so-called "ritualistic civilizations," Aztec art is religious. Aztec society was submerged in the atmosphere, alternately somber and luminous, of the sacred. Every act was impregnated with religion. The state itself was an expression of it. Moctezuma was more than a chief: he was a priest. War was a rite: the representation of the solar myth in which

Huitzilopochtli, the invincible Sun, armed with his *xiuhcóatl*, defeated Co-yolxauhqui and his column of stars, the Centzonhiznahua. The same quality characterized other human activities: politics and art, commerce and artisan-ship, foreign and family relations issued from the matrix of the sacred. Public and private life were two sides of the same vital current, not separate worlds. Dying or being born, going to war or to a festival were religious acts. Therefore, it is a grave error to classify Aztec art as a state or political art. The state and politics had not achieved their autonomy; power was still tinged with religion and magic. Aztec art does not in fact express the tend-encies of the state but those of religion. One will say that this is a play on words, since the religious nature of the state does not limit but rather strengthens its power. The observation is unjust: a religion that is incarnated in a state, as occurs with the Aztec, is not the same as a state that is served by religion, as happens with the Romans. The difference is so important that without it one could not understand the Aztec policy toward Cortés. And one thing more: Aztec art is, literally, religion. Sculpture, poem, and painting are not "works of art"; neither are they representations, but rather incarnations, living manifestations of the sacred. And similarly: the abso-lute, total, and totalitarian character of the Mexican state is not political but religious. The state is religion: chiefs, warriors, and simple *mecehuales* are religious categories. The forms in which Aztec art is expressed, as well as the political expressions, constitute a sacred language shared by the whole society.[1]

The contrast between Romans and Aztecs shows the difference between sacred and official art. The art of the Romans aspires to the sacred. But if the

[1] This is not the place to make a closer examination of the nature of Aztec society and to ferret out the true significance of its art. Let it suffice to note that the dual organization of the society corresponds to the dualism of the religion (the agrarian cults of the ancient towns of the valley and the typically Aztec warrior gods). More-over, we know that the Aztecs almost always used foreign vassals as artisans and builders. All this causes us to suspect that we are in the presence of an art and a religion that, by the accumulation and superimposition of their own and alien elements, conceal an inner schism. There is nothing similar in Mayan art at its height, in "Olmec" art or that of Teotihuacán, where the unity of the forms is free and spontaneous, not conceptual and external, as in the divinity Coatlicue. The living and natural line of the reliefs of Palenque—or the severe geometry of Teotihuacán—permit us to envisage an undivided religious consciousness, a vision of the world that has evolved naturally and not by the accumulation, superimposition, and re-arrangement of disparate elements. Or rather: Aztec art tends toward a syncretism, not fully realized, of opposite conceptions of the world, while that of the more an-cient cultures is merely the natural development of a single and unique vision. And this is another of the barbarous traits of Aztec society in comparison with the ancient civilizations of Middle America.

passage from the sacred to the profane, from the mythical to the political
—as is seen in ancient Greece or at the end of the Middle Ages—is natural,
the leap in the opposite direction is not. In reality, what we are dealing
with here is not a religious state but rather a state religion. Augustus or
Nero, Marcus Aurelius or Caligula, "delights of mankind" or "out-and-out
monsters," are feared or beloved beings, but they are not gods. And the
images with which they aim to make themselves eternal are not divine
either. Imperial art is an official art. Although Virgil has his eye on Homer
and Greek antiquity, he knows that the original unity has been broken for-
ever. The urban desert of the metropolis follows the universe of federations,
alliances, and rivalries of the classic *polis*; the state religion replaces the
communal religion; the inner attitude of the philosophers supplants the old
piety, which worships at the public altars, as in the age of Sophocles; the
public rite becomes an official function, and the real religious attitude is ex-
pressed as solitary contemplation; philosophical and mystical sects prolifer-
ate. The splendor of the age of Augustus—and, later, of the Antonines—
must not cause us to forget that there are brief periods of rest and respite.
But neither the learned benevolence of some men, nor the will of others—be
they named Augustus or Trajan—can resuscitate the dead. An official art, at
its best and highest moments Roman art is an art of the court, aimed at a
select minority. The attitude of the poets of that time can be exemplified in
these verses by Horace:

> *Odi profanum vulgus et arceo.*
> *Favete linguis: carmina non prius*
> *audita Musarum sacerdos*
> *Virginibus puerisque canto ...*

As to the Spanish literature of the sixteenth and seventeenth centuries
and its relation to the house of Austria: almost all the artistic forms of that
period are born at the moment when Spain opens up to Renaissance culture,
feels the influence of Erasmus, and participates in the tendencies that pre-
pare the way for the modern epoch (*La Celestina*, Nebrija, Garcilaso, Vives,
the Valdés brothers, and so on). Even the artists who belong to what Val-
buena Prat calls the "mystic reaction" and the "national period," whose
common attribute is opposition to the Europeanism and "modernism" of
the epoch of the emperor, merely develop the tendencies and forms that
Spain appropriated some years earlier. Saint John imitates Garcilaso (possi-
bly through the "Garcilaso a lo divino" of Sebastián de Córdoba); Fray Luis
de León cultivates Renaissance poetic forms exclusively, and in his thought

Plato and Christianity are allied; Cervantes—figure between two epochs and example of a secular writer in a society of clerics and theologians—"absorbs the Erasmist ferments of the sixteenth century,"[2] besides being directly influenced by the culture and free life of Italy. The state and the church channel, limit, prune, and utilize those tendencies, but do not create them. And if attention is focused on Spain's most purely national crea-tion—the theater—the astonishing thing is, precisely, its freedom and spon-taneity within the conventions of the time. In short, the Austrian monarchy did not create Spanish art and, on the other hand, it separated Spain from the incipient modernity.

Nor does the French example show convincing proof of the supposed relation of cause and effect between the centralization of political power and artistic greatness. As in the case of Spain, the "classicism" of the period of Louis XIV was brought about by the extraordinary philosophical, politi-cal, and vital unrest of the sixteenth century. The intellectual freedom of Rabelais and Montaigne, the individualism of the highest figures of the lyric—from Marot and Scève to Jean de Sponde, Desportes, and Chassignet, and including Ronsard and d'Aubigné—the eroticism of Louise Labé and the "Blasonneurs du corps féminin" bear witness to spontaneity, ease, and free creation. The same must be said of the other arts and even the very life of that individualistic and anarchical century. Nothing could be further from an official style, imposed by a state, than the art of the Valois period, which is invention, sensuality, whim, movement, passionate and lucid curi-osity. This current penetrates the seventeenth century. But everything changes as soon as the monarchy is consolidated. After the founding of the Academy, poets not only have to contend with the vigilance of the Church, but also with that of a State grown grammatical. The sterilization process culminates, years later, with the revocation of the Edict of Nantes and the triumph of the Jesuit party. From this perspective alone the dispute over *Le Cid* and Corneille's difficulties, Molière's troubles and bitterness, La Fontaine's solitude and, finally, Racine's silence—a silence that merits some-thing more than a simple psychological explanation and seems to me like a symbol of France's spiritual situation in the "Grand Century"—acquire true meaning. These examples show that the arts must fear rather than be grateful for a protection that ends by suppressing them on the pretext of giving them guidance. The Sun King's "classicism" sterilized France. And it is not an exaggeration to say that the romanticism, realism, and symbolism

[2] Angel Valbuena Prat, *Historia de la literatura española* (1946).

of the nineteenth century are a profound negation of the spirit of the "Grand Century" and an attempt to resume the free tradition of the sixteenth.

Ancient Greece reveals that communal art is spontaneous and free. It is impossible to compare the Athenian *polis* with the Caesarean state, the papacy, the absolute monarchy, or modern totalitarian states. The supreme authority of Athens is the assembly of citizens, not a remote group of bureaucrats supported by the army and the police. The violence with which the tragedy and the Old Comedy treat of the affairs of the *polis* helps to explain the attitude of Plato, who desired "the intervention of the state in the freedom of poetic creation." One has only to read the tragedians—especially Euripides —or Aristophanes to note the incomparable freedom and grace of these artists. That freedom of expression was grounded on political liberty. And it may even be said that the root of the Greeks' conception of the world was the sovereignty and freedom of the *polis*. "The same year that Aristophanes staged his *Clouds*," says Burckhardt in his *History of Greek Culture*, "there appeared the earliest political memoir surviving anywhere on earth, *On the Athenian State*." Political reflection and artistic creation live in the same climate. Painters and sculptors enjoyed similar freedom, within the limitations of their calling, and the conditions under which they were employed. Unlike what occurs in our own time, the politicians of that period had the good sense to abstain from legislating on artistic styles.

Greek art participated in the debates of the city because the very constitution of the *polis* required citizens' free opinion on public affairs. A "political" art can only spring up where there is the possibility of expressing political opinions, that is, where freedom of speech and thought prevails. In this sense, Athenian art was "political," but not in the base contemporary acceptance of the word. Read *The Persians* to learn what it is to view one's adversary with eyes undefiled by the distortions of propaganda. And Aristophanes' ferocity was always unleashed against his fellow citizens; the extremes he resorted to in order to ridicule his enemies were part of the nature of Old Comedy. This political belligerence of art was born of freedom. No one thought of persecuting Sappho because she sang about love instead of the struggles of the city. It was necessary to wait until the sectarian and shabby twentieth century to know this kind of a disgrace.

Gothic art was not the work of popes or emperors, but of the cities and religious orders. The same may be said of the typical intellectual institution of the Middle Ages, the university. Like the latter, the cathedral was the creation of the urban communes. It has often been said that in their vertical thrust those churches express the Christian aspiration toward the hereafter. It must be added that if the direction of the building, tense and seemingly thrown to heaven, incarnates the *meaning* of medieval society, its structure reveals the *composition* of that same society. Indeed, everything is thrown upward, toward heaven; but, at the same time, each part of the edifice has a life of its own, individuality and character, but that plurality does not break the unity of the whole. The arrangement of the cathedral seems like a living materialization of that society in which, against the backdrop of monarchical and feudal power, communities and guilds form a complicated solar system of federations, leagues, pacts, and contracts. The free spontaneity of the communes, not the authority of popes and emperors, gives Gothic art its double movement: on the one hand, thrown upward like an arrow; on the other, spread out horizontally, sheltering and covering but not oppressing every genus and species and individual in creation. The great art of the papacy is truly that of the baroque period and its typical representative is Bernini.

The relations between the state and artistic creation depend, in each case, on the nature of the society to which they belong. But in general—insofar as it is possible to reach conclusions in a sphere so vast and contradictory—historical examination corroborates the fact that not only has the state never been the creator of an art of real value, but that each time it tries to transform art into a tool for its own purposes, it ends by denaturalizing and degrading that art. Thus, "art for the few" is almost always the bold answer of a group of artists who, openly or with caution, oppose an official art or the decomposition of the social language. Góngora in Spain, Seneca and Lucan in Rome, Mallarmé before the Philistines of the Second Empire and the Third Republic, are examples of artists who, affirming their solitude and repudiating the public of their time, achieve a communication that is the highest to which a creator can aspire: the communication with posterity. Thanks to their efforts, language is not dispersed as a jargon or petrified in a formula but concentrated, acquiring consciousness of itself and its powers of liberation.

Their hermetism—never completely impenetrable, but always open to the one who will venture to cross the undulant and spiny wall of words—is like that of the seed. Immured within it sleeps the life to come. Centuries after their death, the obscurity of these poets becomes light. And their influence is so profound that, more than poets of poems, they can be called poets or creators of poets. The phoenix, the pomegranate, and the Eleusinian corn always figure on their escutcheon.

II. POETRY AND RESPIRATION

Etiemble maintains that the origin of poetic pleasure may perhaps be physi-
ological and, more precisely, muscular and respiratory. To justify his affir-
mation he emphasizes that the measure of the French alexandrine—the time
we take to pronounce it—coincides with the rhythm of breathing. The
same is true of the Spanish and the Italian hendecasyllable. Nevertheless,
Etiemble does not explain how and why we also enjoy verses with longer
or shorter measures. For many centuries the octosyllable was the national
verse of Spain, and even after Garcilaso's reform, the eight syllables of the
ballad continue to be utilized constantly by the poets of our language. Is it
possible to deny the pleasure with which we listen to and say our old octo-
syllable? And what about Whitman's long verses—and the blank verse of
the Elizabethans? The measure seems to depend, rather, on the rhythm of
the common language—that is, on the music of conversation, as Eliot has
shown in a very well-known essay—rather than on physiology. The measure
of the verse is already present in the germ in that of the phrase. The verbal
rhythm is historical. The velocity, lentitude, or tonalities that language ac-
quires at this or that moment, in this or that mouth, tend to crystallize later
in the poetic rhythm. The "rhythm of the epoch" is something more than a
figurative expression, and it would be possible to write a kind of history of
each nation—and of each man—on the basis of their vital rhythm. That
rhythm—the tempo of action, thought, and social life—is also and above all
verbal rhythm.

Lope de Vega's vertiginous and winged velocity becomes in Calderón a
majestic, emphatic promenade through the language; Huidobro's poetry is
a series of verbal discharges, as befits his temperament and that of the gen-
eration following World War I, which had just discovered mechanical
speed; the rhythm of César Vallejo's verse stems from the Peruvian lan-
guage. . . . Poetic pleasure is verbal pleasure and is grounded on the lan-
guage of an age, a generation, and a community.

Etiemble also observes that for André Spire—a theorist of French free verse—poetic pleasure is reduced to a kind of gymnastics, in which the lips, tongue, and other muscles of the mouth and throat participate. According to this ingenious doctrine, each language requires a series of muscular movements in order to be spoken. Verses give us pleasure because they provoke and stimulate pleasing muscular movements. This explains why certain verses "sound good," while others, with the same number of syllables, do not; for the verse to be beautiful, the words must be arranged in the phrase in such a way that it will be easy to pronounce them. Like the runner in an obstacle race, the one who recites a poem jumps from word to word, and the pleasure he derives from this race, which consists in turns and leaps in a labyrinth that irritates and flatters the senses, is no different from that of the fighter or the swimmer. Everything that was said before about poetry as respiration is applicable to these ideas: rhythm is not isolated sound, or mere meaning, or muscular pleasure, but everything together, in indissoluble unity.

III. WHITMAN, POET OF AMERICA

Walt Whitman is the only great modern poet who does not seem to experience inconformity vis-à-vis his world. Or even loneliness; his monologue is a vast chorus. Doubtless there are, at least, two persons in him: the public poet and the private person, who conceals his real erotic inclinations. But his mask—the poet of democracy—is something more than a mask: it is his true face. Despite certain recent interpretations, the poetic dream and the historic one coincide in him completely. There is no break between his beliefs and the social reality. And this fact is higher—I mean, broader and more significant—than any psychological circumstance. Now, the singularity of Whitman's poetry in the modern world can only be explained in the light of another, even greater singularity, which encompasses it: the singularity of America.

In a book[1] that is a model of its kind, Edmundo O'Gorman has shown that our continent was never discovered. Indeed, it is not possible to discover something that does not exist, and America, before its so-called "dis-

[1] *The Idea of the Discovery of America* (Mexico, 1951).

covery," did not exist. One would have to speak of the invention, rather than the discovery, of America. If America is a creation of the European spirit, it began to be outlined in the sea mist centuries before the voyages of Columbus. And what Europeans discovered when they touched these lands was their own historical dream. Reyes has devoted admirable pages to this theme: America is a sudden incarnation of a European utopia. The dream becomes reality, becomes present; America is a present: a gift, a donation of history. But it is an open present, a now that is tinged with tomorrow. The presence and the present of America are a future; by its very nature, our continent is the land that does not exist of itself, but as something that is created and invented. Its being, its reality or substance, consists in being always future, history that is not justified by what is past, but by that which is to come. What establishes us is not what America was, but what it will be. America did not exist; and *it exists only if it is a utopia*, history on the move toward an age of gold.

Perhaps this may not be completely true if one thinks of the colonial period of Spanish and Portuguese America. But it is revealing that as soon as the American creoles acquire consciousness of themselves and oppose the Spanish, they rediscover the utopian character of America and make the French utopias their own. They all see the Revolution of Independence as a return to the original principles, a turning back to what America really is. The Revolution of Independence is a rectification of American history and, therefore, it is the reestablishment of the original reality. The exceptional and truly paradoxical character of this restoration appears clear if one perceives that it consists in a restoration of the future. By means of the French revolutionary principles, America is once again what it was at its birth: not a past, but a future, a dream. The dream of Europe, the place, in space and time, of everything that the European reality could not be except by denying itself and its past. America is the dream of Europe, now free from European history, free from the weight of tradition. With the problem of independence resolved, the abstract and utopian nature of liberal America is again revealed in such episodes as the French intervention in Mexico. Neither Juárez nor the liberals ever thought—as Cossío Villegas points out—that they were fighting against France, but against a French usurpation. The real France was ideal and universal and, more than a nation, it was an idea, a philosophy. Cuesta says, with some justification, that the war against the French must be regarded as a "civil war." The Mexican Revolution was necessary in order to cause the country to awaken from this philosophical dream—which, moreover, concealed a historical reality scarcely touched by the Independence, the Reform, and the Dictatorship—and to find itself, not as an abstract future but as an origin in which three times were to be sought: our past, our present, and our future. The time of the historical accent changed, and this is the real spiritual significance of the Mexican Revolution.

The utopian character of America is even more marked in the Saxon part of the continent. There no complex indigenous cultures existed, nor did Catholicism erect its vast intemporal structures: America was—if it was anything—geography, pure space, open to human action. Lacking historical substance—old classes, venerable institutions, inherited beliefs and laws—reality presented no obstacles except the natural ones. Men did not struggle against history, but against nature. And where there was a historical obstacle—for example, the indigenous societies—it was erased from history and, reduced to a mere natural fact, it was therefore actualized. The North American attitude can be summarized as follows: everything that does not partake of the utopian nature of America does not properly belong to history; it is a natural fact and, therefore, it does not exist; or it exists only as inert obstacle, not as alien consciousness. Evil is outside: it is part of the natural world—like the Indians, the rivers, the mountains, and other obstacles that must be domesticated or destroyed—or it is an intrusive reality (the English past, Spanish Catholicism, the monarchy, etc.). The United States Revolution of Independence is the expulsion of the intrusive elements, alien to the American essence. If the reality of America is to be a constant invention of itself, everything that in some way shows itself to be irreducible or inassimilable is not American. In other places the future is one of man's attributes: because we are men, we have a future; in the Saxon America of the last century, the process is reversed and the future determines the man: we are men because we are a future. And everything that has no future is not a man. Thus, there is no room in reality for contradiction, ambiguity, or conflict.

With complete confidence and innocence, Whitman can sing of democracy on the march because the American utopia is confused with and is indistinguishable from the American reality. Whitman's poetry is a great prophetic dream, but it is a dream within another dream, a prophecy within another prophecy that is even vaster and that nourishes it. America dreams itself in Whitman's poetry because America itself is a dream. And it dreams itself as a concrete, almost physical reality, with its men, its rivers, its cities, and its mountains. That whole enormous mass of reality moves swiftly, as if it had no weight; and, indeed, it lacks historical weight: it is the future that is being incarnated. The reality Whitman sings is utopian. And by this I do not mean that it is unreal or that it exists only as idea, but that its essence, that which moves it, justifies it, and gives direction to its march, gravity to its movements, is the future. Dream within a dream, Whitman's poetry is realistic for this reason alone: its dream is the dream of reality itself, which has no substance other than that of inventing itself, dreaming itself. "When we dream that we dream," Novalis says, "we are about to awaken." Whitman never had consciousness that he was dreaming and always considered himself a poet of reality. And he was, but only insofar as the reality he sang was not something given, but a substance shot through with the future. America dreams itself in Whitman because America itself was dream, pure creation. Before and after Whitman we have had other poetic dreams. All of them—be the dreamer named Poe or Darío, Melville or Dickinson—are really attempts to escape from the American nightmare.

INDEX

Catalog

If you are interested in a list of fine Paperback
books, covering a wide range of subjects
and interests, send your name and address,
requesting your free catalog, to:

McGraw-Hill Paperbacks
1221 Avenue of Americas
New York, N.Y. 10020